F.V.

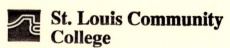

St. Louis Community College

Forest Park
Florissant Valley
Meramec

Instructional Resources
St. Louis, Missouri

THE AMERICAN WORK ETHIC AND THE CHANGING WORK FORCE

Recent Titles in
Contributions in Labor Studies

Trade Unionism and Industrial Relations in the Commonwealth Caribbean: History,
Contemporary Practice and Prospect
Lawrence A. Nurse

Eastern's Armageddon
Martha Dunagin Saunders

A State Within a State: Industrial Relations in Israel, 1965–1987
Ran Chermesh

Culture, Gender, Race, and U.S. Labor History
Ronald C. Kent, Sara Markham, David R. Roediger, and Herbert Shapiro, editors

Infighting in the UAW: The 1946 Election and the Ascendancy of Walter Reuther
Bill Goode

American Labor in the Era of World War II
Sally M. Miller

The American Labor Movement, 1955–1995
Walter Galenson

The American Fund for Public Service: Charles Garland and Radical
Philanthropy, 1922–1941
Gloria Garrett Samson

Black Unemployment: Part of Unskilled Unemployment
David Schwartzman

The Quest for a Living Wage: The History of the Federal Minimum Wage Program
Willis J. Nordlund

Irish Voice and Organized Labor in America: A Biographical Study
L. A. O'Donnell

Economic Liberalization and Labor Markets
Parviz Dabir-Alai and Mehmet Odekon, editors

THE AMERICAN WORK ETHIC AND THE CHANGING WORK FORCE

An Historical Perspective

HERBERT APPLEBAUM

Contributions in Labor Studies, Number 52

GREENWOOD PRESS
Westport, Connecticut • London

Library of Congress Cataloging-in-Publication Data

Applebaum, Herbert A.
   The American work ethic and the changing work force : an
historical perspective / Herbert Applebaum.
      p.   cm.—(Contributions in labor studies, ISSN 0886–8239 ;
no. 52)
   Includes bibliographical references and index.
   ISBN 0–313–30677–X (alk. paper)
   1. Work ethic—United States.   2. Work ethic—United States—
History.   3. Labor market—United States.   4. Labor—United States—
History.   I. Title.   II. Series.
HD8072.5.A663   1998
331.1′0973—dc21   97–49999

British Library Cataloguing in Publication Data is available.

Library of Congress Catalog Card Number: 97–49999
ISBN: 0–313–30677–X
ISSN: 0886–8239

First published in 1998

Greenwood Press, 88 Post Road West, Westport, CT 06881
An imprint of Greenwood Publishing Group, Inc.

Printed in the United States of America

The paper used in this book complies with the
Permanent Paper Standard issued by the National
Information Standards Organization (Z39.48–1984).

10 9 8 7 6 5 4 3 2 1

Dedicated to My Wife, Mika

CONTENTS

INTRODUCTION

THE WORK ETHIC

Human beings are made for work. Working is in our bones and tissues. Homo sapiens emerged as a species in an environment in which working plays a prominent part. Work shaped human beings as the human eye, hand, and brain evolved in response to work performed. The human nervous system, human language, and the human imagination were also shaped by human activities in which work was prominent, if not predominant, in prehistoric times. Work, along with language, helped to distinguish humans from other animals.

Humans take the materials of nature and use tools to fashion useful objects. Objects created by work reflect human culture. The products of the mind and imagination also reflect human culture. Humans see, evaluate, and measure themselves by the things they create through work. They also know themselves by their work, since work enables humans to construct a world that stands between themselves and nature.

The work ethic is the human ethic; to talk about one is to talk about the other. Without work human beings cannot exist. Without work human society cannot exist. Work is not a choice. Work is a necessity; the work ethic is a human survival ethic. It is more than that, but it is at least a necessity for human life. Human beings have to work to survive by growing food, building homes, and making clothes to sustain their bodies and protect them from their natural environment. The human species creates a human-made world to make sense of the natural world and uses the materials of the natural world to make products.

Human beings also create language that enables them to order, describe, and explain both the natural world and their own human order. Humans need order, description, and explanation in order to live in the natural world and to use it for human purpose. Human beings also need culture to create a system of values and behavior, both of which are necessary for interaction with the human and natural worlds. Therefore, work and culture are inseparable. Every society has a culture and a work ethic, whether explicit or not. Work ethics relate to particular human cultures within particular historical, regional, environmental, and economic dimensions. In short, work is necessary for basic physical survival and functioning of human societies. The work ethic is the value system associated with carrying out work in a particular kind of society with specific cultural patterns. A hunting and gathering society has a work ethic very different from that of an industrial or peasant society.

Work ethics differ not only according to overall cultures, such as colonial or modern America, but varies with occupation. One cannot equate the work ethic of a farmer with that of an accountant. Their work settings, work processes, and skills are different. A farmer's work depends on weather conditions, while an accountant can carry on his work in any kind of weather. Work may be central to both farmer and accountant, but for the farmer it is a way of life, a 24-hour, 7-day-a-week occupation, while the accountant leaves the job behind when he goes home. The farmer integrates his work and family life, while the accountant keeps the two spheres separate. The craftsman is more likely to have pride in his work than the common laborer. But within any given occupation, some individuals will be more industrious than others. Each occupation, profession, or job has a set of traditions, rules, customs, and behavior patterns by which members are judged and which reflect the occupational work ethic. Work has an objective and a subjective dimension, with the work process being the objective dimension and the work ethic the subjective dimension.

A strong work ethic involves the belief that work is the core of a moral life, useful to oneself, one's family, and one's community. A strong work ethic stresses building character through the discipline of work. A strong work ethic emphasizes the moral superiority of work over idleness, pride in craft over carelessness, earned income over unearned income.

The work ethic concept is both multidimensional and difficult to measure. Human behavior and the work ethic intertwine, making the work ethic difficult to analyze. Does the work ethic only become relevant when there is choice of work? Does hard work imply a strong work ethic under the constraint of starvation or coercion? Is the work ethic based on cultural, occupational, organizational, or individual dimensions, or all four? This book attempts to answer these questions by discussing work in specific circumstances at particular times and places in U.S. history.

THE WORK ETHIC AND AMERICAN IDEOLOGY

The Puritan Ethic

American social ideology has always included a strong adherence to the importance of work. The work ethic as value landed on the shores of New England with the Puritans and was reinforced as New England became a prominent intellectual center in the colonial period. While pure Puritan theology did not survive the eighteenth century, its work ethic legacy did. Work was the closest thing to a universal religion in colonial New England. Puritans had no tolerance for those who would not work or persons without some visible means of support. Colonial towns and cities had neither the funds nor the patience to support people on the dole.

John Smith, during his exploratory journey in 1614 to "New England," which he named, wrote that those who had a taste of virtue, but no means except their own merits, would succeed in the New World if they were willing to work hard. Later, Puritan leaders like John Winthrop, William Bradford, Cotton Mather, and Increase Mather repeated the admonition about the necessity of hard work for success in the New World. At Jamestown, Plymouth, and Boston, hard work was essential for survival. Settlers needed to clear land, plant crops, and build shelters. Many years of continuous effort were necessary before the security of the early settlements in New England and Virginia was established. Through the industry of their followers and the writings of their leaders, Puritans left a legacy in the belief that hard work, industry, and frugality were pathways to success.

The Frontier

The word "pioneer" evokes images of hard work. The traditions of the frontier are traditions of heroic, backbreaking labor. The United States was a frontier society for three-quarters of its history. Americans pushing westward worked hard to conquer forestlands, mountains, prairies, deserts, and rivers. Most of those who succeeded did it through hard work, persistence, and luck. Sure there were the gamblers and speculators, but they were vastly outnumbered by the countless men and women who farmed the land and built the great cities. The history of the frontier includes the cowboys who tended cattle and the mountain men who trapped furs, the farmers who broke up the tough prairie sod and the go-getters who founded towns, the railroad builders who connected the regions of the country and the miners who brought out from the deep recesses of mountains, coal, copper, lead, silver, iron, and gold. It also includes the Native Americans with their cultural traditions of communal labor and their successful adaptations to the natural environment. Heroic pioneer women managed to sustain home and family by working long hours under the most trying conditions.

Immigrants

Another element that infused American ideology with the virtue and efficacy of work was the immigrant. America has been a land of immigrants who come to these shores for the primary reason, to work. Besides those brought against their will, immigrants were among the most daring and energetic members of the nations from which they emigrated. The dreaded ocean alone demanded strong incentives for undertaking its crossing, drawing from Europe, Asia, and Latin America its toughest, most resolute, most risk-oriented inhabitants. Immigrants did not come to the

United States thinking they would be idle or would succeed without working. Benjamin Franklin told prospective migrants to America to give up any idea that they would get a free ride from the government or that they could be idle and live off the labor of others. One of the lures of America for many early immigrants was the possibility of securing land to farm, and no farmer ever contemplated a way of life without hard work. Later, it was the promise of a job that drew immigrants here, as the growing American economy in the second half of the nineteenth and early twentieth centuries needed hands for its factories and mills. The immigrant provides strong support for America's work ethic.

Individualism and Independence

Throughout our history the belief in the rights of individuals along with the importance of individual independence are themes in American ideology. John Locke, the British philosopher who influenced the thinking of Thomas Jefferson, espoused the idea that every person has the right to his or her own labor. This right conferred independence on the individual, as he could thereby provide for his own survival if he controlled his own work. Independence for the individual was a strong motivator in bringing people to America. They wanted a piece of land to farm or they wished to open a workshop to ply a trade. Wage labor was also an option, as it was a job and a chance to work. Without work there was no independence, and loss of independence meant loss of self-respect. Being poor and idle earns one disrespect on both counts. In short, American ideology is an ideology of equality in which everyone is expected to make a contribution to society by working. Never mind that some have more opportunity than others, or that some have no opportunity, or that some cannot find work through no fault of their own. That is all true. But if one is not working one is not contributing to oneself, to one's family, or to one's society. If a person has nothing else to foster his or her self-respect, to be at work is the least one can do to establish a place in society, no matter how boring or how unsatisfactory their work may be.

The ideology of individualism as applied to work states that individuals can only be secure and successful through individual initiative and the pursuit of individual self-interest through hard work. Regardless of the success rate, the obsession with bettering one's life is a universal goal in American society. Many have failed in this quest, but the quest is always there giving people a reason to work beyond mere subsistence. If workers, farmers, laborers, and even slaves were beaten down they found a way to keep going, to fight back, and to protest. Early on in American history people believed in the right to the labor of one's own person, the John Locke doctrine. Farmers, artisans, tradesmen, workshop owners, and small businessmen pursued their occupations in the expectation of expropriating the products they produced without being subject to the discipline of others. This changed when more and more people, and even the majority, became wage earners who only had their ability to work to bargain with in the marketplace. In the integrated factory, individual output no longer existed since it was the outcome of the organization as a whole. The negotiating power of the two sides in the wage bargain was unequal, with employers having the upper hand. But the worker, skilled and unskilled, asserted his and her right to a living wage and fought many battles over that principle. The idea that persons have rights to their own labor is sacrosanct today, but was not so before the Civil War. The scourge of slavery was a vast contradiction that remained until it was eliminated. African-Americans still struggle to assert their rights to their own labor by demanding equal opportunity in the labor marketplace.

Progress, Technology, and Invention

Belief in progress, technology, and invention has been an important element in American ideology. American success in productivity and its ability to provide its citizens with a high standard of living are based in part on the inventive genius of American innovators. Each period of American history seems to bring forth a new series of inventions and innovations that lead to fundamental changes in the American way of life. There were early textile mills in New England and Philadelphia; the rise of the factory; the advances in steel-making during the nineteenth century; the application of the steam engine, telephone, and telegraph; the series of inventions of farm machinery like the harvester and tractor that revolutionized agricultural output; the automobile in the early twentieth century; the airplane; the television and communications industry; and now the computer and microprocessors that are the wave of the future. With these changes people had to be trained to work with the new technology, to master it, and to adapt it to their way of making a living. Americans perceive each new change in technology, science, and invention as progress.

Technology and invention make some work obsolete, call for new work skills, and always seem to progress the country in the direction of more material comforts, a higher standard of living, and an improvement in the social and economic structure of the nation. Whether it enhances social values, whether it makes people happy or not, it improves the material foundations of American society, which many equate with progress. New technology also brings about unintended negative consequences like more destructive weapons of war, more air and water pollution, more deaths on the highway, more crowding in urban areas, and more chaos, uncertainty, and stress. Americans still believe in the importance of technology and science and view technological advancement as progress. The work ethic accompanies and is affected by technological changes and adapts to new ways of planning and creating products and services.

The Obligation to Work

American culture has always stressed work as an obligation to society. Work is part of the social contract in which society provides protection and guarantees certain rights and freedoms in exchange for a contribution to society through work and participation in the social and political institutions of society. Work fulfills the obligation for the individual to take care of himself and his or her family. Individualism as an ideology combined with the obligation to work and translated into the idea that each person was responsible to find his own way in society, as far as occupation and means of making a living. During most of American history, work as an obligation to oneself and one's society was a given. Self-esteem and independence derived from one's ability to make a living and those who would not or could not work were stigmatized. But while individuals had an obligation to work, up until recent history, government had no reciprocal obligation to ensure that everyone had the opportunity to work. American individualism decreed that people were on their own in finding land to farm, workshops to ply trades, businesses to run, or to labor for employers. This ideology remained prevalent until the Great Depression in the 1930s. President Hoover (1928–1932) tried to stick to the old ideology, maintaining that government had no obligation to guarantee employment. The social situation became more desperate during the last two years of his administration. When President Roosevelt came into office in 1933 he and his advisers realized that if government did not step in to do something about providing work, the country would suffer catastrophic social upheaval. Since FDR, the obligation to work by individuals has been balanced somewhat by the government assuming some obligation to help the private economy provide jobs, as well as putting into place government public works programs that put people to work. The obligation of individuals to work remains strong and powerful, but the obligation of the government to provide work has waned. There have been some attempts by Congress in the past forty years to espouse a policy of guaranteeing full employment, but this idea was never given practical implementation. With the current attacks on big government, it is unlikely that the public would support a policy that says society has an obligation to provide jobs in exchange for everyone's obligation to work.

Andrew Abbott (1989:274) presents a theoretical discussion regarding the nature of work and how it is to be studied. Abbott states that there are four fundamental aspects to the modern social organization of work: (1) the division of labor; (2) the structure of occupations; (3) the structure of work organizations; and (4) the pattern of staffing. These four divisions and their interrelatedness make the study of modern work extremely complex. In earlier times, such as the colonial period in American history, the interrelations between the different aspects of work was more complete. The early division of labor first separated household and family work from artisanal work. The artisanal division of labor then divided persons into occupations whose internal structure was regulated by local law as well as by occupational custom and tradition. Market exchange and traditional or legal status precedent then provided a linking structure between division of labor, occupation, organization, and staffing. The artisan making his own product needed no division of labor, had a definable occupation, and his own organization that he staffed himself or with the help of his family or an apprentice. With the coming of new organizational forms, especially in the nineteenth century with the formation of commercial organizations and in the twentieth, with the rise of the industrial and financial corporations, the early modern occupational structure broke down. Organizations provided the new internal links within the division of labor. Labor unions that linked workers according to occupation and across organizations, modified to some extent the power of corporations and bureaucracies to control the process of work. In the United States, this influence of unions reached its high point just after World War II and into the 1950s, but has since declined, and industrial corporations and public bureaucracies, along with the professions and their organizations, now dominate the way work is conceived and staffed. In addition, the dimensions of gender, race, ethnicity, and age have become important staffing issues and have impacted the way work is viewed and analyzed. On top of all this, the entry of women into the work force in such huge numbers has changed the relationship between work and household that now requires new perspectives that differ from those of the nineteenth and eighteenth centuries. All of these questions are dealt with in Abbott's important article and should serve as a good overview regarding the issues about work that are dealt with in this book.

Assumptions inevitably enter into social science inquiry into any subject. To explain patterns in any part of social life and behavior requires some overall preconceptions, whether explicit or implicit. Curt Tausky (1992) provides a useful review of two prevailing overall assumptions regarding the study of work. He calls the two views the optimistic and the pessimistic orientations. He summarizes the pessimistic perspective as follows: (1) work is inherently unpleasant; (2) available extrinsic rewards such as money, status, and power shape work behavior; (3) words and actions in the workplace serve as a means to "look good" and get ahead; (4) performance and extrinsic reward must be linked; and (5) the least necessary effort is the usual human behavior to attain material rewards (14).

The optimistic perspective is as follows: (1) work is inherently pleasing; (2) available intrinsic rewards such as challenge, growth, and accomplishment shape work behavior; (3) words and actions are directed toward the work; (4) performance and extrinsic reward can be uncoupled if intrinsic rewards are available; and (5) effort increases with tasks that yield intrinsic rewards (14).

The reader should consult this valuable article that makes explicit our often assumed presumptions. While this book embodies analyses and material based on both perspectives, the reader will find that I tend to be a follower of the optimistic viewpoint in this book as well as others that I have written on the subject of work.

Work and the Work Ethic in Present and Future America

What is to become of work and the work ethic? Most people believe that work will always be part of the human condition. However, new technology and new social conditions cry out for new ways to organize work. For the first time in modern history, technology and the computer have created an environment where there may not be the need for everyone to work full time. What needs to be considered by futurists is how the necessary work of society is to be distributed, how it is to be compensated, and whether individuals should be given a choice regarding the type of work they do and how long they wish to do it. Can work in the future be organized so that individuals can exchange some minimum amount of work for their subsistence? Any work beyond that would be by choice and would be based on the principle of gaining pleasure from one's work. Since American ideology regards freedom as one of its core values, Americans are not likely to accept any kind of coerced labor as a means of achieving a just and fair distribution of work. Up to now, the work ethic has been a motivational substitute for coerced labor. Instead of physically forcing people to carry out work tasks, social and political leaders and the owners of enterprises have had the work ethic as a motivator for work, an ethic that appeals to the value of work as a precondition for social acceptance. Many people today seek a work ethic that goes beyond money, that seeks satisfaction from work itself. Will it be possible to create a new work ethic, something like a life ethic that views work as part of a way of life that fits into individual, family, and community values? Or is American culture destined to continue to accept the basic motivation for work as the pragmatic means to make a living while serving as a precondition for social acceptance and self-respect?

ORGANIZATION AND VIEWPOINT OF THE BOOK

The point of view of this book is anthropological in that my interest is in the cultural aspects of the American work ethic and of Americans at work. The anthropological perspective is a humanistic one, more impressionistic than scientific. The scope of this book covers the ideas about work held and practiced by Americans during four centuries of American history.

In his work, *The Peopling of North America*, Bernard Bailyn states that what is needed in American studies are not, at the moment, more technical studies but a fresh look at the whole story (1986:7). In this book I attempt to look at the whole story of the American work ethic, synthesizing it with American culture and Americans at work in the belief that work and its ethic provides an important insight into the culture and characteristics of the United States and its people.

One final caveat: being involved with the overall scope of the work ethic over four centuries, I am dealing with the broad terrain rather than specific features. In sweeping across so broad a landscape I have had to leave out much scholarly work of great importance, but the choice of the overview and space constraints have made such omissions inevitable and I apologize for them.

BIBLIOGRAPHICAL ESSAY

The opening statement on work as an essential element in the evolution of human beings is taken from Kai Erikson, "On Work and Alienation," in *The Nature of Work*, edited by Kai Erikson and Steven P. Vallas (New Haven: Yale University Press, 1990), 20–21. For additional theoretical discussion of the nature of work and its importance to human societies, see Herbert Applebaum, *Perspectives in Culture Anthropology* (Albany: State University of New York Press, 1987), 386–399. Also see Herbert Applebaum, "The Nature of Work: A Philosophical View," *Anthropology Newsletter* 32, no. 6 (September 1991).

An excellent review of the philosophical and ethical questions associated with work is contained in Edmund F. Byrne, *Work, Inc.: A Philosophical Inquiry* (Philadelphia: Temple University Press, 1990). Of particular value is Byrne's discussion of the obligation to work and the reciprocal question of the community's obligation to provide work. Byrne also deals with the modern work ethic as it has been affected by the rise and power of the modern corporation and by the growth of the new computer and robotics technology.

A good analysis of the core American ideology and its transformation in the modern period is George C. Lodge, *The New American Ideology* (New York: New York University Press, 1986). Like Byrne, Lodge discusses the effect on American society of the growth of the powerful corporation.

For an analysis of the modern work ethic and its dimensions and attributes, see Sar Levitan and Clifford M. Johnson, eds., *The Work Ethic—A Critical Analysis* (Madison, WI: Industrial Relations Research Association, 1983).

For an analysis of the work ethic and various alternatives regarding work in the twenty-first century, see Herbert Applebaum, "Work and Its Future," *Futures* 24, no. 2 (May 1992).

A critical re-evaluation of the work ethic is presented by Michael Rose, *Re-Working the Work Ethic, Economic Values and Socio-Cultural Politics* (New York: Schocken Books, 1985).

The Andrew Abbott reference is to "The New Occupational Structure: What Are the Questions?" *Work and Occupations* 16, no. 3 (August 1989), 273–291.

For the reference to Curt Tausky see his article, "Work is Desirable/Loathsome, Marx versus Freud," *Work and Occupations* 19, no. 1 (February 1992), 3–17.

For a more extended analysis of work based on the optimistic viewpoint, see Kai Erikson, "On Work and Alienation," in *The Nature of Work*, edited by Kai Erikson and Steven P. Vallas (New Haven: Yale University Press, 1990), 19–35.

The reference to Bailyn is from Bernard Bailyn, *The Peopling of North America* (New York: Alfred A. Knopf, 1986), 7.

Part I

THE COLONIAL PERIOD

1

THE AMERICAN WORK ETHIC
IN THE COLONIAL PERIOD

Colonial American history is about a land that was wild and unspoiled, about a people full of hope and opportunity, and about a culture brimming over with youth and energy. It was a time when America was greening, with its vast canopy of forests and unspoiled mountains, its rivers and lakes all teaming with fish, and game roaming the grassy plains, woods, and deserts, while at night, only a few sparkles of light appeared from campfires lit by human hands. It was also a land filled with mystery, unpredictability, savagery, and imagined horrors. After nearly two hundred years, colonial Americans in 1790 still only numbered 3,900,000, and most of them lived within fifty miles of the Atlantic Ocean. It was an abundant land nurturing many Native Americans who lived in balance with their environment, but both the land and the Native-American cultures would soon be overrun by men and women imbued with a sense of mission, believing they were favored by Providence to take control of the New World.

Colonial America represents half of U.S. history, two centuries out of four since the founding of Jamestown in 1607. It is also the period when the framework for governing the country was fashioned, a framework which remarkably has withstood the tests, changes, and challenges of societal and cultural transformations over the last two hundred years. Finally, the colonial period was the time when the ideology of work, the American work ethic, took root, and that too has withstood the test of time. Americans still value work and still consider it an obligation to society, to oneself, and to one's family.

One of the striking things about life in colonial America was the informality, as well as the uncertainty in all aspects of life, including work. Work did not proceed according to the clock nor any regular or regimented routine. If the winter was harsh and the harbor froze, the artisan might not have enough materials to carry on his work. Like the artisan, the farmer was faced with uncertainties, being subject to the vicissitudes of weather, varying fertilities of soils, and insects and pests which attacked his crops or livestock. Payments for products were just as informal and as irregular as the work itself. It could be in the form of specie or corn, of tobacco or wheat, or in the exchange of labor services, or a promise to pay at some future date. Life was unregulated by the clock, the government, or even the church. There were few institutions, enterprises, or public entities that could provide regular work or fix the prices of labor or product. Life was precarious and mystical, a continuous adventure, a searching, and a surprise. Yet, people had their families, friends, and neighbors, and more often than not they knew each other since childhood, as most lived in small, rural communities. Even urban areas were comparatively small so that life within cities was based on personal, face-to-face relationships. These communal relationships must have been a comfort for a society that had not yet reduced the environment to scientific analysis and that viewed the natural world as full of wonders, surprises, and coincidences that made the individual feel they were in the hands of forces beyond their control.

Another characteristic of colonial America was the versatility of its people. Women not only raised children and did all the cooking and cleaning for the household, they also made clothing, spun thread, wove cloth, preserved fruits, brewed beer, milked cows, raised poultry, tended vegetable gardens, made butter, candles, and soap, and assisted husbands in their work. Farmers not only mastered husbandry and cultivation, but often possessed carpentry, blacksmithing, and masonry skills. Artisans often farmed and kept animals on small plots adjoining their homes and workshops. Carpenters could also be joiners, sawyers, and furniture-makers. Masons not only laid brick but also made bricks and plastered walls. Blacksmiths not only shoed horses, they made and mended tools, fabricated railings, made and fixed locks, fixed guns, and made nails. Merchants outfitted ships, operated stores with their imports, built and operated warehouses, provided transport, and served as bankers and money lenders. Craftsmen were shopkeepers as well as artisans. People were busy. They were constantly at work, and they were involved in the affairs of their communities.

INDIVIDUALISM VERSUS SOCIAL RESPONSIBILITY

One of the persistent dilemmas of American life has been between individual rights versus responsibility for the public good. These two values have often clashed in ideological struggles, and the conflict made its appearance after the founding of the Massachusetts Bay Colony, when the elders of the Bay Colony found themselves at odds with its merchants, and continues today with the Congress of the United States at odds with the president over the issue of individual rights versus the public welfare.

During the colonial period, the clergy preached against wealth used for individualistic gain that caused the rich to become arrogant and boastful, and to believe that material values were superior to spiritual ones. The clergy preached an ethic based on people working with their own hands to make their living, while the wealthy should not be using their wealth to be idle. Preachers believed that pride was a vice which accompanied extravagant wealth, something that farmers and artisans avoided through steady work. Colonists viewed the artisan and the farmer as contributing to wealth because they produced goods, while the merchant contributed nothing, like water in a pail, which does not increase by being passed from hand to hand.

From the beginning, colonial America engaged in commerce, but people had difficulty adjusting to its effects. There was anxiety that if trade was the motive force for work, there would be an erosion of community. This was based on the notion that work was a social activity performed in the context of community, while commercial activity led to a loss of community obligations and stressed material, private values over community and spiritual values. If priority was given to economic morality, then selling one's labor for more than it was worth or buying another's labor for less than it was worth was justified, and this kind of behavior destroyed harmony between people and lessened the interdependence of individual interests with community interests.

In the 1760s, the English Parliament began to pressure the colonies to pay taxes to the British treasury. The colonists insisted that Parliament could not tax them as they were not represented in Parliament. From the perspective of many colonists, Parliament seemed determined to destroy their local economy, and they reacted to various measures with a nonimportation movement which sought to boycott all British goods coming into the colonies. To carry out this boycott, colonists would have to make sacrifices for the general good, foregoing selfish interests and giving up goods from England. It was a chance to develop domestic manufactures and to encourage moral reform. It was a chance to reflect on their attitudes toward work and how work related to individual self-interest and community interests. The issue defined and highlighted the relationship between work and morality. With the nonimportation movement the colonists could demonstrate their public spiritedness and oppose the oppressive acts of Parliament at the same time.

Merchants particularly were subject to scrutiny since they were so involved with trade. Storekeepers who sold British goods and merchants who smuggled English goods were publicly shamed and denounced. The virtuous wore American homespun. The colonists hoped that the nonimportation movement would eliminate some of the moral problems that they associated with work that was engaged in only for profit and gain. By disciplining themselves they sought to raise self-esteem. A self-sufficient America would be less corrupt. Men's work would lack selfishness, as the nonimportation movement created a sense of community solidarity as an alternative to preoccupation with individual self-interest. Farmers, artisans, free laborers, and apprentices, in contrast to merchants, came to be looked upon as models of patriotism during the Revolutionary War period. The judgment of patriots was that merchants should adhere to the traditional standards of public virtue, that individual interests ought to be sacrificed for those of the whole society.

However, during the late colonial period, many Americans tended to identify the public interest, at least partially, with commercial prosperity. The attention paid to the social aspects of work diminished and commerce was deemed essential for the success of the revolution. All kinds of economic activity provided opportunities for selfishness. With the disruptions of the Revolutionary War, laborers could demand higher wages, farmers could withhold goods from the market, and merchants could charge high prices for goods. After the Revolutionary War, self-interest and the pursuit of economic gain overcame any concern with morality and the public spiritedness of work. Acquisitive and commercial interests were unleashed by the revolution. By the 1780s, a variety of self-conscious interests were clamoring for help and protection from the state governments and the weak Confederation Congress. In the 1780s, the revolution's leaders had a glimpse of what America, in part, was soon to become—a scrambling society dominated by the pecuniary interests of ordinary people—and they did not like what they saw. For many of the revolution's leaders, masses of ordinary citizens displayed licentiousness and self-interestedness in their pursuit of happiness, which threatened the grand experiment in republicanism.

BIBLIOGRAPHICAL ESSAY

For a discussion of the Puritan ethic as it relates to work, see Edmund S. Morgan, "The Puritan Ethic and the American Revolution," in *In Search of Early America: The William and Mary Quarterly, 1943–1993* (Richmond, VA: William Byrd Press, 1993). For a short, but good introduction to work in early America, see Marcus Rediker, "Good Hands, Stout Hearts and Fast Feet: The History and Culture of Working People in Early America," *Labour/Le Travailleur* 10 (Autumn 1982), 123–144. For a more comprehensive look at work in early America, especially the introduction, see Stephen Innes, ed. *Work and Labor in Early America* (Chapel Hill: University of North Carolina Press, 1988).

An excellent study on work and the diversity of work skills among colonial Americans in Springfield is that of Stephen Innes, *Labor in a New Land: Economy and Society in Seventeenth-Century Springfield* (Princeton, NJ: Princeton University Press, 1983). Innes has a number of tables showing various individuals and the wide range of jobs, skills, and occupations practiced and held by Springfield inhabitants.

Good studies of the way of life, the work ethic, and the value systems of early New England communities include: Philip J. Greven, *Four Generations: Population, Land and Family in Colonial Andover, Massachusetts* (Ithaca, NY: Cornell University Press, 1970); Kenneth A. Lockridge, *A New England Town: The First Hundred Years: Dedham, Massachusetts, 1636–1736* (New York: W. W. Norton, 1970); Darrett B. Rutman, *Husbandmen of Plymouth: Farms and Villages in the Old Colony* (Boston: Beacon Press, 1967).

Studies of society and culture in colonial Virginia, including the culture of tobacco growing and working tobacco plantations include: Thomas Jefferson Wertenbaker, *Patrician and Plebeian in Virginia* (New York: Russell and Russell, 1958 [orig. 1910]); Allan Kulikoff, *Tobacco and Slaves: The Development of Southern Cultures in the Chesapeake, 1680–1800* (Chapel Hill: University of North Carolina Press, 1986); Timothy H. Breen, *Tobacco Culture* (Princeton, NJ: Princeton University Press, 1985). On the early history of the founding of the Virginia colony and a study of the economics of tobacco culture using indentured servants and slaves, there is the classic work by Edmund S. Morgan, *American Slavery, American Freedom: The Ordeal of Colonial Virginia* (New York: W. W. Norton, 1975).

For insightful studies of indentured labor in colonial America see the following: One of the most complete studies is David Galenson, *White Servitude in Colonial America: An Economic Analysis* (Cambridge, England: Cambridge University Press, 1981). Russell R. Menard, "From Servants to Slaves: The Transformation of the Chesapeake Labor System,"

Southern Studies 16, no. 4 (Winter), 355–390, presents the most plausible thesis for the change from indentured servitude to black slavery at the end of the seventeenth century. Mildred Campbell presents important information on the backgrounds and occupations of indentured servants in "Social Origins of Some Early Americans," in *Seventeenth-Century America: Essays in Colonial History*, edited by James Morton Smith (Chapel Hill: University of North Carolina Press, 1959). Abbot Emerson Smith, *Colonists in Bondage, 1607–1776* (Chapel Hill: University of North Carolina Press, 1947), deals with many of the social aspects of indentured servitude, including the treatment of indentured servants, their experience in court, and their chances for becoming freeholders after the term of their servitude ends.

A good introduction to what early America must have seemed like physically and psychologically as a wilderness and frontier can be found in Paul A. Carter, "The Dream of the West," in *Revolt Against Destiny: An Intellectual History of the United States* (New York: Columbia University Press, 1989).

On the uncertainties and informalities of life in colonial America, particularly among craftsmen, see Gary Nash, *The Urban Crucible* (Cambridge, MA: Harvard University Press, 1986); also David Freeman Hawke, *Everyday Life in Early America* (New York: Harper & Row, 1988), particularly Chapter 7; and Carl Bridenbaugh, *Early Americans* (New York: Oxford University Press, 1981). Seamen played an important part in colonial seaport towns and for an insight into their way of life, see Marcus Rediker, "The Anglo-American Seamen as Collective Workers, 1700–1750," in *Work and Labor in Early America*, edited by Stephen Innes, 252–286.

For an excellent, beautifully written discussion of the Puritan heritage, there is Vernon L. Parrington's *Main Currents in American Thought*, Vol. I, Book I: *Liberalism and Puritanism* (New York: Harcourt, Brace, 1954); also see Perry Miller and Thomas H. Johnson, *The Puritan Way of Life* (Boston: D. C. Heath, 1967); and Perry Miller, "Errand into the Wilderness," in *In Search of Early America: The William and Mary Quarterly, 1943–1993* (Richmond, VA: William Byrd Press, 1993); and Peter N. Carroll, *Significance of Puritanism and the Wilderness: The Intellectual and the New England Frontier, 1629–1700* (New York: Columbia University Press, 1969).

One of the best discussions of the theme of individual rights and responsibilities to the community can be found in J. E. Crowley, *This Sheba Self: The Conceptualization of Economic Life in Eighteenth-Century America* (Baltimore: Johns Hopkins University Press, 1974). Crowley has an extensive discussion of the nonimportation movement and how it related to colonial attitudes toward work. For an equally excellent discussion of work as it related to individualism and communitarianism during the American Revolution and afterward, see Gordon Wood, *The Radicalism of the American Revolution* (New York: Alfred A. Knopf, 1992), 65–69, 106–108, 247, 250, 418–419. On the issue of distrust of merchants and how they were seen as undermining the communitarian spirit of the Massachusetts Bay Colony, see Bernard Bailyn, *The New England Merchants in the Seventeenth Century* (Cambridge, MA: Harvard University Press, 1955).

For a discussion of the ideology of independence in colonial America, see James A. Henretta, "The Transition to Capitalism in America," in *The Transformation of Early American History: Society, Authority and Ideology*, edited by James A. Henretta, Michael Kammen, and Stanley N. Katz (New York: Alfred A. Knopf, 1991), 223–226.

2

COLONIAL FARMERS

In the beginning America was the land and the land was America. Land was the dream that drew settlers to American shores, the dream of ownership that had eluded most of them in Europe. Land was waiting for them, waiting to be acquired, granted, seized, bargained for, rented, and above all, worked on and accumulated for one's family and heirs. In the beginning land was so abundant there seemed no way to exhaust it or fill it.

Settled land was of little use without backbreaking and continuous work. Work was the key to success. Those who would not work could starve, go back to England, or die in the wilderness. There were shirkers, but they were ostracized, embarrassed, or punished by the tiny communities struggling for a foothold on the edge of a continent. The early American work ethic was agrarian, and the early towns, villages, and urban areas were never far removed in spirit and outlook from the farms which fed them. Early America was fluid. There was little strict division of labor. Almost everyone worked and did many things, combining the work of a farmer with that of an artisan, the work of a planter with that of a trader, the work of a fur trader with that of a shipper. And early America was open to that which was new and novel. The settler may have come as an artisan, but was ready to turn to farming. Yet, in spite of diversity, the land was the foundation of society: "At the beginning of settlement and for many generations thereafter, agrarian society and the leadership that an agrarian society developed played a paramount part in the civilization of North America" (Wright, 1957:1).

Most settlers knew that without work they would not survive. They willingly accepted their responsibilities and worked shoulder to shoulder planting fields, repairing fences, fixing roads, harvesting crops, building fortifications, and accepting guard duty. Even leaders set to work. Tragically, John Carver, first governor of the Plymouth Colony, died because he was not used to the hard work in which he was engaged. Land was worked communally, but after a time, individuals and families secured tenure to their land and decided for themselves, how, where, and what to labor at. The colonies began to prosper under the voluntary regime that farmers and planters imposed upon themselves, working, saving, and investing in land, tools, livestock, and possessions for themselves and their heirs. Within a few years of settlement, the colonial farmers in the separate colonies differed from their English counterparts by how they lived as they expanded into the American wilderness. They were forced to do for themselves what they once depended on craftsmen to do for them. They learned to supply nearly all their wants from the land and the forests, as they built houses, erected fences, tended livestock, made clothing, and fashioned tools. These settlers were a breed captured in the American term, jacks-of-all-trades.

LAND OWNERSHIP

The basic economic unit in eighteenth-century America was the farm. Eighty percent or more of the population depended on farming for their livelihood. A majority of colonial farmers owned their land outright, as land was not a scarce resource and was sold at relatively low prices. Some colonists received land through the headright system, as in Virginia, which granted fifty acres of land to every man who paid for his passage, plus fifty acres for each person brought over. Others received land through the division of common property, which was practiced in New England townships during the early settlement period. Most farmers either inherited their land or purchased it, sometimes after having leased for a number of years. In England, over 80 percent of English farm workers were tenants or itinerant laborers. In the American colonies, only upstate New York maintained tenancy rates comparable to those in Europe. In Massachusetts and Pennsylvania, tenancy was used as an avenue for young people and new arrivals with little capital and a strong capacity for work to acquire funds to purchase a farm of their own. There were areas in the Chesapeake Bay where landless tenants cultivated the poorest lands and practiced subsistence agriculture. But most American farmers were land-owners. It was part of the culture and ideology of being independent.

Basically, there were three types of farming communities in colonial America: frontier, subsistence, and commercial. The feature of the frontier society was high mobility. Few pioneers had large properties, with land more equally distributed than in older areas. Land in subsistence farm areas was cheap, so that even if many pioneers at first were landless, they soon acquired farms. Only one in five families were still without land at the end of the eighteenth century, but few men acquired wealth as these communities produced little surplus. Commercial farm communities contained far more propertyless men than frontier or subsistence communities. In commercial farm areas, farm laborers, indentured servants, and tenants were common, with this landless class making up nearly half the population in commercial regions such as Chester County, Pennsylvania. The presence of far more slaves in the South increased the proportion of landless workers in that region, and the upper class was larger and wealthier and more concentrated than in any of the other colonies.

Clearing the Land

For the early settlers the land must have looked awesome with its enormous forests that stretched beyond the horizon. Small trees cut easily and were used for building or fencing, but large trees defied rapid clearing with ax and saw. John Smith said that in Virginia they "spoiled" the woods, that is, they cut a notch in the tree and peeled the bark. The tree would cease to sprout and within a year or two would decay, and then the farmer would chop the tree down and cut it up for firewood. Some stumps were so large and heavily rooted farmers would plant around them, and later, after rot set in, they were pulled out with the help of oxen.

Clearing land also involved the removal of rock, particularly in New England. It required sixty days of one able-bodied adult to clear the surface rock on a farm of eighty acres. More rocks worked their way up to ground level after the surface rocks were cleared. Farmers hauled small rocks in wheelbarrows and carts, while large rocks were moved on sleds pulled by draft animals. New York and New England farmers sledded stones and boulders to the borders of their fields and fitted them together into stone walls to mark off their property.

Throughout colonial America, cutting trees was one kind of work that farmers took up as easily as they reached for their axes. The trees of the nearby forests and woodlots offered a continuous supply of timber that was converted into everything from firewood to shingles and furniture. In an economy that used wood as the chief source of fuel in both houses and shops, a tremendous amount of timber was needed. Each year the colonies exported large numbers of shingles and many more were used by the colonists for their own homes and buildings. Most farmers fashioned shingles during the off-season. Almost everything shipped or stored in the colonies was packed in wooden casks made by coopers, who bought their wood from farmers who had already cut and shaped the material. The streams of colonial America were dotted with sawmills and gristmills which used the fall of the river, even if it was only a few feet, to power water wheels that transferred the energy of water to run saws and turn millstones.

AGRICULTURAL METHODS IN COLONIAL AMERICA

With lots of land and a shortage of labor, colonials held back from spending labor to improve the soil. It was easier to plant a field for six to ten years until its fertility ran out and then move to another field than it was to manure fields or plant legumes and clover to restore the fertility of the soil. This was the practice in England, where shortage of land forced farmers to improve their soils in the face of falling yields. In the colonies, farmers tried to accumulate enough reserve land to move from field to field. Owners left old land to become overgrown with weeds, bushes, young trees, and "trash" (broken branches, leaves, stones). Agricultural reformers thought this was reprehensible as land allowed to fallow developed a scruffy, unkempt look. With a twenty-year fallow period early Americans cleared less than 50 percent of their land. In 1784, 49 percent of the land was cleared in

Suffolk County, Massachusetts, and in Chester County, a rich agricultural region with markets in Philadelphia and Wilmington, only 40 percent of the land was cleared by 1780.

By European standards, colonial farmers appeared backward, but with an abundance of land, it may have been more rational not to engage in extensive use of fertilizers nor to use multiple plowing, but rather to use the land intensively for a limited number of years and then to let it stand to renew itself. In contrast to the British, colonials appeared wasteful, accepting small yields, not caring sufficiently for livestock, using primitive tools, and resisting innovations. Colonial practices seem to have been consistent with an economy in which capital was expensive and land cheap. George Washington said that because land was cheap and labor expensive, much ground was scratched over and none improved as it ought to have been. Thomas Jefferson added that an acre of land could be bought cheaper than it would have cost to manure it.

The long fallow had an effect on fencing practices among colonial farmers. In England, hedges and stone walls were used as permanent fences. Hedges could be cut for fuel and harbored small game animals. They were neat and pleasing to the eye. George Washington, for one, was fond of hedges as boundary markers between his fields and very particular about their being kept neat and orderly. Most American farmers used worm-rail zigzag fences, which were easy to put up and move as each new field was cultivated. Many considered them unsightly, but they suited American conditions. When American farmers started to use hedges and stone for their fences it marked the passing of the long-fallow agriculture, and the introduction of permanent, continuous crop fields, and the system of soil renewal through manuring, planting clover, and short-fallow methods.

The Colonial Farmer

Despite regional variations in soils and climate, the colonial farmer was able to grow sufficient food to feed his immediate family. The largest portion of a farmer's output was consumed on the farm. Apart from a few areas, perhaps the rice and tobacco regions of the South and farms located near major cities, the outlook and value system of most farm units in colonial America was not oriented toward commercial agriculture. Yet the special circumstance of a land-abundant colonial America permitted the farmer to achieve an unusually high standard of living, certainly as compared with European farmers and peasants.

The need for reciprocal relationships within the rural locality was important in colonial America. Households rubbed up against one another, sharing boundary lines and, sometimes, mutual fences. Farmers joined together to contribute taxes and manpower, to build and maintain roads, and to build churches that linked them to each other. In addition, reciprocal neighboring at social gatherings such as corn husking, sewing bees, dances, and church socials drew people closer. Community formation in colonial America was largely the result of a voluntary joining of free individuals on their own land, unlike European relations on the land, which were marked by entrenched social classes and obligations of leaseholders and tenants to landlords. Status and the work ethic in America were strongly related to ownership of land, with voluntarism and cooperation operating as strong bonds between rural neighbors. To assure that one's children retained their status, parents sought to accumulate land to pass on to them. In all localities, households formed into community structures reflecting the social pressure to own and acquire land and pass it on to one's heirs. Ownership of land equated with independence and control over work and resources, a highly valued ethic in colonial America.

Gregory Stiverson (1976:37–44) has noted that if early American farmers were ranged from bare subsistence at one end to completely commercialized agriculture at the other end, most would cluster nearer the former than the latter. Many northern farmers (the number is a matter of controversy) were not deeply involved in the larger markets of the Atlantic trade between the colonies and Europe. They did not think of themselves as agricultural entrepreneurs out to maximize profits as we would witness agribusiness today. They swapped goods and services with each other and with shopkeepers and merchants. Some of the exchanges were simple and direct barter. More often than not the exchanges took the form of credits and debits recorded in monetary terms, which were not usually paid in cash but entered in each person's account book. Through these numerous exchanges farmers built up complicated webs of credits and debits. Because such debts were individually small and locally owed, they often lacked explicitly stated promises to pay and implied a measure of mutual trust which linked people into strong, local bonds with each other.

Subsistence Model versus Market Model

There are two views on the orientation of colonial farmers toward their work. One is the subsistence model that stresses communitarian and family values over individualistic, profit-maximizing goals among farmers in the northern colonies. In this view, the behavior of northern farm families was not fundamentally concerned with market forces until decades after the colonial period, well into the nineteenth century. There were transactions among colonial farmers involving the barter of commodities and direct exchange of labor among neighbors, but such reciprocal arrangements did not indicate the existence of formal markets. The subsistence model of colonial farmers' work orientation argues that the work ethic and value system of these farmers stressed subsistence and the long-term security of the farm, and that farmers did not try to maximize production of cash crops, but instead, became involved with the market only when they had a good year and produced some surpluses. Subsistence farmers avoided risks and were suspicious of innovations, behavior for which they were criticized by reformers and English observers of colonial American husbandry. Colonial farmers in the North tried to diversify their crops and livestock and the use of their land, and spread their work requirements throughout the year. Their planning was family oriented as far as acquiring land and sustaining heirs for the future.

Market model interpreters of colonial farmers argue that they were latent entrepreneurs, willing to take risks and accept innovations, but that such farmers were frustrated in their drive for profits by high labor costs, primitive farm methods, and poor transportation. While it is hard for anyone to argue that colonial America was a market economy, market-model interpreters see colonial farmers as individuals involved in enterprises that stressed the business aspect more than the family aspect. In this view, colonial farmers were unavoidably involved in a host of market transactions, if for no other reason than weaving cloth, milling grain, and making other household products was difficult on the average farm. Farmers sought independence, but they also wished to improve their living standards by purchasing carpets, furniture, tea sets, wall coverings, and better clothing toward the end of the eighteenth century.

It is probably true that in certain regions in colonial America, farmers were more oriented toward markets than in others. Certainly, southern tobacco and rice planters in the tidewater along the Virginia coast and in South Carolina produced crops for a commercial market. Even on large plantations, subsistence agriculture was important for the sustenance of the work force. In the North, agricultural regions around Philadelphia and Boston, which had urban markets as an outlet for surplus products, were commercially oriented. But for an agrarian society, the distinctions between subsistence and commercial activities were blurred, since production for home consumption and production for sale or exchange were complementary and often involved the same products. Still, most small farmers in the North, South, and in the Middle Colonies placed the subsistence needs of their families and the long-term security of their farms ahead of short-run, income-producing farming. To have done otherwise would have been an invitation to disaster. There was no such thing as absolute self-sufficiency, even among farmers along the frontier, and they had to purchase certain tools and necessities from storekeepers and traders, and take their grain for milling to the grist mill. Nevertheless, most farmers could grow much of what they needed and acquire the rest from friends and neighbors through mutual exchange.

ATTITUDES TOWARD COLONIAL FARMERS

Some of the elite often described farmers in uncomplimentary terms, as "common sort of people," or "the rabble." Others, agricultural reformers, viewed colonial farmers as improvident and wasteful. Still others, persons of a liberal or polite education, viewed farm life as intellectually debilitating, lacking desirable refinements, and practiced by those in the lowest walks of life. But most Americans of all classes regarded agriculture as the ideal occupation and the farmer as the ideal citizen. While urban life was looked upon as corrupting, the farmer was seen as being close to nature, and while he might not get rich, he enjoyed the good life. The life of the farmer was friendly to health, contentment, liberty, and religion, with agriculture viewed as promoting all that was good in human beings. Colonists believed that it strengthened the mind without enervating the body, increasing virtue without introducing vice. Jefferson, in a letter to John Jay in 1783, viewed cultivators of the earth as valuable citizens, vigorous, independent, and virtuous, tied to their country's interests. Over and over, the yeomanry were seen by American leaders as the main prop and support of the state, and to them alone could the freedom of the country be safely entrusted. Farmers stood at the apex of the prestige order, below which were the professionals, then the merchants and artisans, and at the bottom, the laborers, servants, and slaves.

The key to an agrarian culture is an ethic that recognizes the importance of hard, physical labor within a framework of yearly cycles of tasks. Production of agricultural products involves a complex relationship between the actual cultivation of crops and the farmer's cultural values. Each crop dictated a slightly different production schedule. Visits with friends and relatives, even life-cycle events such as marriages and baptisms, had to be fitted into the agricultural work schedule. The tobacco calendar was relentlessly demanding; the cultivation of wheat culminated annually in a harvest that required intense labor and an enlarged work force; animal husbandry required constant concern over the safety and health of the stock, including birthing and veterinary care. Over time, men living within a specific region were judged by the quality of their crops. These standards became an unconscious part of daily life, slowly determining the life style and work schedule so that it became a mark of the local culture. Young people and migrants in the area learned that one grew a certain crop in a certain way in that part of the country. To do otherwise was unthinkable, an antisocial act that ran counter to the way of life of the farming community. At markets and fairs, in newspapers and almanacs, in face-to-face relations at grinding mills or warehouses, farmers reaffirmed a traditional relationship between crop and work culture. A farming mentality developed across particular regions through such exchanges and it encompassed the totality of beliefs regarding the most suitable use of land and the collective view as to the techniques of working the land. A farmer's ideology and values were in large part bound up with his daily work experience. In colonial America, the work ethic of the farmer was an important ingredient in the cultural values of American society.

BIBLIOGRAPHICAL ESSAY

For a general introduction to colonial farming see David Freeman Hawke, "The Farm," in *The Colonial Experience* (Indianapolis: Bobbs-Merrill, 1966). On the agrarian way of life as a cultural system, see Louis B. Wright, *The Cultural Life of the American Colonies, 1607–1763* (New York: Harper & Row, 1957). On the experience of the early Pilgrims and their struggles to sustain themselves through work and other efforts, see George F. Willison, ed., *The Pilgrim Reader: The Story of the Pilgrims as Told by Themselves and Their Contemporaries Friendly and Unfriendly* (Garden City, NJ: Doubleday, 1953). Another excellent study that presents a picture of village and farm life in New England is Sumner Chilton Powell, *Puritan Village: The Formation of a New England Town* (Middletown, CT: Wesleyan University Press, 1963). For the views of John Smith and his complaints about having too many gentlemen and not enough workers, see Aubrey Land, ed., *Bases of the Plantation Society* (Columbia: University of South Carolina Press, 1969), document 2, page 16.

For an overview of agriculture in colonial America, see Edward J. Perkins, "Farmers and Planters," in *The Economy of Colonial America*, 2nd ed. (New York: Columbia University Press, 1988). Also, see John J. McCusker and Russell R. Menard, "Early American

Agriculture," in *The Economy of British America, 1607–1789* (Chapel Hill: University of North Carolina Press, 1991). The McCusker and Menard volume contains one of the most comprehensive bibliographies on colonial America, touching on all aspects of life in the colonies. On the history of agriculture in the North, see Percy Wells Bidwell and John I. Falconer, *History of Agriculture in the Northern United States, 1620–1860*, Publication No. 358 (Washington, DC: Carnegie Institute of Washington, 1925). On the history of agriculture in the South, see Lewis Cecil Gray, *History of Agriculture in the Southern United States to 1860*, Publication No. 430 (Washington, DC: Carnegie Institute of Washington, 1933 [rev. ed. 1958]).

On the nature and the backbreaking effort that it took to clear land, see Howard S. Russell, *A Long, Deep Furrow: Three Centuries of Farming in New England* (Hanover, NH: University Press of New England, 1976). Also see David Freeman Hawke, *Everyday Life in Early America*, (New York: Harper & Row, 1988), 32–34. For a discussion of the difficulties of living in a forest environment, including the problem of clearing the land with a primitive technology, see Charles F. Carroll, "The Forest Society of New England," in *America's Wooden Age: Aspects of its Early Technology*, edited by Brooke Hindle (Tarrytown, NY: Sleepy Hollow Press, 1985), 13–36.

On the technology and the culture of corn cultivation, see Nicholas P. Hardeman, *Shucks, Shocks, and Hominy Blocks: Corn as a Way of Life in Pioneer America* (Baton Rouge: Louisiana State University Press, 1981). Also see David Freeman Hawke on the virtues of corn cultivation in *Everyday Life in Early America*, 37.

For tobacco growing and the culture of tobacco cultivation see, Timothy H. Breen, *Tobacco Culture* (Princeton, NJ: Princeton University Press, 1985); also Timothy H. Breen, "The Culture of Agriculture: The Symbolic World of the Tidewater Planter, 1760–1790," in *Saints and Revolutionaries: Essays on Early American History*, edited by David D. Hall, John M. Murrin, and Thad W. Tate (New York: W. W. Norton, 1984). Another excellent study of growing tobacco and its culture is by Gloria L. Main, *Tobacco Colony: Life in Early Maryland, 1650–1720* (Princeton, NJ: Princeton University Press, 1982).

On the cultivation of wheat see John T. Lemon, *The Best Poor Man's Country: A Geographic Study of Early Southeastern Pennsylvania* (New York: W. W. Norton, 1976). Also see Perkins, "Farmers and Planters," 62–63. On the importance of millers and their grist-mills in colonial rural areas, see John J. McCusker and Russell R. Menard, "Early American Agriculture," 321–325.

For a discussion of agricultural methods among colonial farmers, particularly the use of the long-fallow method and zigzag fencing procedures, see Richard L. Bushman, "Opening the American Countryside," in *The Transformation of Early American History*, edited by James A. Henretta, Michael Kammen, and Stanley N. Katz (New York: Alfred A. Knopf, 1991), 239–256. For a detailed discussion of farming methods in the colonial period and some of the criticisms by contemporary observers of colonial farmers, see Harry J. Carman, ed., *American Husbandry* (New York: Columbia University Press, 1939). On George Washington's and Thomas Jefferson's comments on colonial agriculture, see McCusker and Menard, "Early American Agriculture," 295, 305–306, n. 22. On George Washington's fondness for hedges as boundary markers, see James Thomas Flexner, *Washington: The Indispensable Man* (New York: Penguin Books, 1984), 50.

On subsistence and market orientations in colonial agriculture, see Gregory A. Stiverson, "Early American Farming: A Comment," *Agricultural History*, no. 50 (1976), 37–44. On the subsistence model of colonial agriculture, its foremost advocate is James A. Henretta, and his ideas can be found in "Families and Farms: Mentalité in Pre-Industrial America," *William and Mary Quarterly* 35, no. 1 (January 1978), 3–32; and in his 1980 "Reply to James

T. Lemon's Comment on Mentalité in Pre-Industrial America," *William and Mary Quarterly* 37, no. 4 (October 1980), 696–700. For the market model see James T. Lemon, *The Best Poor Man's Country: A Geographical Study of Early Southeastern Pennsylvania* (New York: W. W. Norton, 1976); and Lemon's "Comment on James A. Henretta's 'Families and Farms: Mentalité in Pre-Industrial America,' " *William and Mary Quarterly* 37, no. 4 (October 1980), 688–696. For other comments on the issue see Carole Shammas, "How Self-Sufficient Was Early America?" *Journal of Interdisciplinary History* 13, no. 2 (1982), 247–272; another is by Bettye Hobbs Pruitt, "Self-Sufficiency and the Agricultural Economy of Eighteenth-Century Massachusetts," *William and Mary Quarterly* 41, no. 3 (July 1984), 333–364; and another comment on the issue from Joyce Appleby, "Commercial Farming and the 'Agrarian Myth' in the Early Republic," *Journal of American History* 68, no. 4 (March 1982), 833–849. For Timothy H. Breen's views regarding those of Henretta and Lemon, see "Back to Sweat and Toil: Suggestions for the Study of Agricultural Work in Early America," *Pennsylvania History* 49, no. 4 (October 1982), 241–258. As Breen's title suggests, he believes that the actual work of farmers should be studied if we are to gain insights into colonial American agriculture.

For attitudes toward colonial American farmers see Jackson Turner Main, *The Social Structure of Revolutionary America* (Princeton, NJ: Princeton University Press, 1965), 209–211. For the Jefferson quote on farmers see his *Writings* (New York: Library of America, 1984), 818. Other views of yeomen farmers can be found in Wesley Frank Craven, *The Southern Colonies in the Seventeenth Century* (Baton Rouge: Louisiana State University Press, 1949), and in Thomas Jefferson Wertenbaker, *Patrician and Plebeian in Virginia* (New York: Russell and Russell, 1958 [orig. 1910]). And for a viewpoint from a contemporary, on the virtues of farming and farmers, see Michel-Guillaume Jean de Crevecoeur (J. Hector St. John), *Sketches of Eighteenth-Century America*, edited by Henri Bourdin et al. (New Haven, CT: Yale University Press, 1925).

For additional analysis and description of farmers in colonial society, see Alan Kulikoff, *The Agrarian Origins of American Capitalism* (Charlottesville: University of Virginia Press, 1992), 34–42. Kulikoff makes the following comments regarding colonial farmers:

> Urban workers shared with yeomen a republican producer ideology, an insistence on looking at themselves as economically independent and struggles to control their own labor . . . yeomen owned land, the means of production, property that ensured their independence and endowed their skills with great economic meaning. . . . They participated in commodity markets with regularity—but only to sustain noncommercial neighborhood networks. . . . (36)

> The new American reality of plentiful land combined with the inherited goals of the descendants of settlers led ordinary white families to forge a new class system in rural America based upon widespread landownership. During the last half of the eighteenth century, between two-thirds and three-quarters of householders were freeholders who owned land in places as disparate in social structure as Connecticut, eastern Massachusetts, Long Island, eastern New Jersey, and tidewater Virginia—a far greater proportion than in England. (39)

3

COLONIAL CRAFTSMEN

In colonial America the terms artisan, craftsman, tradesman, and mechanic were frequently used interchangeably; thus they are used so in this chapter. Artisans or craftsmen were men who owned their own tools, possessed a skill, and served an apprenticeship to learn their trade. They were a heterogeneous group; some owned their own shops, some worked for wages in the building and shipbuilding industries, and some were journeymen who worked for wages in the shops of master craftsmen.

Colonial times in America were times of limited mechanization and craftsmen worked with a few simple tools to directly manipulate their raw materials. They purchased their own supplies—wood, bars of iron, cloth, leather, brass, silver and gold. The rhythms of work were intermittent, with physical work, socializing, and breaks for talk or a drink blended together. Craftsmen worked slowly, not seeing any reason for haste in any particular job. They constantly changed tasks or stopped work to deal with the flow of people who came through their shops. The work week was frequently interrupted by religious holidays, weddings, funerals, feasts, and other community or neighborly activities. In the craft system, work and leisure intermingled so that awareness of being part of a larger social community permeated the workshop.

THE ARTISAN WORK ETHIC

The work ethic so central to colonial society rested on the habits and traditions of artisans and craftspersons, as well as that of farmers. Artisan work was task oriented rather than time oriented, with craftsmen usually working in their own homes or lofts, setting their own pace of work. They might spend Monday and even Tuesday at the tavern or at some recreational activity and then work at a rapid pace the rest of the week through Saturday. Work patterns were irregular, varying from trade to trade, shop to shop, week to week. Moderation, integrity, and industry were the ethics of artisan work rather than speed, taking advantage of others, or manipulation of the market.

Artisans desired to earn a decent living, not to experience the poverty of the laboring poor of Europe. Their sense of pride, desire for recognition, and desire to contribute to the communities in which they worked and resided were of great importance to artisans. Many members of the elite considered artisans to be manual workers and therefore inferior, which clashed with the artisans' self-image as contributors to society. To merchants, lawyers, and wealthy landowners, craftsmen and mechanics were people belonging to the lower orders, neither worthy nor capable of aspiring to social leadership. Those in positions of leadership in the colonies expected artisans and working people to accede to the wisdom and guidance of the wealthier, better educated, and better bred elite. However, this all changed with the American Revolution, during which artisans and laborers helped make up the ranks of the Sons of Liberty as well as being in the forefront of the nonimportation movement. After the Revolution, artisans and mechanics wanted to share in the nation's politics and government, and they wanted respect as men of independence.

In order to assert his self-respect, the artisan emphasized his economic and social independence, meaning that he could maintain himself through his own labor and fend off any need for poor relief. Besides economic rewards, artisan independence meant that he could control his hours of work, have an autonomous existence outside the workplace, and enjoy respectability in his community. The artisan ethic also involved the notion of belonging to a trade, of being part of a corporate body, and of having a community outlook. This traditional ethic stressed the mutuality of craftsmen in their relationships with each other and a joint responsibility to serve their communities. This was challenged in the late eighteenth century and in the nineteenth century by the rise of a laissez-faire ethos that celebrated individualism, competition, and the acquisitive spirit.

E. P. Thompson, the British historian labeled the older, artisan view and its reflection in social structure the "moral economy." In this economy, the work of artisans, tradesmen, and craftsmen carried social responsibilities tied to the good of the community. This system put limitations on artisan behavior. The community held him responsible for his conduct, his products, and his contribution to society. Artisans in Philadelphia complained in 1779 when Robert Morris wanted to ship grain out of the colony during a food shortage. They argued that while it was his property, all property was social in origin and carried with it responsibilities to the community. To the artisan, property was legitimate if it was the product of visible labor. Locke derived his concept of property from a belief that private property was a natural right flowing from each individual's property in his own labor. Locke tied the legitimacy of property directly to individual labor, stating that men should accumulate only enough to meet their needs, leaving the rest for others.

Howard Rock singled out a colonial journal, *The Independent Mechanic*, as a source of writings on the craftsman's work ethic. The journal encouraged artisans to live an honest and industrious life, condemning drunkenness, fighting, and vices. The journal warned artisans against living on credit and told them to contract only for what they could produce. Artisans were exhorted to cherish a harmonious family life, not to depend on wealth for happiness. In order to have a clear conscience, artisans were told not to practice fraud and to be free of poverty through the application of their own industry. In making its case for a moderate, sober, and family-centered life for artisans, *The Independent Mechanic* contrasted this proposed conduct for artisans with the pernicious values associated with the upper classes; values that led to idleness, disdain for work, and debauchery.

The journal singles out three aspects of the artisan's ethic. One was the Puritan work ethic, which valued work undertaken not for selfish gain and luxury, but rather in the spirit of industry and frugality oriented toward the common good. The second was the value of a free, egalitarian, and republican government that could set the moral direction for the nation, which was based on the participation of mechanics and farmers as the true guardians of republican virtue. The third was the belief in artisan self-control and self-reliance that would lead to economic independence for himself and his family.

The artisan work ethic included joy of creativity in work, something more than just pride in one's work. The extra designs that were worked into a wagon or a brass lock had no functional value but expressed the individuality and the spontaneity of the craftsman. Master masons would carve designs into the facades of buildings, furniture makers would carve elaborate designs in a table top, and wheelwrights would carve scrollwork into finished wagons. All of these were individual forms of creativity in the making of products, which otherwise were governed by rules based upon the traditions and practices of the craft.

Artisans and craftsmen performed work for its own sake, beyond the ulterior motivation as a means to a livelihood. Colonial craftsmen, with their Calvinist leanings, largely believed that God willed them to a calling and that work was good, not only because of the rewards it brought, but because the act of work permitted them to fulfill the social role that God and the community had assigned to them. They worked as craftsmen because their fathers and grandfathers had worked as craftsmen and had instilled in them the craft work ethic. If a colonial American became a mason or a cabinetmaker it was because everyone in his community expected him to follow the path of his forebears, and he could expect to find fulfillment in his community by doing what the rest of the community expected of him. A craftsman knew his role in life, and in following this path he was anchored to a way of life.

Before the spirit of acquisitiveness and competition which marked the rise of industrialism in the nineteenth century, craftsmen in the colonial period believed that the individual had to defer individual advantage in favor of the welfare of the community. There were two communities to consider for the craftsman. One was his occupational group and the other was the urban area or rural community in which he resided. The craftsman's values required him to act in such a way as not to injure the interests of his fellow craftsmen in his particular trade. He was also tied to a set of rules in the larger community and he had a strong sense of place, whether he lived in a city such as Boston, New York, or Philadelphia, or in a small village where he might be a blacksmith or a weaver. Membership in the citizenry of the city or the village was prominent in the identity of the artisan, since his entire welfare and that of his family was bound up with the welfare and success of the town or city in which he resided.

This moral universe was the ideal. Actual practice departed from the ideal, especially as changes took place in colonial society. The ideal was that the apprentice would move up the ladder to the status of journeyman and eventually become a master. But as the eighteenth century drew to a close, many found themselves stuck in the position of journeyman. A permanent class of journeymen arose, with no hope of becoming masters. The apprenticeship system began to break down as youths chafed under the regime of the indenture contract, and many ran away or refused to complete or honor their contracts. Masters, for their part, were willing to give up these contracts as they found it a burden to provide room and board for their apprentices and journeymen. They preferred hiring employees to whom they had no obligation other than paying wages.

Another departure from the ideal came in the form of inferior workmanship. It is often assumed that because articles in colonial times were made by artisans and craftsmen that they were always of the highest quality. But inferior goods were made and sold in colonial days. Casks of false sizes, made of green staves were often passed off on unsuspecting purchasers. There was bad flour, poorly tanned leather, and bad repair work. In 1725, Boston officials burned 61,000 shingles because they were not made "according to law." City governments framed laws and ordinances to guarantee that consumers would receive good quality products and honest weights and measures. There were official viewers, surveyors, and inspectors to reduce cheating and misrepresentation. Honest craftsmen often took measures of their own against fraudulent claims or bad workmanship.

Many artisans proved inadequate to the enterprise of being master craftsmen. The master had to operate a workshop, purchase tools and raw materials, design the product, instruct the apprentices, supervise the journeymen, procure commissions for work, and then sell the product. The quality of workmanship and materials, every step in the producing process, and all dealings outside the shop were his responsibility. The master was also responsible for the education, housing, and maintenance of his apprentices, the boarding of his journeymen, as well as the health, comfort, and moral welfare of his entire household, including strangers who lived within it. It is no wonder, that despite the small-scale nature of the average craftsman in colonial times, many artisans could not manage to stay out of debt or keep their enterprises from failing.

THE ARTISAN COMMUNITY

The structure of the craft hierarchy—masters, journeymen, and apprentices—was based on a value system that stressed long years of practice and experience to acquire craft skills. The education and training of a craftsman required repeated performance to thoroughly master the ways and harmony of motion by the hand employing tools to work on materials. Only years of experience would impart to the apprentice/trainee the subtle movements of hand coordinated with the eye, the knowledge of materials and how they could be transformed, and the use of the right tool to be applied to the particular task. In addition to skills, apprentices learned the entire system of values regarding workmanship, dedication to craft, honesty in performance, and responsibility to customer and community.

Apprentices

Just as in Europe, part of the tradition of artisans and craftsmen in colonial America was the training and certification of artisans based on the system of apprenticeship. Traditionally, the skills of a trade or craft passed from father to son. In addition, artisans took on outsiders as apprentices to be helpers and trainees. Just as in Europe, the apprentice's parents normally paid the artisan a fee for agreeing to assume responsibility for teaching their son a marketable skill. The parties negotiated a contract similar to an indenture. It required the artisan to feed and house the youth and to teach him a useful trade in return for labor. Contracts often stipulated a term from four to seven years, or when the apprentice reached the age of twenty-one. The contract often specified instruction in reading, writing, and arithmetic. The apprentice was to keep the master's secrets, faithfully serve, not waste his master's goods, not commit fornication, nor marry during the term of service. He was not to play cards, dice, or other unlawful games, nor was he to buy or sell any of his master's goods. He was not to absent himself from his master's service without permission, nor attend alehouses or playhouses. The apprentice, if he was industrious, sought to learn his trade so he could hire out as a journeyman, save some money, and eventually set up shop as a master.

The regime for apprentices was harsh and difficult for youths bursting with energy. While most masters were probably decent family men with a sense of responsibility for their apprentices, there were many hard masters and the courts endeavored to support the claims of abused apprentices. A New York judge released James Jamison from his contract with Henry Broughton in 1718, when they learned that Broughton had disfigured Jamison, who was in danger of losing his eyes from Broughton's brutality. Many apprentices ran away. Benjamin Franklin was one such apprentice, fleeing from the injustice and abuse of his own brother, a printer to whom Franklin was apprenticed by his father. Hours of work were long, averaging twelve to fourteen per day. By running away an apprentice could escape from the tyranny of a bad master and from the many restrictions imposed by the terms of the apprenticeship indenture.

The American Revolution symbolized a challenge to patriarchy that released young people from close supervision and created an environment that provided a base for youths to assert their independence. In the decades following the Revolution, the authority of the master over apprentices increasingly came under attack. The master's superior knowledge was called into question by the rise of alternative sources of knowledge such as manuals dealing with the various crafts. The master also had to contend with revolutionary rhetoric that was absorbed by apprentices who asserted claims to liberty and equality. Republican ideology did not square with the absolute supremacy of the master over his apprentices. There was an increase in the number of runaway apprentices. In time, both masters and apprentices gave up the indentures as both agreed that the apprentice should stay only so long as he wanted. No longer were masters totally responsible for apprentices and no longer did the apprentices owe masters absolute fidelity until they turned twenty-one. In the new order both master and apprentice would be free from entanglements, and in being free, each had to stand alone. The apprentice had to make his own way, and the master was free of the obligation of providing room and board, and could hire journeymen and apprentices for wages only.

Journeymen

The journeyman was the man in the middle, above the apprentice, but not yet a master, a craftsman who was not independent, who worked for wages, and who often depended on the master for room and board as well as for income.

There was a growing gulf between journeymen and masters in wealth and social status. Masters made out well, but journeymen did not nearly do so well, working for wages to earn their subsistence. In New York, 72 percent of masters had 150 dollars worth of personal property, while only 8.4 percent of journeymen did. Over one-fourth of masters owned a house but only 2 percent of journeymen did. Many, though not all, journeymen faced the prospect that they would never become masters. In New York's Sixth Ward, three-quarters of all artisans under the age of fifty were still journeymen, while in Philadelphia, in some trades, 80 to 90 percent of artisans were still journeymen.

Years after their apprenticeship journeymen might secure a loan or get help from family and friends, to set up as a master. The majority, however, remained journeymen and were constantly on the move to find work. Some masters were hard on the journeyman; some were too bad off financially to pay journeymen their wages on a regular basis. In the South, journeymen faced competition from slave artisans who were carpenters, coopers, and blacksmiths. After the American Revolution, journeymen established their own craft associations, which acted as benevolent societies, collecting funds to aid families of sick and deceased members. Journeymen struggled against competition from immigrants and half-trained apprentices, people the masters were willing to hire at low wages. Journeymen resorted to collective actions, including appeals to the public, walkouts against individual masters, and turnouts (strikes) against all masters of a particular trade. Journeymen came to see masters as selfish, uncaring men, bent on enriching themselves at the journeymen's expense. By their actions, some masters had broken the bonds that once united all craftsmen as a producing class.

Masters

Masters saw themselves as the protectors of their respective trades, believing that they had the knowledge and foresight to set the conditions of work, along with the compensation and conduct of journeymen and apprentices. Masters formed their own associations, dealt with raw material suppliers, negotiated with apprentices and journeymen, and arranged for the sale of their products. They sought to protect their craft against unfair or unwanted regulation, though they lobbied Congress for tariff protection against foreign goods, particularly English imports. Early in the eighteenth century, New York and Philadelphia required a fee from masters who desired to set up a trade or craft within the city. Boston and Newport also regulated the entrance of craftsmen into their cities.

Master craftsmen developed a professional spirit and a desire for exclusiveness that impelled them to form associations for mutual benefit. The first and most sustained of such associations was the Carpenter's Company of Philadelphia, founded in 1724. Later in the century, organizations were set up by carpenters in New York, cordwainers and tailors in Philadelphia, and a number of other master craftsmen in other cities. They participated in parades commemorating the American Revolution, in which all the members of a particular craft, including journeymen, apprentices, and masters, marched together. Masters were active in the political life of their cities, running for and occupying many of the important administrative offices. Masters believed that through a combination of ambition, skill, discipline, and good management, they could advance the crafts and trades toward greater profits and productivity. They believed that it was their duty to protect the crafts against the dangerous inroads threatened by factory production and to fend off unfair or unwanted regulation. Finally, the masters assumed the heavy responsibility of reminding both their own craft communities as well as society as a whole of the central place that artisans occupied in the founding and maintenance of freedom and republicanism in America.

CONCLUSION

Who was the colonial artisan? In preindustrial colonial society he was a workman who possessed specialized skills that set him apart from the common laborer. Those skills were his most valuable possession, for they gave him varying degrees of independence, mobility, and status. In the ritualistic language of the apprenticeship indentures, the craft skills to be learned were the "arts and mysteries" of the craft, art in the sense of technical skills, and mystery in the sense of spiritual values, specialized privileges, and a sense of morality. The craftsman, with his leather apron, was more than a mere producer of goods. He represented a work ethic that stressed quality, fairness, and independence. That at least was the ideal. But any realistic treatment of the colonial craftsman must take into consideration that there was a hierarchy of crafts, that some artisans became wealthy while others were able to obtain only a modest living or remained poor most of their lives. Research reveals that most journeymen never made it into the ranks of the masters and eventually were relegated to a permanent class of wage earners in constant search for work and in conflict with masters. In spite of the deviations from the ideal, however, the world of the colonial craftsman stands as a landmark of a work ethic that wedded morality to manual labor and individual industry to community service.

BIBLIOGRAPHICAL ESSAY

For an overview of the colonial craftsman in America see Carl Bridenbaugh, *The Colonial Craftsman* (Chicago: University of Chicago Press, 1950). Also, see the volume prepared by the Winterthur Museum, *The Craftsman in Early America*, edited by Ian M. Quimby (New York: W. W. Norton, 1984). And for a picture of craftsmen in New York, one that could be applied to the entire colonies with respect to their work processes and their work ethic, see Howard Rock, *Artisans of the New Republic: The Tradesmen of New York City in the Age of Jefferson* (New York: New York University Press, 1979). Another view of the colonial craftsman along with a discussion of source material can be found in Thomas J. Schlereth, "Artisans and Craftsmen: A Historical Perspective," in *The Craftsman in Early America*, edited by Ian M. G. Quimby, 34–61. On women in the brewing craft, see Laurel Thatcher Ulrich, *A Midwife's Tale: The Life of Martha Ballard, Based on Her Diary, 1785–1812* (New York: Vintage Books, 1991), 73, 264, 313.

For a discussion of the economic value of craft products and the role of artisans and craftsmen in the economy of colonial America, see Edwin J. Perkins, "Artisans and Merchants," in *The Economy of Colonial America*, 2nd ed. (New York: Columbia University Press, 1988). On the role of the artisan in rural environments, see Jean B. Russo, "Self-Sufficiency and Local Exchange: Free Craftsmen in the Rural Chesapeake Economy," in *Colonial Chesapeake Society*, edited by Lois Green Carr, Philip D. Morgan, and Jean B. Russo (Chapel Hill: University of North Carolina Press, 1988), 389–432. Also on the rural craftsman, see Carl Bridenbaugh, *The Colonial Craftsman*, 1–64.

On the work ethic among artisans and craftsmen see Carl Bridenbaugh, *The Colonial Craftsman*, (Chicago: University of Chicago Press, 1950), 125–154. For the discussions on the work ethic in the *Independent Mechanic*, see Howard Rock, *Artisans of the New Republic*, 302–319. For other aspects of the artisan work ethic, see Rock, ibid., 7–9, 303–304, 309. On the dedication of artisans to the communitarian spirit see Gary Nash, "Artisans and Politics in Eighteenth-Century Philadelphia," in *The Craftsman in Early America*, edited by Ian W. G. Quimby, 69–71. On the artisanal work ethic in general, see "The History of Work in the West: An Overview," by Edward Shorter, in *Work and Community in the West*, edited by Edward Shorter (New York: Harper & Row, 1973).

On artisans and craftsmen in cities and urban areas, see the following: Eric Foner, *Tom Paine and Revolutionary America* (New York: Oxford University Press, 1976); Gary Nash, "Up From the Bottom in Franklin's Philadelphia," *Past and Present*, no. 77 (1977), 57–83; Gary Nash, *The Urban Crucible: The Northern Seaports and the Origins of the American Revolution* (Cambridge, MA: Harvard University Press, 1986). Benjamin Franklin's "Autobiography," in his *Library of America: Writings* (New York: Viking Press, 1987), 1307–1469; Carl Van Doren, *Benjamin Franklin* (New York: Penguin Books, 1991), 37–125; Darrett B. Rutman, *Winthrop's Boston* (Chapel Hill: University of North Carolina Press, 1965), 181–190. For a picture of a Boston shoemaker, see Alfred F. Young, "George Robert Twelves Hewes (1742–1840): A Boston Shoemaker and the Memory of the American Revolution," *William and Mary Quarterly* 38, no. 4 (October 1961), 561–623. Finally, there is Carl Bridenbaugh, *The Colonial Craftsman*, 65–124.

For an overview of apprentices, journeymen, and masters, with excerpts from original material about their lives, see Paul A. Gilje and Howard B. Rock, eds., *Keepers of the Revolution: New Yorkers at Work in the Early Republic* (Ithaca, NY: Cornell University Press, 1992). On the tradition of fathers and son in the same craft, see Robert Blair St. George, "Fathers, Sons and Identity: Woodworking Artisans in Southeastern New England, 1620–1700," in *The Craftsmen in Early America*, edited by Ian. M. G. Quimby. On the apprenticeship system in colonial America and beyond, see W. J. Rorabaugh, *The Craft Apprentice: From Franklin to the Machine Age in America* (New York: Oxford University Press, 1986). Material on Stephen Allen, sail maker and later mayor of New York City, can be found in Gilje and Rock, *Keepers of the Revolution*, 27–33, 122–128. For a discussion of the deterioration of the apprenticeship system, see Rorabaugh, *The Craft Apprentice*, 32–34, 42–43, 55–56. The figures on the percentages of journeymen in New York and Philadelphia come from Howard Rock, *Artisans of the New Republic*, 265, and from Eric Foner, *Tom Paine and Revolutionary America*, 280, n. 24.

For an overview of colonial artisans in the second half of the eighteenth century, see Howard B. Rock, Paul A. Gilje, and Robert Asher, eds., *American Artisans: Crafting Social Identity, 1750–1850* (Baltimore: Johns Hopkins University Press, 1995). The Introduction by Paul Gilje (xi–xx) discusses many of the ideas contained in Chapter 3 of this book and provides a good bibliography in the notes (198–201). For slave artisans in the colonial period, see the essay in the volume cited above by James Sidbury, "Slave Artisans in Richmond, Virginia, 1780–1810," 48–62.

An excellent review of the work ethic among colonial artisans is provided by David Brody in his essay, "Time and Work During Early American Industrialism," in *Labor History* 30 (Winter 1989), 5–46, and was reprinted in David Brody's volume of essays, *In Labor's Cause: Main Themes on the History of the American Worker* (New York: Oxford University Press, 1993), 3–42. Brody presents a number of significant ideas in his extremely well-researched essay. One point that he makes is that colonial America contained a productive system in which the demand for extra hands and specialized skills was irregular but vital, and therefore, labor constituted the most important item of exchange (7).

Brody also states that before the American Revolution, the artisan labor force was substantially a labor force of masters. Lacking any effective guild regulation, the master was simply an artisan who had managed to set up for himself. The term master meant any self-employed artisan. A study by Billy Smith, "The Material Lives of Laboring Philadelphians 1750 to 1800," *William and Mary Quarterly* 38, no. 2 (1981), 197, 200, cited by Brody (9), concludes that half or more of the taxable cordwainers and tailors in Philadelphia functioned as masters on the eve of the Revolution. Roughly half of the printers in Philadelphia were also masters. Brody singles out the large number of self-employed among both artisans and manual workers. Many construction artisans were contract workers, employed by the day or by the job. In port cities, much of the needed manual work was performed through respectable forms of self-employment. Cartmen and porters were licensed tradesmen, granted a privilege in exchange for close regulation (9). Brody concludes that to the degree that self-employment prevailed, the incentives for industriousness spread through the artisan economy. Self-employment was a condition fostered by the rapidity of colonial settlement and economic growth. Those who were not self-employed but were dependent on others for wage employment were looked down upon. Finally, Brody points to the large reliance upon bound labor (indentured servants and slaves) in the colonial artisan economy. Slaves made up 30 percent of New York City's laboring population in 1746. The same was true of Philadelphia up until the Seven Years' War. Bound workers made up nearly half the labor force of Philadelphia's handicraft economy in the pre-Revolution years. Brody concludes that "the compulsions for industriousness ran exceedingly strong through the American craft economy, operating directly on the self-employed and, through their power over everyone else, penetrating down into the entire labor system" (13).

In the text, it is pointed out that toward the end of the eighteenth century, a gulf began to develop between masters and journeymen regarding their outlook, interests, and goals. One reflection of this gulf was the fact that journeymen began to form their own organizations.

David Brody (1993, *In Labor's Cause*, 20) states that a big part of self-employment was grafted on to wage labor as the journeymen split off from their masters. This happened where the product could be reckoned by the piece. Thus, journeymen unions issued price lists that they expected all journeymen to abide by. This preserved the notion that they were not paid for their time, but for the product they produced. These arrangements led to a fundamental loss for the artisan since he did not control the product, which belonged to the manufacturer or merchant. But the artisan did retain what seemed to him the essence of his independence. He owned his tools, he worked on his own premises, he was subject to no man's supervision and he set his own pace and schedule. He received, more truly than the hired journeyman who worked for wages, a price for his work. It was a price over which he bargained and the time he spent on his work was his own.

4

SERVITUDE:
WHITE AND BLACK

Some people may believe that the continent on the other side of the Atlantic Ocean from England in the seventeenth century was waiting for anyone wishing to start a new life and they could easily sail over, acquire a piece of land, and become successful. No doubt some people living in England at the start of the seventeenth century had similar thoughts. The reality, however, was that people could not simply pick themselves up and go off to British America. Most Englishmen did not have the money. That is why during the seventeenth century more than half the migrants were indentured servants. In the Chesapeake, the percentage may have been as high as 70 or 75 percent.

INDENTURED SERVANTS, THEIR ROLE IN COLONIAL AMERICA, AND THEIR WORK ETHIC

The indentured servant, both male and female, entered into a contract of servitude called an indenture. The contract required that the migrant agree to work for a designated master for a fixed period of time. In return, the migrant received passage to a specific colony along with food, clothing, and shelter for the term of the contract. At the conclusion of the term, the indentured servant was to receive "freedom dues," that is, tools, food, a suit of clothing, and in some cases land. The contract could be sold by the master during the term of service. The indenture did not make the servant a slave, for it was the servant's labor, not his or her person, that was temporarily owned by the master. At the end of a specific term, generally three to five years, the servant was free. Still, indentured servitude was a less free and a more strict obligation to work as compared with other forms of labor contracts—apprenticeship, wage labor, and contract labor. On the other hand, indentured servitude was less strict and more free than slave labor.

"What Virginia needed, what it had always needed, was a large, inexpensive labor force, workers who could perform the tedious tasks necessary to bring tobacco to market" (Breen, 1980:129). Seventeenth-century Virginia solved the need singled out by Breen with imported, white, indentured servants. Whether Virginia planters preferred white servants over slaves made little difference since they had no choice. Before the 1680s, there was no reliable, inexpensive source of black slaves.

While indentured servants were important in the Chesapeake, New England imported few indentured servants. In most areas of New England, the labor supply for farming came from the family members of farmers.

In the Middle Colonies there were sizable flows of indentured servants, but these occurred mainly in the eighteenth century. A large proportion of these migrants came from Germany. Pennsylvania attracted German sects because of the colony's policy of religious toleration. The influx of Germans into Pennsylvania was so large that Benjamin Franklin estimated that in the middle of the eighteenth century they constituted a majority of the colonists.

Many servants arrived in the colonies without contracts and served according to "local custom." Servants by custom tended to be young, sixteen on the average, compared to servants with contracts. Servants by custom served longer terms, were less skilled, and were more likely illiterate. They were of lower social origins, less knowledgeable about opportunities in the New World, and were easy marks for the unscrupulous merchant or ship captain. Although a large proportion of yeomen and skilled artisans were among the migrants who came with written contracts (indentures), it was often the youth who came without contracts to perform field labor.

Colonial white servitude was distinct from slavery by the legal rights of servants as Englishmen and Englishwomen, as well as by their limited term of service. However, servants were subject to strict enforcement of their contracts by colonial courts and were subject to harsh punishment for attempts to avoid them. White servitude was present in colonial America before slavery and was the main labor source in the Chesapeake during most of the seventeenth century. The southern colonies typically had high levels of immigration and high proportions of unfree workers as they did not have a native-born population that reproduced itself until the end of the seventeenth century. There were too few women in the colony.

Work Routines of Indentured Servants

Of the various kinds of plantation labor that indentured servants had to perform, the one that was most difficult and exhausting was the preparation of new land for planting: trees had to be felled, trimmed, and dragged away; bush had to be cleared and the soil turned over for the first time without the benefit of good plows, and sometimes, without draft animals. Indentured servants made to perform this work groaned under this unaccustomed burden. One of Robert Beverley's indentured servants, Robert Clark, agreed to serve his master one year longer, if he could be released from "workeing in the ground, carryeing, or fetching railes or loggs" (Smith, 1947:257). Some servants who had a trade and wished to avoid the burden of field labor, and could make their indentures before leaving England, could include a provision that they should work only at their craft and not at field labor. In a Pennsylvania case, the judge ordered a master to keep his servant at his trade of weaver, according to his indenture, and not to employ him at field labor, under penalty of having to set the servant free.

A large proportion of servants were not bred to agricultural labor and thus found it an extreme hardship. The English husbandman or the German farmer found no great difficulty with farming work. This, however, was not true for the tailor, shoemaker, or weaver who was forced to work in the tobacco, corn, or wheat fields. It was worse for vagrants and beggars who were picked up in London or other British cities and transplanted to the New World to work at hard farm labor. They suffered much and received little sympathy. White indentured servants who had been idle in England and had to adapt to work in the colonies did not normally survive the first year of "seasoning" in the colonies. Tradesmen who had a sedentary occupation found the work hard. If they survived, many were able to adapt to life on the farm, and when they were free they could take up farming if they could acquire a piece of land.

The Work Ethic of Indentured Servants

A substantial number of indentured servants, perhaps 35 to 40 percent in the samples available, listed their occupations as farmers or skilled craftsmen. If this was representative of the former occupations of servants, then one may suppose that they brought a strong work ethic with them when they migrated to the New World. Their aspirations as servants must have been to complete their terms and take up their former occupations. Even former laborers must have hoped to acquire a piece of land to farm, since their indentured service could have prepared them for hard work, along with skills in the cultivation of tobacco and corn. If they were servants to artisans then they could have learned a craft such as coopering (making barrels), shoemaking, carpentry, or blacksmithing. The servants-in-husbandry system, on which the indentured system was modeled, was like an apprenticeship system designed to teach young men and women about farming and farm life. The major difference was that the servants in England served for a year or two and then switched masters, whereas the term in the colonies was fixed at three to five years and sometimes four to seven years, with obligations to a single master. The principles of both systems were in theory to train the servants in the arts of husbandry, and to furnish masters with a needed labor supply. In the colonies, the labor supply aspect was dominant, and the training aspect depended on the good will of the master, which in many cases was lacking. At least some percentage of servants had the knowledge of husbandry or learned it during their servitude and were able to secure land and become planters in their own right.

The work ethic of many indentured servants must have included the aspiration to become landowners. The question is how many were able secure land at the end of the term of service. Indentured servants were supposed to receive "freedom dues" at the end of their term of service. It was an important element in the indenture

system since it determined whether a servant would have a chance for a useful life
after servitude.

In Virginia, until 1675, opportunities for freed indentured servants to acquire
lands were substantial. After that date, their chances declined. Large planters who
acquired more and more land dominated the production of tobacco, and thus the
price of land was driven up and the availability of land fell. It became difficult for
latecomers such as former servants to acquire land and make a go of it. Many court
cases involved indentured servants demanding their freedom dues and masters
refusing to grant it to them, using various means such as forged documents to take
advantage of their servants.

On achieving freedom, servants not given land free and clear had three options—
to work for wages, to lease land, or to work as a sharecropper on another's land. To
become a freeholder, a servant had to pay surveyor's fees, fees for a patent, and the
purchase price of the land. Land had to be cleared, a house had to be built, and
provisions had to be secured to survive at least one growing season. Prospective
landowners would also need tools, seed, and livestock. All this required capital, and
capital was one thing former servants did not have. Wage labor, sharecropping, and
leaseholding offered men a chance to accumulate enough capital to get started on
their own and to sustain themselves in the meantime. Those who could not afford
to pay rent or who did not wish to sharecrop, worked for wages. Wages could
amount to up to 1500 pounds of tobacco a year, plus shelter, food, and clothing,
and could serve as a means of accumulating enough capital to get started as a small
farmer.

From Indentured Servitude to Black Slavery

A large absolute decline in the number of servants migrating to the Chesapeake
and an increase in the number of slaves available during the 1680s and 1690s
produced a sharply increasing ratio of slaves to servants in the Chesapeake. Planters
probably abandoned the use of white servants reluctantly. The supply of servants
dried up because of the declining opportunities in the Chesapeake for freed servants
to acquire land, which was part of their aspirations and their work ethic. Meanwhile,
opportunities in England were improving as real wages appear to have risen in the
final decades of the seventeenth century. In addition, more recently settled colonies,
including North and South Carolina and Pennsylvania, were competing for servants
and offering land and greater opportunity than existed in the increasingly stratified
Chesapeake. It was not the demand side that caused the transition to black slavery
as much as it was the supply side, with the shortage of white servants and whites
who chose other colonies to migrate to instead of the Chesapeake.

Three factors are usually cited as to why slavery became dominant in the
economy of southern plantation society. These are (1) alternate sources of labor
were scarce; (2) European labor was more expensive than black labor; and (3)
Africans could endure the rigors of the southern climate. While each of these factors
played somewhat of a role in the introduction of slavery, no one of them or their
joint sum is an adequate explanation. Planters preferred the slave labor system to

the free labor system, even when free labor was relatively abundant and even in climates such as in Virginia and Maryland, which were as congenial to Europeans as to Africans. The answer lies instead in the degree of force available to masters who wanted and needed to transform old modes of labor into a new discipline of work. Centuries of tradition shielded European laborers from the degree of force that was permitted against African-American slaves. A certain amount of force was used with indentured servants, but the degree of force involved was not much greater than what was traditional in European society. Furthermore, it was monitored by the courts and constrained by the nature of the contract covering indentured servants. The change to slave labor involved a change in the mode of work and a change to the master-slave relationship based on a new system of force that contrasted with the master-servant relationship or the employer-employee relationship in eighteenth-century colonial America.

Black Slavery and the Plantation System of Work

Slavery was a system of perpetual servitude and lifetime labor for others. Unlike white servitude it was an indefinite term of servitude and the condition of servitude was hereditary for all offspring of slave families. Slavery was prevalent in colonial America where there was a staple crop, such as tobacco in the Chesapeake and rice in South Carolina. To establish slavery in Virginia it was not necessary for planters to enslave anyone, but only to buy men and women who were already enslaved and who were brought to America by others who risked the costs of transportation over the ocean. Slaves were present in Virginia as early as 1619 and the courts recognized property in men and women and their progeny at least as early as the 1640s.

Black slavery never flourished in New England as it did in the South. There were only a few hundred blacks in New England in 1680 and not more than 3 percent of the population in the eighteenth century. Blacks were not treated very differently from white servants, except that they and their children had to serve for life. Puritans had an ambivalent attitude toward slavery. They declared that there should be no slavery among themselves, but they were willing to accept it for others. Theophilus Eaton, one of the founders of New Haven and a very pious Puritan, seems to have owned black slaves before 1658, justifying it by reference to the Bible. During the Pequot Indian War of 1637, some of the Pequot captives were shipped aboard the *Desire* to Providence to be exchanged for slaves. Emanuel Downing, John Winthrop's brother-in-law, advocated exchanging Narragansetts captured in war for slaves. Thus, for some early New Englanders, enslavement was justified as spoils of war.

Black Slavery and the Work of Slaves

Black slaves were the second-largest group of workers in colonial America, after yeomen farmers, and they represented 20 percent of the colonial work force. They functioned mainly as field hands, house servants, and artisans. In the Chesapeake and North Carolina, slaves constituted 38 percent of the population, while in South

Carolina they outnumbered whites by roughly 50 percent. In the North, only New York, Newport, and Providence had slave populations over 10 percent, with the vast majority of northern blacks involved in domestic service. In Philadelphia, slaves resided in the homes of more than one in five families, and constituted 8.8 percent of the population; artisans owned half of Philadelphia's slaves. The *Pennsylvania Gazette* carried advertisements listing slaves who qualified as carpenters, millers, distillers, bakers, shipbuilders, blacksmiths, and sailmakers.

So much of slave life was expressed in toil that it is appropriate to speak of the slaves' world of work as giving expression to their self-view, their relations with other slaves, and their encounters with masters. In the eighteenth century, there were three types of slave work—field work, household work, and artisan work. The location or setting of a slave's work was as important as the work routine because it controlled the slave's degree of access to colonial society. Field work and household duties cut slaves off from the outside world, whereas artisan slaves sometimes traveled beyond the plantation's boundaries.

The planters' problem was to instill discipline into a slave population that remained bound to traditional methods and ethics of work based on their African backgrounds. The black work ethic was associated with preindustrial people, while the Anglo-Saxon work ethic was adapted to a commercial outlook. The plantation system served as a halfway house between their agricultural past and their industrial future for African-Americans. Slaveholders got enough work out of their slaves to enable the system to survive. One of the factors that accounted in part for the viability of the slave system was that slaves of both sexes worked, along with children who became full-time workers when they reached an age between 11 and 14. Older slaves worked as long as they were physically able.

Competence in growing tobacco was acquired slowly by the field hands who were divided by age, sex, and strength. Boys became full hands in their late teens and both men and women probably reached their greatest physical strength during their early twenties, the age when prices of field hands peaked. Women, considered less productive than men, counted as three-quarter hands. Between the ages of twenty and thirty-five, men continued to be very productive, while old men and old women worked until they became habitually ill or lame. Elderly slaves were taken from the fields and given responsibilities in the house or slave quarters, or were set to tending livestock. Retirement was rare. Every slave except one worked up to age sixty-five on Robert Carter's plantation.

The gang system never became dominant in tobacco because it required careful cultivation. The planting of seedlings and the topping of the tobacco plant were operations that involved skill and judgment and therefore could not be subjected to gang labor. Replanting, however, could be based on a division of labor, with one group pulling up the seedlings, another group putting them into baskets, and a third group doing the replanting. Other tasks, such as curing tobacco and packing it into barrels also required care, as one mishap in these operations could spell ruin.

Almost all slave women worked in the fields. Only on the largest plantations, where many slaves had to be clothed, did slave women escape the drudgery of ordinary field work to do sewing. Female slaves owned by Jefferson, Washington, and Robert Carter, who were used in domestic service, made up one-sixth of their female slaves. Carter's women slaves included ninety-seven field hands, six domestics, twelve spinners, seamstresses, and weavers, and two women who served as midwives and nurses; one was a cooper.

Between 5 to 10 percent of slaves in the South could be expected to be hired out during any given year. Those hired out were primarily field hands, then domestics and artisans. Sometimes, planters hired out slaves away from family and friends as a means of punishment. In some cases, slaves preferred living with those who hired them rather than with their own masters. Slaveholders worried about the treatment of their slaves by temporary masters and their condition when they were returned. Mechanics and craftsmen were sometimes allowed to choose their own masters to hire out to and make their own arrangements. They could live almost like free blacks, except that they had to surrender a large part of their wages to their owners. Skilled slaves developed an independence of spirit and a thirst for freedom and knowledge of the world to such an extent that many became runaways and participated in insurrectionary plots.

Overseers tried to get slaves to work steadily and productively. They were in the middle between masters and slaves. Despite their responsibilities, they had little authority over the slaves. Usually single men in their twenties, overseers rarely held the same position for more than a year, and slaves knew that overseers were neither permanent nor vested by the master with great authority. Overseers either allowed slaves to control their pace of work, hoping they would produce more because they were satisfied, or drove the slaves very hard, forcing them to work even when they were ill, using the whip frequently to increase production and the size of their share. When overseers directed with a light hand, masters complained of low productivity. When they drove the slaves hard, masters thought the overseers too vicious.

Small planters who worked alongside their slaves had greater authority than overseers over their charges. In such an environment the master, rather than his slaves, controlled the pace of work. Still, slaves who lived on small plantations possessed leverage. Each slave was more important to the master than a single hand on a large plantation. If a slave on a small farm was mistreated he could reduce the size of his master's crop significantly by running away for a few days during planting or harvesting season.

Slave work proceeded around the changing seasons. They worked hard at certain times and at other times they worked at a slow, methodical pace. Overseers and masters drove slaves hard during the long summer of replanting, weeding, and harvesting tobacco, but after slaves hung tobacco in the tobacco house, masters had to find new work for them to keep them busy. Slaves who worked together developed their own pace of work. Each member of the group had his own responsibility, his own place in the daily routine, and when one member was ill or could not work, the group's work rhythms were disrupted and work slowed or halted. Masters and overseers had few weapons to induce the slaves to work at a satisfactory pace. If they paid constant attention to their slaves they were seen as being too solicitous. If they whipped them into submission they might create a sullen, dissatisfied group. Incentives and relatively lax management might produce results, but as most masters became resigned to slave strategies they used a combination of the lash and incentives to motivate their slaves to greater effort.

While masters had a monopoly of power, slaves were able to maintain their own pace of work in the fields, and a semi-autonomous life in their own quarters. Masters tried to keep families together, but when they believed necessity dictated certain decisions, they did not hesitate to sell slaves away from their kinfolk. The vast majority of slaveholders were too small to worry about slave families or to hire doctors to minister to slave illnesses. The small planters worried mainly about their tobacco crops and slaves were a means to that end by giving unquestioned obedience. While small masters might work alongside their slaves, they considered blacks to be inferior, to be consigned to servitude for life, and to be unworthy of equal social status with whites. Most masters were content to leave slaves alone in their quarters at night, as long as they gave a steady, productive effort during the daytime in the fields.

Every region had its own unique system of slavery. In the low country region of South Carolina and Georgia, where the cultivation of rice was the key staple, the distinctive feature of the work routine was the use of the task system. Under the task system, the slave was assigned a certain amount of work for the day, and after completing the task he could use his time as he pleased. In the low-country rice economy there was a division between the master's time and the slave's time. Slaves received the opportunity to grow their own products because of the establishment of the daily work requirement. By the mid-eighteenth century the basic task unit was one-quarter of an acre. Other activities, such as pounding rice and grain, were also tasked. Providing fences was tasked at splitting 100 poles of twelve feet in a day.

The working conditions of slave artisans differed significantly from that of field hands. They took pride in their craftsmanship and their being exempt from field work. Some learned several trades. By the 1760s and 1770s, slave craftsmen were being hired out or were allowed to make such arrangements themselves. Artisan slaves, unlike field hands, often worked in groups that included whites. In 1761, Thomas Fleming, while building a schooner, hired seven whites and five black men to work on it, with the whites receiving three to five pounds, and the slaves two to five pounds. At the Snowden Ironworks in 1766, more than three-quarters of the employees were slaves, which included thirty-four black artisans and fifteen slave women. Black colliers made charcoal, black founders molded metal, black finders heated the iron pigs, black hammermen pounded metal into blooms, and black chafers drew the pigs into bars. Women slaves at the ironworks mined coal and worked as domestics. Charleston's slave population earned wages in skilled crafts. By the 1770s, the majority of the city's population were slaves who participated in over fifty occupational categories. Many of these slaves exercised a fair degree of independence in their work lives, hiring out to third parties and dividing their wages with their owners.

Frontier regions were fluid environments conducive to permitting slave participation in all facets of life. The South Carolina frontier had slaves working at clearing land, hunting, cultivating fields, raising cattle, building fences, and engaging in all forms of carpentry. More often than not they worked alongside whites. Free blacks were a feature of the frontier, many of whom were mulatto children manumitted along with their mothers by white masters who were also their fathers. Whites and blacks were also brought together in military groups, in hunting bands, and in bandit gangs within the wilds of the South's western boundaries in the 1760s and 1770s.

Slavery and the Work Ethic

The big problem for planters throughout the colonial South was how to motivate their slaves to work. Blacks saw slaveholders as people who lived on other people's labor and who did not work themselves. Basically, the planters came to believe that black slaves would work only under compulsion. Many slaves, perhaps a majority, believed that by fulfilling their work obligations they had earned the right to decent food, garden plots, adequate clothing, fair discipline, and most importantly the right to privacy in their own quarters where they could develop a sense of community. In their own quarters slaves were able to lighten their burden of oppression by promoting group solidarity and building some sense of self-esteem.

Despite the often-repeated charge of slaveowners that slaves were lazy, they could and did work hard. But they resisted that regularity and routine which planters tried to impose upon them. Slaves developed their own notions of work and leisure patterns that suggested some African cultural influence. The African tradition, like the European peasant tradition, stressed hard work and condemned laziness. The Puritan ethic, which many slaveowners espoused but did not practice themselves, called for steady, routine work as a moral duty, and this the slaves would not swallow no matter how hard and by what methods the slaveowners tried to force it down their throats. Slaves worked in their own garden plots and willingly worked late into the night or on Sundays to give themselves and their families more food. In addition they fished and hunted and trapped animals. In this way they expressed concern for their families. Some slaves voluntarily worked for masters on Sundays or holidays in return for money or goods.

Masters had few incentives to offer slaves in order to get them to work harder or with more zeal. Indentured servants had their freedom to look forward to, along with a plot of land. Slaves had none of that. For masters to offer freedom to slaves was to lose the whole advantage of slavery. Most often, the master sought to inflict pain at a level so high as to instill fear in slaves. If slaves could not be made to work hard for fear of losing their liberty they would be made to fear losing their lives. Not that a master wanted to lose his property by killing his slave. However, the masters reasoned that, in order to get work out of men and women who had nothing to gain by working hard except the absence of pain, they had to be willing to beat, maim, and even kill to force discipline upon the slaves. Masters knew that their society would back their actions. Virginia laws stated that runaways could be killed and that the public would compensate the master for loss of slaves thus killed. If the slave was caught he could be punished by dismembering, which it was hoped would result in terrifying others from running. It was not an idle threat, as many slaves had ears, fingers, and toes cut off, or were branded with an *R* for running away.

Was it possible for slaves to have a work ethic other than doing as little as possible? They might have had some ethic or motivation relative to one another. Rather than compete with one another to work hard, which could only benefit the master, they probably chose to work together collectively to establish their own pace. This appears to be what happened, since masters who recorded their thoughts, like Landon Carter and William Byrd, continually complained how they could not get their slaves to work harder. Slaves and masters must have come to some mutual understanding of what was to be a sufficient day's work. The master could use force, and did use force, to get what he considered a fair day's work from his slaves. But slaves had their own weapons. They feigned sickness, misunderstood orders, misused tools or livestock, and they ran away. If there was one continuous theme regarding work among slaves, it was that they had a solidarity and an obligation to each other to support the group as much as possible in imposing their own rhythm and pace of field work. Masters did use some incentives, like offering small gifts or extra food or clothing, to induce slaves to work harder. They also offered a few slaves the position of slave driver, a position comparable to that of a foreman. However, what little evidence exists suggests that masters were not able to break the solidarity of the slaves, who maintained their sense of collectivity both in the fields and in their quarters.

Certain questions persist for which there are no answers due to lack of evidence. Did slaves spur each other on to greater effort when they worked in gangs? Did slaves think that by benefiting their masters they would benefit themselves, since the master then would have greater means to be more generous to them? That slaves did and could work hard was demonstrated often during harvest time or during those hours when they worked on their own garden plots. However, within the system of slavery, which rested ultimately upon force, it would be difficult to postulate any effective incentive system. Even if masters wished to employ such a system, it would not overcome the lack of motivation to work hard when working hard could not alter the basic, inhumane status of a slave as a piece of property.

BIBLIOGRAPHICAL ESSAY

One of the best overall descriptions and analysis of the white indentured servitude system can be found in David Galenson's *White Servitude in Colonial America: An Economic Analysis* (Cambridge, England: Cambridge University Press, 1981). An older study, but one that is still very solid and based on good substantiation is Abbot Emerson Smith, *Colonists in Bondage, 1607–1776* (Chapel Hill: University of North Carolina Press, 1947). Another older but sound study of indentured servitude is by Marcus Wilson Jernegan, *Laboring and Dependent Classes in Colonial America, 1607–1783* (Chicago: University of Chicago Press, 1931).

For estimates of the number of indentured servants in the population of the Chesapeake colonies, see Wesley Frank Craven, *White, Red and Black: The Seventeenth-Century Virginian* (Charlottesville: University of Virginia Press, 1971), 5. Also see Russell B. Menard, "British Migration to the Chesapeake Colonies in the Seventeenth Century," in *Colonial Chesapeake Society*, edited by Lois Green Carr, Philip D. Morgan, and Jean B. Russo (Chapel Hill: University of North Carolina Press, 1988), 102, 105–106. Statistics on the numbers of indentured servants who migrated to the New World and their countries of origin can be found in Richard Dunn, "Servants Recruitment and Employment of Labor," in *Colonial British America*, edited by Jack P. Greene and J. R. Pole (Baltimore: Johns Hopkins University Press, 1984). The quotation by Timothy Breen is from *Puritans and Adventurers* (New York: Oxford University Press, 1980), 129. Lewis Cecil Gray, *History of Agriculture in the Southern United States to 1860*, Publication no. 430 (Washington, DC: Carnegie Institute of Washington, 1933 [rev. ed. 1958]) is another source of information on indentured servants and their numbers.

On the transportation of indentured servants to the New World see Abbot E. Smith, *Colonists in Bondage*, 210–217; and Jernegan, *Laboring and Dependent Classes*, 50–51.

For the former occupations of indentured servants, see Galenson, *White Servitude in Colonial America*, 34–35, 173; and Mildred Campbell, two references: "Social Origins of Some Early Americans," in *Seventeenth-Century Americ: Essays in Colonial History*, edited by James Morton Smith (Chapel Hill: University of North Carolina Press, 1959); and " 'Middling People' or 'Common Sort'? The Social Origins of Some Early Americans Reexamined," *William and Mary Quarterly* 35, no. 4 (1978), 499–524.

On the treatment of indentured servants by their masters, see Edmund S. Morgan, *American Slavery, American Freedom: The Ordeal of Colonial Virginia* (New York: W. W. Norton, 1975), 117, 126–127. Also see Carl Bridenbaugh, *Jamestown, 1544–1699* (New York: Oxford University Press, 1980), 55–56. For a description of an indentured servant who was so mistreated that it led him to murder his master and mistress, see Timothy H. Breen, James H. Lewis, and Keith Schlesinger, "Motive for Murder: A Servant's Life in Virginia, 1678," *William and Mary Quarterly* 40, no. 1 (1983), 106–120. Galenson, *White Servitude in Colonial America*, 172, also discusses the treatment of indentured servants. For indentured servants' protest against their conditions, see Timothy Breen, *Puritans and Adventurers*, 134–135, 141. For the full quotation on the contract between Robert Beverly and his servant, Robert Clark, regarding "workeing in the ground," see A. E. Smith, *Colonists in Bondage*, 257.

On the work routines of indentured servants, see A. E. Smith, *Colonists in Bondage*, 257–258. Also see Lois Green Carr and Lorena S. Walsh, "Economic Diversification and Labor Organization in the Chesapeake, 1650–1820," in *Work and Labor in Early America*, edited by Stephen Innes (Chapel Hill: University of North Carolina Press, 1988), 144–188. On the work of indentured servants on a particular farm, see Lois Green Carr, Russell R. Menard, and Lorena S. Walsh, *Robert Cole's World: Agriculture and Society in Early Maryland* (Chapel Hill: University of North Carolina Press, 1991), Chapters 2 and 3.

On the issue of "freedom dues" for indentured servants and the proportions of servants who were able to secure land, see A. E. Smith, *Colonists in Bondage*, 239–242, 299; and Russell Menard, "From Servant to Freeholder: Status Mobility and Property Accumulation in Seventeenth-Century Maryland," *William and Mary Quarterly* 30, no. 1 (January 1973), 37–64.

On the transformation from indentured servitude to black slavery and the supply theory as to its causes, see Russell R. Menard, "From Servants to Slaves: The Transformation of the Chesapeake Labor System," *Southern Studies* 16, no. 3 (1977), 355–390. Also see Galenson, *White Servitude in Colonial America*, 117, 154, 162, 167–168, 174. For another view of the use of black slavery rather than indentured servants in plantation agriculture, see Robert W. Fogel, *Without Consent or Contract: The Rise and Fall of American Slavery* (New York: W. W. Norton, 1989), 34–36.

On the attitudes of whites toward the first blacks brought into the colony, see Philip Bruce, *Economic History of Virginia in the Seventeenth Century*, vol. 2 (New York: Macmillan, 1986), 108–109; see also Timothy H. Breen, *Puritans and Adventurers*, 146.

On the slave trade, see Philip D. Curtin, *The Atlantic Slave Trade: A Census* (Madison, WI: University of Wisconsin Press, 1969), 87, 119, 140. Also see Richard S. Dunn, *Servants and Slaves*, 165–166. For an overview of black slavery in colonial times, including the slave trade, see Winthrop D. Jordan, *White Over Black: American Attitudes Toward the Negro, 1550–1812* (New York: W. W. Norton, 1968), 57; also see Jordan's article, "Enslavement of Negroes in America to 1700," in *Colonial America: Essays in Politics and Social Development*, edited by Stanley N. Katz (Boston: Little, Brown, 1971). For attitudes of New Englanders toward slavery, see Jordan, *White Over Black*, 67–71.

On the cultivation of tobacco and the use of slave labor, see Allan Kulikoff, *Tobacco and Slaves: The Development of Southern Cultures in the Chesapeake, 1680–1800* (Chapel Hill: University of North Carolina Press, 1986). Also see Edmund S. Morgan, *American Slavery, American Freedom*, 26–27, 309–310, 332–336. On rice cultivation and black slavery in colonial South Carolina, see Peter H. Wood, *Black Majority: Negroes in Colonial South Carolina from 1670 Through the Stono Rebellion* (New York: Knopf, 1974).

On slavery and work routines in the cultivation of tobacco, see Richard Dunn, *Servants and Slaves*, 166, 179–180; Edmond S. Morgan, *American Slavery, American Freedom*, 310; Kulikoff, *Tobacco and Slaves*, 11–12, 403, 411–412, 417. The quote by Landon Carter on not being able to work when the weather was bad, is from Jack P. Greene, ed., *The Diary of Colonel Landon Carter of Sabine Hall, 1752–1778* (Charlottesville: University of Virginia Press, 1965), 158. The attitudes of masters toward servants and slaves is from Morgan, *American Slavery, American Freedom*, 319–321. For a contemporary description of slaves at work in tobacco fields in Virginia, see Hugh Jones, *The Present State of Virginia*, edited with an Introduction by Richard L. Morton, The Virginia Historical Society (Chapel Hill: University of North Carolina Press, 1956 [orig. 1734]), 36–38. For a view of overseers, see Kulikoff, *Tobacco and Slaves* 410; and William K. Scarborough, *The Overseer: Plantation Management in the Old South* (Athens: University of Georgia Press, 1984). For Jefferson's view of overseers, see Jack McLaughlin, *Jefferson and Monticello: The Biography of a Builder* (New York: Henry Holt, 1988), 127–128, 141–143. For further discussions of slaves and their work routines, see Gerald W. Mullin, *Flight and Rebellion: Slave Resistance in Eighteenth-Century Virginia* (New York: Oxford University Press, 1972), 37–38.

For population statistics, see Robert W. Fogel, *Without Consent or Contract*, 29–30; 33–34. Also Edwin J. Perkins, *The Economy of Colonial America* (New York: Columbia University Press, 1988), 98. For slave population in Philadelphia, see Gary B. Nash, "Slaves and Slaveowners in Colonial Philadelphia," *William and Mary Quarterly* 30, no. 2 (April 1973), 243, 250.

On the work ethic of slaves see Eugene D. Genovese, *Roll, Jordan, Roll: The World the Slaves Made* (New York: Pantheon Books, 1974), 286–287, 298, 303, 309, 312, 314, 391–393. Also see John W. Blassingame, *The Slave Community* (New York: Oxford University Press, 1972), 39, 42.

On the slave artisan, see Kulikoff, *Tobacco and Slaves*, 397–401; also McLaughlin, *Jefferson and Monticello*, 95–98, 103, 112–113. Also see Perkins, *The Economy of Colonial America*, 106.

On rice cultivation and the task system see, Philip D. Morgan, "Work and Culture: The Task System and the World of Lowcountry Blacks, 1700–1800," *William and Mary Quarterly* 39, no. 4 (October 1982), 563–599. Also, Philip D. Morgan, "Task and Gang Systems:

The Organization of Labor on New World Plantations," in *Work and Labor in Early America*, edited by Stephen Innes (Chapel Hill: University of North Carolina Press, 1988), 189–220.

For a picture of the shared work experiences of both whites and blacks during the eighteenth century, see Mechal Sobel, *The World They Made Together: Black and White Values in Eighteenth-Century Virginia* (Princeton, NJ: Princeton University Press, 1987). See Chapter 4, "Shared English and African Experiences of Work," 44–53. It is also valuable to look at Chapter 2, "English and African Perception of Time," 21–29; as Sobel points out perceptions of time affect all other values, especially the work ethic and the manner in which work is carried on. For another study of the relationship between time and the slave economy of the South, see Mark M. Smith, "Old South Time in Comparative Perspective," *American Historical Review* 101, no. 5 (December 1996), 1432–1469. Smith points out that clock consciousness and time also existed among slave systems and was not confined to industrial, free wage labor capitalism (1433).

On the renting out of slaves, see James A. Henretta, "The Transition to Capitalism in America," in *The Transformation of Early American History: Society, Authority, and Ideology*, edited by James A. Henretta, Michael Kammen, and Stanley N. Katz (New York: Alfred A. Knopf, 1991), 231–234.

5

COLONIAL WOMEN

WOMEN'S WORK IN THE COLONIAL ECONOMY

In studying colonial women one focuses on the household where their lives were centered. As daughters, wives, and mothers, white women devoted their energies to being homemakers and caring for their children, just as husbands were raising crops, crafting products, and working for wages. The family played a central role in shaping colonial America. Family and household were intertwined and household manufactures, in which women played a key role, were an essential contribution to the colonial economy. Women lived and developed a work ethic within a feminine, domestic circle where their work was normally carried on separately from their husbands; their infants were delivered by midwives, the sick were cared for by female neighbors, and they exchanged and bartered products and services with other women.

Household tasks were not easily accomplished and their nature varied with the wealth and size of the family and its place of residence. Cooking, cleaning, and washing were, as always, female prime responsibilities. So was the caring for children and the caring for and making of clothing. On farms, women raised chickens, tended vegetable gardens, ran the dairy, made cheese and butter for family use or for barter and sale. While men butchered hogs and cattle in the fall, women supervised the salting and smoking of meat so the family would have an adequate supply for the winter. They gathered, dried, and preserved fruits and berries and sometimes oversaw the making of hard cider, the standard drink in the colonies. In towns and cities, women performed these chores on a lesser scale, raised a few chickens and a cow or two, cultivated a kitchen garden, and preserved beef and pork purchased at the local market. Only the wealthiest women with numerous servants escaped tiring, physical labor.

In colonial times, the division of labor within the family reflected the division of labor in colonial society as a whole. For the most part, production for sale was the province of the male and household production was the domain of the female. Each spouse had an area of clear authority over resources, children, and servants. This was by no means absolute, especially in farming. Work roles in colonial America were quite flexible and expectations about work functions of the sexes periodically expanded. Gender roles on farms normally overlapped during certain critical periods in the growing cycle. In artisan families, the craftsman's wife might assist him from time to time with the work or with keeping his accounts. There were a few occupations that a woman might enter by the apprenticeship route— millinery work, dress and mantua making, hairdressing, embroidery, and making artificial flowers. Despite cultural, legal, and economic restrictions, women played a major role in the internal economy of the colonies from New England to Pennsylvania and from Delaware to South Carolina. While the household was their domain, they were involved in a variety of activities that were an extension of the feminine sphere—sewing, housekeeping, teaching small children, nursing, and selling food or clothing. In addition, many colonial women owned dry goods, millinery, and grocery shops, inns and taverns, and a variety of businesses that were initially established by their deceased husbands or other relatives. The husband was the property owner in colonial America and the woman was generally without property or political rights. If she inherited property it passed on to the husband into whose household she moved after marriage. A woman might carry on her husband's shop or farm after his death and be the property owner if she did not remarry, but this was an infrequent event as most women did remarry, especially in the seventeenth century when males far outnumbered females.

The difference in work activities in the family differentiated men and women as social beings. Agriculture and gardening were technically similar, but agriculture was male work since it was production for the market and gardening was considered female work as it was production for the family table. Similarly, weaving and sewing were done by both men and women, but men sewed and wove as craftsmen, while women sewed and wove at home for the family. As commodity production developed, men's work was considered to be in the public sphere while women's work was in the private sphere. When the family needed goods essential for the household, women moved into production for exchange, selling or bartering their extra products. If the husband was a small shopowner, the woman would help in production or selling. The gender division of labor was perpetuated generationally through the training of children for the work proper for their sex. Daughters assisted their mothers starting around age seven and by age twelve they were full apprentices learning housewifery tasks.

The lives of early American housewives were distinguished by the tasks they performed and by the economy and family responsibilities that tied each man and woman to a household, a village, or a town. The skilled work of a wife included the specialized skills of the household as well as assisting her husband on the farm or in his trade. Since most productive work was based within the family, there were many opportunities for a wife to wind quills if she was a weaver's wife, to keep shop if she was a merchant's wife, and to plant corn if she was a farmer's wife. Almost any task was suitable to a woman as long as it furthered the welfare of her family and was acceptable to her husband. There was social complexity as well as diversity of women's work in colonial America that allowed a fluid rather than a rigid gender division of work.

THE WORK ETHIC OF FREE WOMEN IN COLONIAL AMERICA

It may seem remarkable, but to some extent, given the fluidity of early America, women seemed to have played a more diversified role in that society than they would up to the twentieth century. Evidence suggests that women in colonial America were quite versatile and active. The system of household manufactures, under which the husband's craft was practiced in or near the home, gave the wife or daughter an opportunity to learn the trade and assist in it. The small scale of farming meant that wives and daughters were engaged in all aspects of agriculture, except for the very heavy work. There were a surprisingly large number of women innkeepers and women engaged in the barter trade, selling surplus butter and cheese. There was also the active role of women in nursing and caring services, especially the midwives.

The work ethic of colonial American women was a family ethic. Not only was her work largely centered on the household and within the family group, but her social outlook and her way of life revolved around the family. Work for women in colonial times was both an obligation and a responsibility for maintaining her household and her family. Without her labor, involving the preparation of food, the care and making of clothing, and the upkeep of the family shelter, the basic needs of food, clothing, and shelter would not have been provided. In addition, the work ethic of colonial women was a nurturing ethic. Not only did she bear and rear her children, but she was expert in the arts of caring—providing nursing and medical care, the education of children, the maintenance of ties with neighbors and kin, and participation in church and community affairs. The work ethic of colonial women cannot be separated from her feminine ethic, that is, her role as a woman, providing the fundamental services supporting her family and its resources, plus her own creative impulses as an individual in the manner in which she understood and met her family's needs. It was all of one piece—the female ethic, the work ethic, the family ethic—which made up the life of the average colonial woman in America.

While colonial households did furnish most of what they required from their farms, the work ethic of both women and men was interdependence rather than self-sufficiency. There were exchanges between households with women helping each other and offering services and products. Martha Ballard sent a side of veal to one family and borrowed a quarter of veal from another. She settled one account by offering two days work by her daughter, Dolly. Girls would come and go between their own houses and that of neighbors, spinning, washing, caring for the sick, milking, and cleaning. Mrs. Peirce, a New England woman, threaded a loom so the daughter of her neighbor, Mrs. Phelps, could do some weaving.

The female work ethic was also a communal ethic. In farm communities, both males and females helped furnish their households communally with products they had difficulty producing by themselves. These activities included berrying, nutting, breaking wool, fishing, husking, house raising, barn raising, and quilting. Such communal work was joined with sociability. For women living on isolated farms, quilting bees and spinning frolics in the North and barbecues and corn husking in the South were opportunities for outside contacts.

It is significant that New England Puritans regarded the soul as feminine, and viewed women as passive, nurturing, emotional, and vulnerable. Women who were agressive or who tried to break out of the social boundaries of the household were viewed as threats by the dominant male society. In New England, toward the end of the seventeenth century, there is evidence of tension between men and women and a breakdown in familial social control mechanisms. Signs of this tension were revealed in the witchcraft accusations and the rising numbers of prosecutions for sexual offenses and increasing rates of premarital pregnancy. The sharp rise in premarital pregnancy revealed a trend in the increasing autonomy of young women. Such behavior was considered a deviation from the feminine ethic as the Puritan church viewed it and was considered a threat to the social order. While fornication involved an equal number of men and women, more women faced prosecution for that offense than men and 75 to 80 percent of accused witches in New England were female. The relationships of men and women, based on the aggressive male ethic and the nurturing female ethic, was the model for the general social hierarchy. Disruptions in those relations were considered a threat to society. Women's misdeeds were seen as more disruptive than men's because such misbehavior by women involved insubordination to male superiors and thus a challenge to the hierarchy. Furthermore, since women were responsible for the transmission of culture to their children, their misdeeds were a threat to the social order.

Despite the increasing forms of rebellious and "sinful" activity by colonial women, and despite the fact that one out of eight colonial women were thought to have committed the crime of premarital fornication, most women probably preserved their virginity until marriage. Three-fourths of colonial women were never charged with any crime, and the great majority of females did not become innkeepers, shopowners, or school marmes. Most mothers and daughters attended regular church services, observed the orthodox moral standards, and remained submissive, dependent, and modest. Their work ethic was part of the feminine ethic that stressed mothering, nurturing, and dedication to the needs of their families.

WORK ETHIC OF SLAVE WOMEN

Slave women's work involved two basic relationships, one with their master's family that revolved around the production of commodities or housework, and one with other slave family members, friends, and coworkers. In the former relationship slave women were subordinate members of the master's household; in the latter they were treated as family members—wives, mothers, and parents.

Among free families of colonial America, the division of labor was based on the position of the husband as household head and property owner, with the wife's work consisting of fulfilling the family's needs within the framework of the household economy. Unlike the free family, the slave family was not able to work out its own or any similar division of work, since both husband and wife had obligations to their master that took priority over any commitments they had to each other. The master's heavy hand extended into the personal relations of the slave family since the offspring of slave families were the property of the master. The master's exercise of power compromised the authority of slave parents. Masters could intrude upon and even violate the ties of love and unity between slave family members by treating slaves as units of property that could be sold away from their family. Slave women were vulnerable to sexual abuse by masters and overseers whether they were married or not, and slaves who defended their families against such attacks were severely punished. One slave recalled that his mother had been assaulted by an overseer. His father beat up the overseer and received 100 lashes and had his ear cut off.

Slaveowners found it practical and necessary to allow and recognize slave marriages and to acknowledge the existence of the slave family. Slave families were permitted to maintain their own gardens and their own animals, giving them a measure of independence and self-determination within certain narrow bounds. Despite the obligations to masters, slaves had to construct their own particular gender division of work during their free time. The gender division of labor for slaves was based on complementary work. Women did the cooking, cleaning, child-rearing, sewing, and nursing. The men hunted, trapped, worked in gardens, repaired the cabins, and cared for their few animals.

Whereas in the free family, the white homemaker interacted with the public sphere through her husband and had her work determined by him, the enslaved homemaker was directly subordinated to her owner, a nonfamily member. Enslavement created a distinctive family form for slaves. The slave woman was employed outside her family, outside of homemaking, usually in field work, or for the white homemaker, or both. She worked in the fields next to slave men. In the master's house she did homemaking for her mistress and often for her fellow slaves. She was forcibly made a member of the public economic sphere, not as property owner, but as property of others. As a member of the public slave sphere she had to fend for herself. She was treated as an individual and punished as an individual, not as a woman, and she did not enjoy the normal protection and punishment of women by their husbands or fathers.

The institution of slavery in America clearly differentiated white and black womanhood. The white woman's marriage contract and position as mother was recognized by society at large, while the marriage contract of the enslaved black woman was often violated. While white and black communities both placed married women under the authority of their husbands and fathers, the black woman was enslaved to her master and his family, and this forced the black woman to act independently from her husband. Unlike the white homemaker, the black homemaker's work was not determined by her husband. The slave woman was more burdened than the enslaved man because she served two masters instead of just one. While she could sustain the essence of the feminine ethic, that of homemaker, her male counterpart was denied a public arena where he could act out his masculine ethic. The sphere of slavery prevented him from consistently acting as the masculine head of household, as provider and protector of his wife or daughter.

BIBLIOGRAPHICAL ESSAY

A fine, overall survey of women in American history and their work ethic is the study by Julie A. Matthaei, *An Economic History of Women in America: Women's Work, the Sexual Division of Labor, and the Development of Capitalism* (New York: Schocken Books, 1982). Another excellent general history study of women's work in American history is by Carol Groneman and Mary Beth Norton, *To Toil the Livelong Day: America's Women at Work, 1780–1980* (Ithaca, NY: Cornell University Press, 1987). In addition to the two titles above, there is the comprehensive study by Barbara Mayer Wertheimer, *We Were There: The Story of Working Women in America* (New York: Pantheon Books, 1977). An earlier, but still valuable study of women's work is by Edith Abbott, *Women in Industry: A Study in American Economic History* (New York: D. Appleton, 1910).

An up-to-date study of male and female work in colonial New England and their comparative wages can be found in Gloria L. Main, "Gender, Work, and Wages in Colonial New England," *William and Mary Quarterly* 41, no. 1 (January 1994), 39–66.

A comprehensive study of women's work in seventeenth-century New England was done by Lyle Koehler, *A Search for Power: The "Weaker Sex" in Seventeenth-Century New England* (Urbana: University of Illinois Press, 1980).

For a discussion of the social and economic role of women in Salem, Massachusetts, and the accusations of witchcraft, see Paul Boyer and Stephen Nissenbaum, *Salem Possessed: The Social Origins of Witchcraft* (Cambridge, MA: Harvard University Press, 1974). For an analysis of the Puritan concept of the soul as feminine, see Elizabeth Reis, "The Devil, the Body, and the Feminine Soul in Puritan New England," *Journal of American History* 82, no. 1 (June 1995), 15–36.

For a contemporary colonial view of women as homemakers dependent upon their husbands, see Cotton Mather, *Ornaments for the Daughters of Zion: Or the Character and Happiness of a Virtuous Woman* (Cambridge: S & B Green, 1692; 3rd ed., Boston: Kneeland & Green, 1741).

On premarital sex and pregnancy in New England, see Daniel Scott Smith and Michael S. Hindus, "Premarital Pregnancy in America, 1640–1971: An Overview and Interpretation," *Journal of Interdisciplinary History*, 5, no. 4 (1974–1975), 537–570. On the same subject and the attitudes of colonial society toward female misdeeds, see Mary Beth Norton, "The Evolution of White Women's Experience in Early America," *The American Historical Review* 89, no. 3 (June 1984), 593–619.

A classic in the study of a midwife in colonial times is that of Laurel Thatcher Ulrich, *A Midwife's Tale: The Life of Martha Ballard, Based on her Diary, 1785–1812* (New York: Vintage Books, 1991). Another study of women in northern New England, which depicts their social and economic roles in colonial society, along with their work, is by Laurel Thatcher Ulrich, *Good Wives: Image and Reality in the Lives of Women in Northern New England, 1650–1750* (New York: Vintage Books, 1982).

For a view of the work of southern women on a plantation in colonial Maryland, see Lois Green Carr and Lorena S. Walsh, "The Planter's Wife: The Experience of White Women in

Seventeenth-Century Maryland," *William and Mary Quarterly* 34, no. 4 (October 1977), 542–571. For a full-length book study of women's work in seventeenth-century Maryland, see Lois Green Carr, Russell R. Menard, and Lorena S. Walsh, *Robert Cole's World: Agriculture & Society in Early Maryland* (Chapel Hill: University of North Carolina Press, 1991).

An older but still excellent study of the work of southern colonial women is that of Julia Cherry Spruill, *Women's Life and Work in the Southern Colonies* (Chapel Hill: University of North Carolina Press, 1938).

For a view of black women's work in colonial Virginia, see Carole Shammas, "Black Women's Work and the Evolution of Plantation Society in Virginia," *Labor History* 26, no. 1 (Winter 1985), 5–28.

For a study of the position of women in colonial society and how their status related to the ideology surrounding the American Revolution, see Linda K. Kerber, *Women of the Republic: Intellect and Ideology in Revolutionary America* (Chapel Hill: University of North Carolina Press, 1980). Another study dealing with the same subject is that of Mary Beth Norton, *Liberty's Daughters: The Revolutionary Experience of American Women, 1750– 1800* (Boston: Little Brown, 1980).

We can gain a view of the status of women in colonial America through an interesting study by Mary Beth Norton. She examined the claims of widows and family members of loyalists. The documents presented to the British courts by these women revealed much about their lives and attitudes, which Mary Beth Norton captures in a way that enables her to present a picture of colonial women's lives. The study is called, "Eighteenth-Century American Women in Peace and War: The Case of the Loyalists," and it was reprinted in *A Heritage of Her Own: Toward a New Social History of American Women*, edited by Nancy F. Cott and Elizabeth H. Pleck (New York: Simon and Schuster, 1979).

For a picture of the domestic economy in colonial America and the place of women in it, see, Richard B. Sheridan, "The Domestic Economy," in *Colonial British America: Essays in the New History of the Early Modern Era*, edited by Jack P. Greene and J. R. Pole (Baltimore: Johns Hopkins University Press, 1984).

Carl Bridenbaugh in his study, *The Colonial Craftsman* (Chicago: University of Chicago Press, 1960 [orig. 1950]), 105–107, discusses women in trades and women taking over businesses from craftsmen husbands.

On housewifery duties and the training for such work, see Edwin J. Perkins, *The Economy of Colonial America* (New York: Columbia University Press, 1988), 141–142, 148–150; also Gloria Main, *Gender, Work, and Wages*, 48.

William Marshall describes his wife at work. This can be found in Julie A. Matthaei, *An Economic History of Women in America: Women's Work, The Sexual Division of Labor and the Development of Capitalism* (New York: Schocken Books, 1982), 37, with reference to the original source on page 336, n. 1.

For a view of the medical professional and role of women in it, there is the excellent study by Laurel Thatcher Ulrich, *Good Wives*, 31, 40, 49, 53–55, 58, 64–65. There is also information about southern midwives in Julia C. Spruill, *Women's Life and Work*, 274–275.

On the communal aspects of women's work, see Ulrich, *Good Wives*, 21–22, 24–26, 38–41; and Mary Beth Norton, "Eighteenth-Century American Women," 38–39.

For a study of women in commodity production, namely butter making, see Joan M. Jensen, "Butter Making and Economic Development in Mid-Atlantic America, from 1750 to 1850," in *Women and Power in American History*, vol. I, edited by Kathryn Kish Sklar and Thomas Dublin (Englewood Cliffs, NJ: Prentice-Hall, 1991). For a study of women shoe binders in the colonial period, see Mary H. Blewett, "The Sexual Division of Labor and the Artisan Tradition in Early Industrial Capitalism: The Case of New England Shoe-making," in *To Toil the Livelong Day* edited by Carol Groneman and Mary Beth Norton.

For women as innkeepers, see Spruill, *Women's Life and Work*, 300–303; and Matthaei, *Economic History of Women in America*, 57–58.

For the work ethic of slave women, see Matthaei, *Economic History of Women in America*, 80–85, 93–97; also Jan Lewis, "Women and the American Revolution," *Organization of American Historians Magazine of History* 8, no. 4 (Summer 1994), 23–26. For a description of a slave mother at work, see John W. Blassingame, ed., *Slave Testimony: Two Centuries of Letters, Speeches, Interviews, and Autobiographies* (Baton Rouge: Louisiana State University Press, 1977), 132–133.

After the American Revolution, as the young United States began to develop capitalist elements in its economy, women were no longer strictly confined to household production, but their activities, like that of their husbands, were more and more oriented toward the market. For a picture of this process, including that of the activities of women, see James Henretta, "The Transition to Capitalism in America," 221, 224–225. For a statement on looms in Hallowell, Maine, see Henretta, 224. On barter between colonial women, see Henretta, 224.

6

THE AMERICAN REVOLUTION
AND THE AMERICAN WORK ETHIC

LABOR AS A UNIVERSAL BADGE OF HONOR

While the cries of liberty and equality rang in the towns and countrysides of colonial America in 1776, the wheels of eighteenth-century history slowly trundled out another and equally important message—work was expected of all citizens and the fancied life of the leisured classes was not to be tolerated in democratic, revolutionary America. Before this idea ran its full course in the nineteenth century, there were few who dared publicly proclaim that they did not work for their livelihood. Gordon Wood's thesis about the American Revolution includes the idea that Americans during and after the Revolution regarded aristocratic leisure with contempt and turned labor into a universal badge of honor.

John Adams concluded in 1790 that the main issue of any society would forever be who shall do the work. Adams answered that question by holding to the distinction between gentry and commoners, believing that leisure must be the portion of the few who would serve in government. Others, like Benjamin Rush, asserted that all men and women in society ought to work, adding sarcastically that a man bred as a gentleman cannot work because his hands and legs are rendered useless by having others to work for him. Rush argued that those who perform no work and live by the fruits of other men's labor had no right to make laws as they are too far removed from the people at large.

Abraham Bishop, mayor of New Haven, a 1778 graduate of Yale and a lawyer, sought to convince common people through speeches and pamphlets that they ought not feel inferior to the wealthy classes. There was a long tradition in England, carried over to the colonies, that fostered the idea that elites were best qualified to govern society. Bishop conceded that the aristocracy were the best informed, best educated, and most versed in history and political science. However, Bishop believed that for these very reasons they were not equipped to rule society. His argument ran counter to Plato's belief that those who had to work were unfit to rule since they could not devote their full time to learning the art of governing. Bishop believed that the well educated were extraordinary and therefore dangerous and that ordinary people should not be ruled by extraordinary people. The gap between the way of life of the aristocracy and working people, he contended, meant that the wealthy could never understand the experiences of the common people, and therefore the rich and powerful were not fit to rule over the mass of ordinary folk.

In the decades following the American Revolution, the assault on gentry idleness was coupled with a heightened appreciation of the dignity of labor. Property became associated less with the authority of its possessor and more with the labor that produced and improved it. The claims of speculators and absentee landlords came to have less legitimacy than the claims of those who had worked on the land. New moral value was given to work on the land that tended to overshadow mere legal title to land. Gordon Wood has argued that the real revolution that took place in the eighteenth century was the attack on the colonial American aristocracy and the raising of the rhetoric of work against the rhetoric of idleness and leisure.

WORKING PEOPLE AND POLITICS DURING AND AFTER THE AMERICAN REVOLUTION

In the wake of the American Revolution, artisans, traders, mechanics, and farmers were tired of being dismissed as individuals who were narrow, parochial, and common. They were no longer willing to defer to anyone's political leadership but their own. In the early 1790s, the tradesmen, mechanics, and industrial classes of society organized themselves into mechanics associations and Democratic–Republican societies that came to comprise the heart and soul of the Republic Party, the party of Jefferson. Everywhere, artisans, laborers, small businessmen, and farmers directed their egalitarian anger at aristocrats who had scorned them. Inspired by the American Revolution, and for half a century afterward, ordinary men challenged the rule and pretensions of the gentry.

The American Revolution was the opening wedge for the emergence of gains for the workingman and the commoner, gains that were later consolidated by the advances of Jeffersonian republicanism and Jacksonian democracy. The Revolution and the sweep of democracy that followed it, laid the foundation for an extension of the franchise to universal male suffrage by 1830 and for the greater approval of, and esteem for, the man who toiled, whether on the farm or in the workshop. In spite of the gains of working people with regard to suffrage and being able to achieve some advances in representation in the cities, the offices of both state and federal governments continued to remain in the hands of the wealthy and the elite. In Maryland, for example, under its new constitution of 1776, one had to own 5,000 pounds of property to run for governor and 1,000 pounds to run for state senator. This excluded 90 percent of the population from holding office. The new constitutions that were drawn up in all states from 1776 to 1780 were not much different from the old ones. Although property qualifications for voting and holding office were lowered in some instances, in Massachusetts they were increased. Only

Pennsylvania abolished them totally. Edmund Morgan stated that the involvement of the lower ranks in the Revolutionary War should not obscure the fact that the contest itself was generally a struggle for office and power within members of the upper class—the newly rich against the established rich. James Madison pointed out that most of the political battles during and after the Revolution were not fought between the class with and the class without property, but among different groups of property holders—rich planter and poor; merchant creditor and farmer debtor; banker creditor and artisan borrower. It was mainly in the cities where members of the working class played an active role in the political process. In Newburyport, Massachusetts, for example, 86 percent of adult males were eligible to vote in 1785, as compared with 60 percent in 1773.

After the Revolutionary War the voters did not repudiate those wealthy leaders who had led the movement for independence. However, because of the change in the basis of apportioning representation, these men constituted a small and less powerful group within the representative bodies. In democratic Massachusetts men from the wealthy class had furnished over half of the representatives. By 1784 this percentage had dropped to 22 percent, and there were corresponding decreases in other states. Less than one in five of the delegates to the colonial assemblies in the third quarter of the eighteenth century had been yeoman farmers or artisans, but in the aftermath of the Revolutionary War these social groups now constituted a majority in some of the northern legislatures and a powerful minority in the southern assemblies.

IDEOLOGY OF WORK AND THE AMERICAN REVOLUTION

During the 1790s, Jeffersonian Republicans like Matthew Lyon labeled the gentry men brought up in idleness, as contrasted with mechanics and farmers, who were the industrious part of American society. Jeffersonian Republicans in the North saw society divided between those who worked and those who lived not by their labor but by their cunning. William Manning, a New England farmer writing under the name of A Labourer, stated that the revolutionary struggle and its aftermath was between the many and the few, between those who worked and those who did not. Those who "live without labour," a phrase used by Manning to identify the wealthy, managed the government and laws, controlled the newspapers, and manipulated banks and credit. Manning said that the elite were always arguing for the advantages of education in order to make places for men in power to live without work. Manning wanted to form a Society of Labourers comparable to the Order of Cincinnati, a society made up of Revolutionary War military officers. In the early decades following the Revolution, craftsmen and manufacturers shared common resentments toward the elite who held them in contempt. Later, rich employers and masters would distinguish themselves from journeymen and laborers.

In 1792 Connecticut artisans joined in a massive petition drive against the state's system of taxation, which they believed was unfair to the working man. It was an effort that enlisted over 1,400 artisans in every craft and spread to more than twenty towns throughout the state. One of the leaders of this protest was Walter Brewster, a shoemaker residing in Canterbury who wrote a series of essays that he signed The Mechanick on Taxation, which helped prepare the way for the protest. Brewster was an ideologue whose views on public affairs reflected the new ideas about work and the workingman that followed in the aftermath of the American Revolution. He believed that men were selfish by nature and that those who controlled the most property would control the most political power. In relatively democratic Connecticut, the 600 offices above town level were filled by only 400 different men because of plural officeholding in the 1750s. In any one year over half of these officials were members of the one hundred most prominent families. John Adams commented that in any village in New England, representatives of the people, though freely elected, generally descended from generation to generation in three or four families at most. The rich managed to get elected year after year to the state councils, a body unresponsive to the problems of the common man. The great mass of ordinary men voted for members of those families who had proved their success in economic affairs, which marked them for the management of the affairs of the state. This was the tradition of deference as well as the tradition of power associated with wealth. During and after the American Revolution, this tradition was challenged by farmers and mechanics and those who did the work of colonial American society.

Brewster trusted the national government no more than he trusted Connecticut leaders. However, he did believe that men like Jefferson and Paine, employing the force of reason, would someday create a virtuous republic where honest labor would be accorded respect. Above all, he believed that reason would dictate that the crucial role of the artisan and the farmer would be recognized and that whatever was repugnant to the laboring interest was also repugnant to the common interest of the American republic.

There was a legacy from England that saw artisans as men of inferior status and lesser ability, and that is why men like Manning, Brewster, and Bishop were constantly telling the laboring people that they should stop feeling inferior and stop deferring to the wealthy and letting them monopolize the seats of power. The *Oxford English Dictionary* (1881), for example, defined *mechanic* as "belonging to or characteristic of the lower orders; base, coarse, vulgar." Samuel Johnson's *Dictionary of the English Language* (1755) described a mechanic as "servile, of mean occupation." Alexander McDougall, a noted major general in the Continental Army, was looked down upon because he began his career as a milkman and as an apprentice sailor. Merchants, lawyers, and landowners considered mechanics to be base and contemptible, neither worthy nor capable of aspiring to political or economic leadership. They were expected to accede to the wisdom and guidance of the wealthy, who were better educated and better bred. Hence the rhetoric of ideas about work after the Revolution was the truly revolutionary notion that everyone should work. Even in the South people had to maintain that pose of being at work. The popular biographer Parson Weems (1809:203–214) pictured George Washington as a man who worked, as a farmer identified with labor, and as a man praised for his industry. Even modern biographers of Washington describe him as rising early and working hard all day managing his plantations. Weems spoke about idleness as a crime and argued against the notion that "labour is a low-lived thing, fit for none but poor people and slaves." Weems also helped make Benjamin Franklin a hero for artisans and working people.

Edward Everett of Massachusetts, congressman, governor of Massachusetts, U.S. minister to England, and president of Harvard, said that all value was in labor and that "man was a working being." According to Everett gentlemen and professionals as well as artisans, farmers, and common laborers all did an honest day's work. He tried to merge all workers, laborers, and gentlemen, however varied their occupations, into one interest group. In his writings and speeches, Everett tried to dissolve the distinction between intellectual and physical work and between the liberal and mechanical arts.

Foreign visitors particularly noted that in American society work was considered honorable. De Tocqueville remarked,

> Among democratic peoples where there is no hereditary wealth, every man works for his living, or has worked, or comes from parents who have worked. Everything therefore prompts the assumption that to work is the necessary, natural and honest condition of all men.

De Tocqueville goes on to say that not only is it no dishonor to work in America, but that

> It is regarded as positively honorable; the prejudice is for, not against, it. . . . American servants do not feel degraded because they work, for everyone around them is working. There is nothing humiliating about the idea of receiving a salary, for the President of the United States works for a salary. (1969:550–551)

Nothing separated Americans coming out of their Revolution more from Europeans than their attitude toward work and their egalitarian sense that everyone must participate in it. Theodore Sedgwick, son of a prominent Federalist, said that to live without some regular employment or industry was not reputable in the new American Republic. Sedgwick concluded that the whole body of Americans were working people and that everyone in America had an occupation. Beginning with the 1820 census, every adult male was asked what his occupation was. All Americans were making a living, a leveling idea that was unprecedented in history and one that no other society had duplicated up to that time. In future America, new distinctions would arise between manual and mental work, between blue-collar and white-collar workers. However, in the decades following the Revolutionary War, all who made a useful contribution to society were considered to be working. Every nonslave American was presumed to be working at something, and therefore every nonslave American was considered to be free.

In the years immediately after the Revolutionary War, republican ideology extolled the virtues of an honest, hardworking citizenry, and this idea gave mechanics a new sense of self-worth. Artisans and journeymen united under traditional craft symbols in new mechanics societies and during public celebrations. This trend reached its apex in the great parade celebrating the ratification of the United States Constitution in 1788. Borrowing English craft symbols, masters, journeymen, and apprentices marched together in a new political setting. This unity, however, proved to be short-lived as the craft work structure soon would break down, with masters becoming employers, wholesalers, and retailers, while journeymen and apprentices remained employees and wage workers for all of their lives.

Along with commitment to the public good, republican artisans and farmers expected to expand their economic horizons now that the fetters of British mercantilism were lifted. The new republic held out the promise that however humble one might be, he could rise in the social order. America was rich in raw materials which, combined with the initiative and enterprise of hard-working farmers and artisans, offered opportunity for people to become independent. American cities began to grow. New York's population expanded from 33,000 in 1790 to 197,112 in 1830. This expanded the mechanic's world and allowed artisan enterprises to extend beyond the traditional family workshop. For successful masters this meant new avenues to wealth. For the journeyman, the picture was different. While revolutionary ideology encouraged them to seek independence, most of them remained wageworkers all of their lives and they had to struggle against masters, even engaging in strikes to try to gain a living wage. Revolutionary ideology also had an impact on youths. Young men attacked the hierarchy of the workshop and ran off before completing their apprenticeship. They refused to concede deference to their elders, revolting against the traditional patriarchy. Masters hired apprentices to use as semiskilled workers and abdicated their responsibility for these young men. Apprentices, in turn, freed from paternalism, developed a rough egalitarianism of the streets and a rowdy youth culture.

CONCLUSION

The American Revolution could not have unfolded when or as it did without the self-conscious actions of working people who became convinced that they must either create power where none existed or watch their position deteriorate. The history of the Revolution is in part a series of popular, collective actions and challenges to the claims of wealthy merchants, landowners, and professionals that their rule was legitimized by custom, law, and divine will. Ordinary people took over, sometimes violently, the power and procedures of constituted authorities. Lower classes, particularly in the cities, forced their way onto the political stage, not so much through the formal mechanisms of electoral politics, as through street demonstrations, mass meetings, and extralegal committees that assumed governmental powers and intimidated enemies. This reordering of political and social power required a mental breakthrough, for it challenged the model of social relations established by the elite, who asserted that the educated and the wealthy had superior wisdom and public-mindedness and that the proper role of the lower classes was deference toward their betters. Thus, the American Revolution was a revolution of ideas, and, as both John Adams and Thomas Paine declared, it represented a change in the minds and hearts of the American people. In the new land of America there was a conflict between rich and poor, between aspiring farmers and wealthy entrepreneurs, and, as James Madison expressed it in *The Federalist*, between those with property and those without property, the basis of class conflict in the republic. But the diversity and expanse of life following the Revolutionary War was too large to be encompassed within the tight ideological bounds of the traditional systems of elite control. Therein lay the promise of creating a genuinely democratic society.

BIBLIOGRAPHICAL ESSAY

The best discussion I have found regarding the American Revolution and the concept of work as a badge of honor is in Gordon Wood's latest book on the American Revolution. Wood's thesis regarding the radicalization of American society as a result of the American Revolution is that it created an ideology that everyone had an obligation to work and to contribute to American culture in that way. The main discussion can be found in Part III, and more particularly in the chapter within that part called "The Assault on Democracy." See Gordon S. Wood, *The Radicalism of the American Revolution* (New York: Alfred A. Knopf, 1992), 229–305.

An excellent essay that relates work and the American Revolution, specifically the Puritan Ethic and the American Revolution, can be found in Edmund S. Morgan's article entitled "The Puritan Ethic and the American Revolution," *William and Mary Quarterly* 24 (January 1967), 3–43. Morgan's thesis is that each part of the struggle against Great Britain reinforced American values of frugality, industry, sacrifice for the community and the importance of work and one's calling as a contribution to the community.

For an analysis of the American Revolution with regard to social classes and social changes, see James A. Henretta, *The Evolution of American Society, 1700–1815* (Lexington, MA: D. C. Heath, 1973). Henretta describes the various social classes involved in the Revolution and the struggles by farmers and artisans to find their place in the social and political spheres of colonial America and the young republic. He also points to the fact that a number of groups, particularly women, slaves, indentured servants, and those without property, were left without power in the new social structure that emerged from the Revolution. Henretta discusses the notion of deference and how it continued to be a potent force in the election of leaders in the various states. Both the continuance of deference and the various qualifications for voting combined to restrict the electorate and guarantee the election of those with wealth and influence. There were property qualifications not only for voting but also for holding office and this resulted in an elite holding most of the major offices, at least until the period of Jacksonian democracy. The distribution of wealth in the young republic continued to favor the largest landowners and merchants, especially after the confiscation and sale of loyalist land, which fell mostly to those already holding large estates. Henretta discusses the conflicts between commercial and subsistence farmers, with the commercial farmers seeking free and untrammeled workings of the market mechanism, while the subsistence farmers were being squeezed by high prices of manufactured goods and high taxes. This resulted in a number of actions by farmers, the most potent being Shays Rebellion.

During and after the Revolution gentlemen of leisure served in political offices without pay. The most prominent example was George Washington, who served both as commander in chief of the Continental Army and as president of the United States without pay. See James

Thomas Flexner, *Washington: The Indispensable Man* (New York: Penguin Books, 1984), 59, 212. There was debate about whether those in public service should be paid. Those arguing against paying public officials said that honor and the opportunity to serve was enough compensation. Those arguing for payment stated that those who were not independently wealthy, which was most of the population, would not be able to serve, and thus, most of the political offices would be filled by the rich. On the subject of George Washington as a working farmer in colonial times, see Mason L. Weems, *The Life of Washington* (1809), edited by Marcus Cunliffe (Cambridge, MA: Cambridge University Press, 1962), 203–214.

On the subject of deference and how it was affected by the Revolution, see Richard R. Beeman, "Deference, Republicanism, and the Emergence of Popular Politics in Eighteenth-Century America," *William and Mary Quarterly* 49, no. 3 (July 1992), 401–430.

For a discussion of artisans in Connecticut and their struggles for political and economic recognition, see James P. Walsh, " 'Mechanics and Citizens': The Connecticut Artisan Protest of 1792," *William and Mary Quarterly* 42, no. 1 (January 1985), 66–89.

On the role of mechanics in the politics of the new republic following the Revolutionary War, see Alfred F. Young, "The Mechanics and the Jeffersonians: New York, 1789–1801," in *The Labor History Reader*, edited by Daniel J. Leab (Urbana: University of Illinois Press, 1985), 66–95.

For a fascinating study of an artisan who participated in the Revolutionary War, see Alfred F. Young, "George Robert Twelves Hewes (1720–1840): A Boston Shoemaker and the Memory of the American Revolution," *William and Mary Quarterly* 38, no. 4 (October 1981), 561–623.

On the attitude that artisans and mechanics were base and servile and not fit for political office, see Howard Rock, *Artisans of the New Republic: The Tradesmen of New York City in the Age of Jefferson* (New York: New York University Press, 1979), 4.

For a discussion of Parson Weems, the biographer of Franklin and Washington, and how he viewed them as men who worked and as models of industriousness, see Gordon Wood, *The Radicalism of the American Revolution*, 283, 414, n. 26. On the views of Edward Everett of Massachusetts, see Wood, *The Radicalism of the American Revolution*, 284–285.

With reference to the view of De Tocqueville that in America work was an honorable thing and that everyone was expected to be working, including the president, see Alexis de Tocqueville, *Democracy in America*, edited by J. P. Mayer (New York: Harper & Row, 1969 [orig. 1833]).

On the activities of artisans and mechanics in cities, see Gary Nash, *The Urban Crucible: The Northern Seaports and the Origins of the American Revolution* (Cambridge, MA: Harvard University Press, 1986).

For a discussion of the colonial artisan's participation in the Revolution, see Carl Bridenbaugh, "The Craftsman as a Citizen," in *The Colonial Craftsman* (New York: Dover Publications, 1960 [orig. 1950]), 155–181.

Gary Nash discusses artisan participation in the politics surrounding the Revolution in Nash, *The Urban Crucible*, 227–233.

For a discussion of artisans in New York and their participation in the revolutionary movement, see Paul A. Gilje and Howard B. Rock, eds., *Keepers of the Revolution: New Yorkers at Work in the Early Republic* (Ithaca, NY: Cornell University Press, 1992).

For a quotation from Jefferson describing artisans as "the yeomanry of the city," see Young, "The Mechanics and the Jeffersonians," 94.

For a discussion of the youth culture and the breakup of the traditional relationship between masters and apprentices following the Revolutionary War, see Paul A. Gilje, *The Road to Mobocracy: Popular Disorder in New York City, 1763–1834* (Chapel Hill: University of North Carolina Press, 1987). See also Gilje and Rock, *Keepers of the Revolution*, 4–6.

On the participation of Philadelphia's artisans in the events leading up to the Revolution, see Gary Nash, *The Urban Crucible*, 240–246. For another view of Philadelphia's working people see Eric Foner, *Tom Paine and Revolutionary America* (New York: Oxford University Press, 1976).

A general view of the artisans of Charleston can be found in Richard Walsh, *Charleston's Sons of Liberty: A Study of the Artisans, 1763–1789* (Columbia: University of South Carolina Press, 1959).

On the thesis that the American Revolution was a revolution in ideas and values, see Hermann Wellenreuther, "Labor in the Era of the American Revolution: A Discussion of Recent Concepts and Theories," *Labor History* 11, no. 4 (Fall 1981), 573–600.

For an interpretation of the American Revolution from the point of view of working people, farmers, artisans, laborers, and others, and from the point of view of the disadvantaged members of colonial society, see Howard Zinn, *A People's History of the United States* (New York: Harper Perennial, 1980), 76–101.

On the use of crowds and mobs during and after the American Revolution to enforce and project demands of working people, see Paul A. Gilje, *The Road to Mobocracy*, 39–92.

Michael Zuckerman, in his article "A Different Thermidor: The Revolution Beyond the American Revolution," in *The Transformation of Early American History: Society, Authority, and Ideology*, edited by James A. Henretta, Michael Kammen, and Stanley N. Katz (New York, Alfred A. Knopf, 1991), 170–193, discusses at length the issue of the individual versus the community and how it related to the American Revolution. Zuckerman points out that revolutionary ideology lay in its drive for social regeneration through civic virtue. Many of the patriots sought to establish a state whose virtue would be in a polity without partisanship, an economy without individualism, and a society without sectarianism. Republican liberty was an attribute of societies whose citizens were virtuous, and virtue lay in the willingness of individuals to subordinate their private interests to the public good. Commerce was often inimical to virtue, for it often led men to an undue infatuation with their own immediate interests in the marketplace (Zuckerman, "A Different Thermidor," 172–173). Zuckerman adds that Americans could only imagine that the gains of the greedy would be at the expense of the public welfare. Before the Revolution there was no systematic moral sanction for competitive self-seeking in early America (178). Avowals of virtuous simplicity intensified in the years after 1750. Professions of republican submission of self to society came to a crescendo in the final decades before the break with Britain. As opulence grew, Sam Adams asserted that the citizen "owes everything to the commonwealth" (180). Zuckerman states that surely there were Americans who put their own interests before the general welfare. Otherwise, there would have been no necessity for protesting too much the priority of communal good over partisan interest (178, 181). The ideas and ideals of American culture as it entered upon the rebellion in 1776 were those of republican communalism. The norms of the nation as it entered upon the nineteenth century were very different (190).

Zuckerman spells out, with many references, the fact that in the aftermath of the American Revolution, Americans turned from the ideology of public virtue to the ideology of individualism and pursuit of private self-interest (182–193).

Pauline Maier discusses the same issue of private versus public interests, with a slightly different slant, viewing the conflict of ideas as that between an older, traditional view of classical republicanism that involved deference toward the elite and their ability to rule, as against a new liberal ideology of individualism, self-interest, and competition that arose after the Revolution. See her article, "The Transforming Impact of Independence, Reaffirmed,

1776 and the Definition of American Social Structure," in *The Transformation of Early American History*, edited by James A. Henretta, Michael Kammen, and Stanley N. Katz, 194–217. Maier sums up the issue as follows:

> The Federalists of 1787–88 and the Federalist Party of the 1790s allegedly remained faithful to this archaic vision. They sought to establish "a patricianled-classical democracy" in which the people would defer to gentlemen of wealth, education, and leisure, who alone were capable of disinterested leadership. But independence, according to this interpretation, released "pent-up forces" that imperiled the Federalists' social vision. It brought into politics "new men" whose attitudes were founded . . . in a "period of striking economic growth" during the half century before independence. These "tradesmen, mechanics and newly launched merchants" developed an appreciation for self-interest and a "liberal vision of society" totally incompatible with classical republicanism and its injunctions to selfless deference. (206)

Part II

THE NINETEENTH CENTURY

7

THE AMERICAN WORK ETHIC
IN THE NINETEENTH CENTURY

OVERVIEW

The territory of the United States mushroomed in size between 1800 and 1860. From a nation squeezed between the Atlantic Ocean and the Appalachian Mountains, it swept like a gale across the plains of the Midwest, over the Rocky Mountains, and reached the Pacific Ocean. By 1860, there were miners and ranchers in California, farmers in Oregon, railroad builders in the Rockies, town boosters in Nebraska and Kansas, and cattle drovers in Texas. The Louisiana Purchase of 1803, the acquisition of Florida in 1819, the establishment of Oregon in 1836, and the taking of land from Mexico in 1846 extended the territory of the United States to make it a continental power. Settling the West and the Far West was the result of hard work by pioneers willing to give up their way of life in the East. They struggled against harsh conditions on tough prairie land, forbidding mountainous terrain, and the hostility of Native Americans. Still, they succeeded in making the prairie, the mountains, and the Far West a treasure house of resources and new states, where the energies of a youthful, vital population could find new opportunities.

Nineteenth-century America was a society of mixed values and social transition. It was the century when the traditional values of craft and the new values of industrial factory work coexisted and struggled for supremacy. It was the century that started out with the agricultural population predominant and ended with the wage worker predominant. It was the century when the leisurely work styles of the artisan gave way to the pressured, time-oriented styles of the industrial worker.

Americans were optimists in the nineteenth century, believing in irresistible progress based on human achievements in science, technology, and knowledge. Americans also embraced the theory of evolution. Thinkers and academics preached that evolutionary forces were creating higher forms of life from lower ones in the natural world, and more organized social structures from less organized ones in the social world. Darwin and Spencer were popularized, and on all sides progress and evolution seemed confirmed by social improvements in the nineteenth century.

During the last quarter of the nineteenth century, rapid changes permeated the social fabric of American culture. One invention followed another—the telegraph, the telephone, the electric light, the typewriter, the automatic air brake, the electric motor—and transformed American homes, farms, factories, and offices. The corporate form of business became dominant, enabling large concentrations of capital to be centered in nationwide businesses that expanded into international markets. Business thrived and the federal government encouraged it with land grants, subsidies, a banking system, and an enlarged money supply.

America was growing, swelled by waves of immigrants landing on its shores. The population of the country grew from 5 million in 1800 to 12 million in 1850, to 32 million in 1860, to 62.9 million in 1890, and reached 75.8 million in 1900. The undeveloped state of transportation initially inhibited the growth of national and regional markets. It cost more to move goods overland than it did to transport them over the ocean. With canal building in the 1820s and 1830s, and railroad and bridge building in the 1840s, 1850s, and 1860s, local markets were knitted into regional markets and national markets. Freight rates fell drastically and merchandise flowed swiftly westward and eastward.

A NEW WORK FORCE

While the farm population grew during the nineteenth century, the nonagriculture population grew even faster. By the Civil War wage earners represented 40 percent of the working population. Thread, yarn, and textiles moved from the spinning wheel and loom in the home to the mule spinner and powered loom in the factory. Factory workers produced steam engines, textile and sewing machines, milling machines, metal products, machine tools, stoves, firearms, springs, bolts, and wires. Construction workers built factories, housing, and roads. Armies of laborers found employment on canals and railroads.

Towns and cities grew to accommodate the growing numbers of factories, workshops, and mills. In 1840, when the population of the United States was 17 million, only 8.5 percent lived in urban areas. By 1860 there were nearly 400 towns and cities, with New York having a million people and Philadelphia more than half a million. Cities needed housing, utilities, and streets, as well as sewer and water systems and transportation systems to get people into and out of the cities. The cities needed warehouses to store goods. These needs created jobs for the skilled trades as well as unskilled porters, carters, teamsters, drivers, laborers, and warehousemen. In the port cities, seamen and dockworkers found work. Women and children entered the work force, particularly in the textile mills. In 1812, Albert Gallatin reported that eighty-seven cotton mills in the United States employed 3,500 women and children and only 500 men.

From the 1820s, more and more work was "put out." The putting-out system was especially widespread in the clothing and shoe industries. Merchants supplied the raw materials, paid the worker by the piece, and then marketed the product. In the 1830s, 18,000 Massachusetts women braided straw hats at home for wages, while another 12,000 or 13,000 women worked at home making paper boxes, hoopskirts, shirts and collars, artificial flowers, ladies' cloaks, and other products. The countryside surrounding American cities was a vast scene of household manufacturing. Household industries also provided work for thousands of men, women, and children processing agricultural products such as pork, hides, cheese, soap, tallow, and leather.

FACTORIES

America's industrial revolution had rural origins. In New England, where large-scale water-powered manufacturing first became widespread, early factories usually were located outside cities in hamlets or in communities scattered along hinterland streams because coastal cities lacked adequate water power. This was true of America's vanguard manufacturing establishment—the textile mill.

The factory system for cotton spinning and weaving became firmly established in New England after the War of 1812, when imports from England ceased. By 1840 there were 1,200 cotton factories in the United States. By 1850 there were over 1,500 woolen mills in the northern states. Most of them were small, individually owned enterprises with few sets of machinery, employing country people from neighboring villages. In Connecticut, the factory system spread to take advantage of the energy from almost every waterfall. These small factories produced machine tools, firearms, furniture, the Hitchcock chair, wooden clocks, and other household products. In Rhode Island, Samuel Slater introduced machines into his textile factories and operated on a much larger scale. Slater employed whole families in his factories. Lowell mills in Massachusetts in the 1820s and 1830s hired young, unmarried Yankee women from the countryside, paid them relatively high wages, and offered them food and board. As time went on, however, mill owners cut wages and raised rents, and conditions deteriorated to the point where the women engaged in strikes to protest. By the 1840s, the Yankee women were going back to their farm families and were replaced by Irish immigrants.

During the nineteenth century there were tensions between the customs of working people used to the artisan's work ethic and the demands of an industrial system based on a strict timed and disciplined work regime. These tensions between the old and the new gave rise to protests among workers in factories, mines, construction projects, and railroads. Forms of protest included absenteeism, slowdowns, spontaneous riots, and organized strikes as men and women resisted the industrial work ethic. This new ethic embodied in the regimentation of the factory included an authoritarian command structure over work. The artisan's leisured pace of work was increasingly supplanted by the new demands of factory production based on speed and efficiency.

The productivity of its working people made the United States the leading industrial nation by the end of the nineteenth century. While the factory was the most visible manifestation of industrialism, as late as 1860, more wage earners worked in farmhouses and small workshops than in factories, and most used hand tools, not power-driven equipment; handicrafts were still dominant up to 1860. In New York and St. Louis, less than 10 percent of wage earners worked in manufacturing, while in Baltimore and New Orleans only 8 and 3 percent respectively worked in manufacturing. Newark, one of the most industrialized cities in the mid-nineteenth century, had 25 percent of its employed as industrial workers.

Iron making before the Civil War was a rural-based industry, located near iron ore deposits and near forests for raw material to make charcoal. The industry moved westward toward western Pennsylvania and Ohio in the 1830s and 1840s. Some iron manufacturers in the South used slave labor. In the presteam age, falling water was needed for power, which was another reason for locating iron-making mills in countryside towns. Iron was the miracle material of the nineteenth century—abundant, cheap, and useful. It was perfect for jobs requiring great strength in proportion to weight—beams and columns for mill buildings, and trusses for bridges. Several thousand iron bridges were built in America between 1840, when iron began to replace wood and stone, and 1880. Then iron was in turn superseded by steel. The iron bridge helped Americans cross thousands of streams and rivers to reach new land and markets as the frontier moved west. Entrepreneurs, largely self-taught craftsmen, built these early bridges. The craftsman-millwright-founder, who learned his skills by apprenticeship, built as many bridges as the educated engineer during this period.

While the new regimen in factories and mills was heavy handed and filled with all kinds of rules, life was very different for workers in the handicrafts. The artisan worked according to his own rhythm. He was task oriented and worked until completing a given job. His day was a blend of work, fellowship, and breaks. The casual workplace of the artisan was in transition in the 1830s and 1840s. By 1850, shops were substituting machinery for hand equipment. In printing, employers were trading in screw presses for steam-driven ones. By the closing decades of the nineteenth century, wage workers no longer referred to themselves as journeymen. Distinctions of skill endured, but manual workers thought of themselves as workers, just as employers no longer thought of themselves as masters, but businessmen and manufacturers. Workplaces grew larger, machines replaced hand tools, and standardized products spilled out of factories corporately owned and hierarchically structured.

CONCLUSION

The nineteenth century nourished a mixture of work ethics that often clashed and remained unresolved until the march of industrialism imposed a new regime of authority and discipline in the workplace. The work ethic of artisans persisted throughout the nineteenth century even while wage labor and industrialization became dominant. Craftsmen continued to be prominent in construction, in the metal trades, in newspaper and printing enterprises, in the needle and leather trades, in jewelry, in furniture, in woodworking, in the railroad crafts, and in tool and machine manufacture. What defined the artisan's ethic was quality of workmanship, rhythm of work, and a sociable environment in the workplace. As factory production encroached on the crafts, artisans became factory artisans, no longer making the entire product. They still used hand methods, but they became specialists rather than generalists. They were no longer self-employed producers dealing with customers, but wage workers dealing with owners of capital. The craftsman's work ethic of independence gave way to a work ethic of dependence.

The influx of immigrants starting in the 1840s brought with it a population not used to, nor accepting of, the work discipline of the factory. Many were peasants used to the rhythms of farm work, and they did not easily take to the regimen of continuous work. They worked with alternate bouts of intense labor and idleness. They did not take well to factory speed-up, and they had more loyalty to their church, community, and family than to their employers. It was a long struggle before these workers succumbed to the rules of the factory, a struggle not completed until well into the twentieth century.

Farmers still made up the majority of the population in the nineteenth century, in spite of growing industrialization. Farmers expanded as the country pushed westward, with wheat and corn dominant in the Midwest, ranching in the Southwest, and fruit and vegetables in California. Southern plantation agriculture also pushed west until interrupted by the Civil War. Farming rested on the use of family labor, the need to choose appropriate crops for a particular region, and the mixture of subsistence and commercial activities. As farming became increasingly market oriented it affected the farmer's work ethic. He had to be more of a manager and he had to deal with debt when he needed to buy new machines to compete in the marketplace. The work ethic of the independent, self-sufficient and self-reliant farmer was giving way to a work ethic of calculation, profit, and dependency on banks, railroads, and crop storage companies. Being squeezed between low prices for what they sold and high prices for what they bought, farmers organized Farmers' Alliances and the Populist Political Party in the 1880s and 1890s in an effort to restrict the power of banks, railroads, and monopolies. However, they were never able to create sufficient power to offset that of the rising industrial and financial corporations that came to dominate the United States economy after the Civil War.

There were in the nineteenth century, as in all American experience, the unskilled, manual workers who had nothing to offer but strong hands and backs. These workers built canals and railroads, loaded ships and warehouses, cleaned streets and carried away city garbage. They worked in mines and on ranches and they filled all the unskilled jobs in the factories and mills. Unions considered them unorganizable because of their ethnic differences. Many lived on the margins of society, were single men housed in camps and shantytowns, and were part of the unskilled labor pool swelled each year by waves of immigrants.

Into this mixture, one must add the work of slaves, who performed all the different kinds of work that free workers performed, except that they received no wages and were themselves involuntary, coerced labor. Their ethic was one of survival, since they had no hope that hard work could improve their lot or gain their freedom. Slaves had to learn to preserve for themselves time for their own families and time to work in their gardens or in their cabins for the comfort of their families.

Finally, there was the work of women, mostly in their households, but increasingly in the public sphere in factories and mills. On the farm, women did what they always did—helping with the harvest and planting, being responsible for the dairy cows and chickens, making clothing for the family, rearing children, and caring for the household. In the cities, women were mainly homemakers, but their role was essential for the viability of the family and the rearing and education of the children. Toward the end of the nineteenth century, women began to enter certain industries like textiles and clothing in large numbers, and they began to find white-collar work in offices and professional work as teachers and nurses.

Thus, in the nineteenth century there was a mixture of work ethics, including wage workers, craftsmen, slaves, the unskilled, immigrants, farmers, and women. No one work ethic fit all of these groups. It was the industrialized society that reduced most workers to wage workers and that eventually would impose a time-centered discipline in the workplace. This would homogenize the mixture of work ethics of the nineteenth century into the profit-oriented, marketplace, consuming, and producing work ethic of the twentieth century.

BIBLIOGRAPHICAL ESSAY

There has been much debate about the transition between the eighteenth and nineteenth centuries that led from a tradition-oriented society based on farming and crafts to a commercial and industrial society based upon capitalist economic institutions. There is no question that the American Revolution expanded both the freedoms of the colonial population as well as its ability to develop and expand its own resources. This expansion of resources was accompanied by an expansion of values and ideology, along with a geographical expansion westward and an opening of opportunities for new avenues to wealth. Eventually, the process led to a capitalist society in which wage earners would be more prominent than farmers and artisans and manufacturing more significant in its economic power than farming. When and how this transformation began to occur is a matter of interpretation, and a good survey of the literature and the ideas associated with this transformation can be found in Michael Merrill, "Putting Capitalism in Its Place: A Review of Recent Literature," *William and Mary Quarterly* 52, no. 2 (April 1995), 315–326.

For an overview of the social and economic transformations that occurred during the nineteenth century between the presidencies of Thomas Jefferson and that of William McKinley, see Walter Licht, *Industrializing America: The Nineteenth Century* (Baltimore: Johns Hopkins University Press, 1995). Licht focuses on industrialization as both a product and an agent of change leading to the development of a new political and economic order put into place by the start of the twentieth century. Henry Steele Commager draws a comprehensive picture of nineteenth-century American values and culture in "The Nineteenth-Century American," in *The American Mind* (New Haven, CT: Yale University Press, 1959), 3–40.

For a review of the attitudes toward work and workers in the nineteenth century before the Civil War, see Nicholas K. Bromell, *By the Sweat of the Brow: Literature and Labor in Antebellum America* (Chicago: University of Chicago Press, 1993), especially 15–60. A fine, short introduction to the study of work and workers in the nineteenth century is contained in an article by Merritt Roe Smith, "Industry, Technology, and the 'Labor Question' in 19th-Century America: Seeking Synthesis," *Technology and Culture* 32, no. 3 (July 1991),

555–570. This article not only contains a useful summary regarding the main issues in the study of work and workers in the nineteenth century, but also provides many useful references for further study and reading. On the statement regarding the founding of the first factories in rural areas, see Jonathan Prude, "Town-Factory Conflicts in Antebellum Rural Massachusetts," in *The Countryside in the Age of Capitalist Transformation*, edited by Steven Hahn and Jonathan Prude (Chapel Hill: University of North Carolina Press, 1985), 71. Prude's essay provides valuable insights into the kinds of communities in which the early factories were located and their social and economic outlook. He points out that what was characteristic of the early factory towns in America is that while market transactions were frequent and a buoyant consumerism was taking root, the sense of a whole-hearted commitment to profit maximization had only limited consensus. Local yeomen, for all their involvement with buying and selling, still retained many conventions of household production. They relied less on hired workers than on family members, and on receiving and giving neighborly assistance during busy seasons. Farmers in these factory communities ventured into the market not to get rich but to acquire the goods and services needed to preserve their households. Artisans, shopkeepers, and their small retinue of employees evinced similarly noncommercial perspectives. Despite their widening connection with distant customers, handicraftsmen did most of their business with fellow townspeople and their customers were still almost always nearby inhabitants (75). This picture applies to the first three or four decades of the nineteenth century, a picture that would drastically change after the Civil War.

Another important review of work and working people which I have drawn upon in Part 2 is a study written by Bruce Laurie, *Artisans into Workers: Labor in Nineteenth-Century America* (New York: Hill and Wang, 1989). Laurie deals with the basic change that occurred during the nineteenth century as the industrialization of society encroached upon and undermined the craft basis of work and drew people into factories and mills where work was regimented, disciplined, and subdivided.

Herbert Gutman was responsible as a pathbreaking historian in bringing to light the struggles between the traditional craft-oriented organization of work and the new industrial order. Gutman pointed to the value system brought to America by immigrants with their peasant backgrounds and how this value system clashed with the values of the factory and the mill. Gutman's ideas can be found in two works: "Work, Culture and Society in Industrializing America, 1815–1919," *American Historical Review* 78, no. 3 (June 1973), 537–603; a volume of essays, *Work Culture and Society in Industrializing America: Essays in American Working-Class and Social History* (New York: Alfred A. Knopf, 1976).

Another important study from which I have derived many ideas and facts is by Daniel T. Rodgers, *The Work Ethic in Industrial America, 1850–1920* (Chicago: University of Chicago Press, 1978). Rodgers, with flowing prose and wit, presents material showing how men and women reacted to the industrialization of America in the second half of the nineteenth century. He also reveals the discrepancies between the belief system of leaders of the society and employers, and the realities of life for workers and employees. Rodgers presents an analysis of the work ethic and how it relates to industrial technology, along with its consequences for workers in industrialized settings.

For a good introduction to the prevalence of the belief in evolution and progress in the last quarter of the nineteenth century, see the introduction by Perry Miller, ed., *American Thought: Civil War to World War I* (New York: Holt, Rinehart and Winston, 1962). Also see Ray Ginger, ed., *American Social Thought* (New York: Hill and Wang, 1961), specifically the chapters on John Dewey and Charles Horton Cooley.

In dealing with the nineteenth century, one inevitably must deal with the movement west and the idea of the frontier. For a classical, though much debated theory about the significance of the frontier to America society, see Frederick Jackson Turner, *The Frontier in American History* (New York: Henry Holt, 1962 [orig. 1920]). The discussion and commentaries on Turner's great theory are too many to be cited here. But two reviews that may be consulted are George Rogers Taylor, ed., *The Turner Thesis: Concerning the Role of the Frontier in American History* (Boston: D. C. Heath, 1956); and "The Dream of the West," in Paul A. Carter's book, *Revolt Against Destiny: An Intellectual History of the United States* (New York: Columbia University Press, 1989), 1–19.

The period of the Jacksonian presidency, 1828–1836, was an important one for the rise of worker consciousness and the development of workingmen's parties and labor unions. A good review of worker attitudes during that period can be found in Maurice Neufeld, "Realms of Thought and Organized Labor in the Age of Jackson," *Labor History* 10, no. 1 (Winter 1969), 5–43. Books dealing with Jacksonian democracy include: Marvin Meyer, *The Jacksonian Persuasion* (New York: Vintage, 1960); Robert V. Remini, *The Age of Jackson* (New York: Harper & Row, 1972); Arthur Schlesinger, Jr., *The Age of Jackson* (Boston: Little, Brown, 1945). Edward Pessen has questioned whether the Jacksonian party deserved or earned the loyalty of labor support. See Edward Pessen, *Jacksonian America: Society, Personality and Politics* (Homewood, IL: Dorsey, 1969); and Edward Pessen, "Should Labor Have Supported Jackson," in *The Labor History Reader*, edited by Daniel J. Leab (Urbana: University of Illinois Press, 1985), 96–106.

For the review of the early factory system and its introduction into Lowell, Massachusetts, see the following works by Thomas Dublin: *Women at Work: The Transformation of Work and Community in Lowell, Massachusetts, 1826–1860* (New York: Columbia University Press, 1979); *Farm to Factory: Women's Letters, 1830–1860* (New York: Columbia University Press, 1981); and *Lowell: The Story of an Industrial City* (Washington, DC: U.S. Department of Interior, 1992).

Attitudes and responses of workers to the new factory system are excellently portrayed in David A. Zonderman, *Aspirations and Anxieties: New England Workers and the Mechanized Factory System, 1815–1850* (New York: Oxford University Press, 1992).

On the early shoe industry in Lynn, Massachusetts, see the following: Alan Dawley, *Class and Community: The Industrial Revolution in Lynn* (Cambridge, MA: Harvard University Press, 1976); Paul G. Faler, "Cultural Aspects of the Industrial Revolution: Lynn, Massachusetts, Shoemakers and Industrial Morality, 1826–1860," in *American Workingclass Culture: Explorations in American Labor and Social History*, edited by Milton Cantor (Westport, CT: Greenwood Press, 1979); Paul G. Faler, *Mechanics and Manufacturers in the Early Industrial Revolution: Lynn, Massachusetts, 1780–1860* (Albany: State University of New York Press, 1981).

On the specific process of turning artisans into wage workers, two studies are particularly significant. One dealing with the artisans of Cincinnati is by Steven J. Ross, *Workers on the Edge: Work, Leisure and Politics in Industrializing Cincinnati, 1788–1890* (New York: Columbia University Press, 1985). The other is by Susan E. Hirsch, *Roots of the American Working Class: The Industrialization of Crafts in Newark, 1800–1860* (Philadelphia: University of Pennsylvania Press, 1978).

For a general overview of early industrialization in the nineteenth century, see Bruce Levine, Stephen Brier, David Brundage, Edward Countryman, Dorothy Fennell, and Marcus Rediker, *Who Built America: Working People and the Nation's Economy, Politics, Culture, and Society.* Vol. 1 (New York: Pantheon Books, 1989), 239–240, 249, 251–252, 259–260, 266.

On the early factory system in Connecticut and the establishment of early factories in the countryside because of the need to utilize the waterpower of streams, see Samuel Eliot Morison, *The Oxford History of the American People*, Vol. 2: *1789–1877* (New York: Mentor, 1972), 232. For the textile industry of the South, see Bruce Laurie, *Artisans into Workers*, 32–33.

On the construction industry in the nineteenth century, and particularly the use of the balloon method of framing housing, see Bob Reckman, "Carpentry: The Craft and Trade," in *Case Studies on the Labor Process*, edited by Andrew Zimbalist (New York: Monthly Review Press, 1979), 80–81. Also see Daniel J. Boorstin, *The Americans: The National Experience* (New York: Vintage Books, 1965), 148.

On the importance of iron as a crucial material between the Civil War and the 1890s and the use of iron in the building of truss bridges, see Eric Delony, "The Golden Age of the Iron Bridge," in *Invention and Technology* 10, no. 2 (Fall 1994), 8–23.

On the labor movement in the 1820s, see Bruce Laurie, *Artisans into Workers*, 74, 78–79, 83–86. For the labor unrest in the post–Civil War period, see Walter Licht, *Industrializing America*, 166–174.

On farmers, farming and the farmer's work ethic, see Richard Hofstadter, *The Age of Reform: From Bryan to F.D.R.* (New York: Alfred A. Knopf, 1955). Also see Thomas J. Schlereth, *Victorian America: Transformations in Everyday Life, 1876–1915* (New York: Harper Perennial, 1991), 34–45. For insights into the trials faced by farmers confronted by big business, see the novel by Frank Norris, *The Octopus*, The Library of America Edition (New York: Library Classics of the United States, 1986 [orig. 1900]), 553–1098. The novels of Willa Cather such as *My Antonia* are also excellent for insights into the farming life of the late nineteenth century. On the Populist Movement of farmers in the last two decades of the nineteenth century, see Lawrence Goodwyn, *Democratic Promise: The Populist Movement in America* (New York: Oxford University Press, 1976). Also Norman Pollack, *The Populist Response to Industrial America* (Cambridge, MA: Harvard University Press, 1976). On one of the leaders of the Populists, see C. Vann Woodward, *Tom Watson, Agrarian Rebel* (New York: Oxford University Press, 1963).

On the increase in the size and influence of industrial establishments, see Boorstin, *The Americans: The Democratic Experience*, 145–157, 309–332. Also see Thomas Cochran and William Miller, *The Age of Enterprise* (New York: Macmillan, 1942). On the great fortunes that were made after the Civil War, see Matthew Josephson, *The Robber Barons* (New York: Harcourt Brace Jovanovich, 1962).

On the cigarette industry, see Laurie, *Artisans into Workers*, 117–118. On the cigar industry, see Patricia Cooper, "Women Workers, Work Culture and Collective Action in the American Cigar Industry," in *Life and Labor: Dimensions of American Working-Class History*, edited by Charles Stephenson and Robert Asher (Albany: State University of New York Press, 1986).

On American immigrants, see Maldwyn Allen Jones, *American Immigration* (Chicago: University of Chicago Press, 1970). For an impressive discussion of American ethnic groups and their historical backgrounds, see Thomas Sowell, *Ethnic America: A History* (New York: Basic Books, 1981). On immigrants also see Bruce Laurie, *Artisans into Workers*, 122–123.

On the American labor movement during the last two decades of the nineteenth century see Joshua Freeman, Nelson Lichtenstein, Stephen Brier, David Bensman, Susan Porter Benson, Bret Eynon, Bruce Levine, and Bryan Palmer, *Who Built America: Working People and the Nation's Economy, Politics, Culture, and Society.* Vol. 2 (New York: Pantheon Books, 1992), 113–129. Also see Harold U. Faulkner, *Politics, Reform and Expansion, 1890–1900* (New York: Harper & Row, 1959), 87–91. Also see Bruce Laurie, *Artisans into Workers*,

148–158. On labor unrest in the late nineteenth century, see Walter Licht, *Industrializing America*, 169–186.

For an economic survey of the nineteenth century, see Jeffrey Madrick, *The End of Affluence* (New York: Random House, 1995), 22–33, 38–55. Jeffrey Madrick, in this book, is seeking to find the causes of the present-day decline of America's growth, and in order to do so he examines the historical trends in American economic history. As such he provides an excellent review of the economic background to work in the nineteenth century.

For a picture of living conditions for working Americans in the last two decades of the nineteenth century, see Jerome M. Clubb, Erik W. Austin, and Gordon W. Kirk, Jr., *The Process of Historical Inquiry: Everyday Lives of Working Americans* (New York: Columbia University Press, 1989).

8

FARMERS IN THE
NINETEENTH CENTURY

THE AGRARIAN WORK ETHIC—IDEAL AND REALITY

The Ideal

During the colonial period and at least until the first half of the nineteenth century, American values were largely shaped by country life. Even spokesmen for city people realized that their audience had largely been reared on the farm. For many American writers and leaders, including Thomas Jefferson and Hector St. Jean de Crevecoeur, the yeoman farmer was admired for his honest industry, his independence, his spirit of equality, and his ability to produce and enjoy a simple abundance.

As the nineteenth century unfolded American farmers were drawn into the commercial aspects of farming and were concerned with making money, but those who saw farm life as an ideal stressed the nonpecuniary, self-sufficient aspects of American farm life. The American mind was attached to rural living and held the yeoman farmer as the ideal man and the ideal citizen. Praise for the virtues of farmers and the special values of rural life were coupled with the belief that agriculture was uniquely productive and important to society and had a right to the protection of government. The yeoman who owned a small farm and worked it with the aid of his family was seen as the incarnation of the simple, honest, independent, healthy human being. As he lived in close communion with nature his life was believed to have a wholesomeness and integrity not possible for city populations. The farmer's well-being was both physical and moral, not merely personal but central to civic virtue. Since the yeoman was believed to be both happy and honest and since he had a secure, propertied stake in society as a landowner, he was believed to be the best and most reliable sort of citizen.

Among the intellectual classes of the eighteenth century in both Europe and America, the agrarian ideal had universal appeal. Agrarianism was linked to a formal philosophy of natural rights. The application of natural-rights philosophy to land tenure became very popular in America. The writings of John Locke contained the argument that the land is the common stock of society to which every man has a right. Jefferson called it a fundamental right to labor in the earth. Since occupancy and use of land are the true criteria of valid ownership, labor expended in cultivating the earth confers one's title to it. And since government was created to protect property, the property of working farmers has a special claim to be fostered and protected by the state. It was hoped by many, the Jeffersonians in particular, that with the development of the western lands the great inland regions would result in a preponderance of yeomen and therefore would insure the health of the republic.

The agrarian ideal was a powerful ideology because the United States in the first half of the nineteenth century consisted predominantly of literate and politically enfranchised farmers. The agrarian ideal which took form in the colonial period did correspond to many of the realities of American agricultural life at that time. There were commercial elements in colonial agriculture from the earliest days, but there were also large numbers, perhaps the majority, of independent farmers who had substantial self-sufficiency and who gave their children a strong belief in the traditions of farming and household industry. For a long time the commercial potentialities of agriculture were held in check by poor transportation, and only those farmers near towns and rivers were able to produce on a scale for urban regions. However, the small urban population (Philadelphia, the largest city had only 40,000 people at the end of the eighteenth century) provided a limited domestic market. Outside the South, operations above the size of the family farm were held back by the absence of a force of farm laborers. At the beginning of the nineteenth century, when Americans were still largely confined from the Atlantic seaboard to the eastern edge of the Appalachians, the agrarian ideal largely conformed to the realities of colonial agriculture.

The Reality

Between 1815 and 1860 the character of American agriculture was transformed. The rise of native industry created a home market for agriculture, while at the same time demand arose abroad for American cotton and for American food. A network of turnpikes, canals, and railroads linked the planter and the western farmer to these new markets. Eastern farmers began to cultivate more thoroughly the nearby urban outlets for their products. As the farmer moved on to the flat, rich prairies of the Midwest he found opportunities for use of machinery that did not exist on the small farms in the East. Western farmers began to use horse-drawn mechanical reapers, steel plows, wheat and corn drills, and threshers. The cash crop converted the yeoman farmer into a small entrepreneur and farmers more and more gave up their self-sufficiency. They continued to be independent because they owned their own land and they were hard-working and frugal in the old tradition. But they no longer grew or manufactured what they needed as they concentrated on the cash crop and bought more of their supplies from the country store. To take full advantage of mechanization, they bought as much land as they could. To mechanize fully, they borrowed cash. When they could not afford machines they hired itinerant jobbers with machines to do ploughing or threshing. The shift from self-sufficiency to commercial farming was completed in Ohio by 1830 and in Indiana, Illinois, and Michigan by 1850. Instead of living in isolation, the farmer now found himself surrounded by jobbers, banks, stores, middlemen, horses, and machinery. In so far as this process was unfinished by 1860, the Civil War and its demand brought it to completion. The agrarian ideal of self-sufficiency and independence now gave way to the growing American cult of opportunity, career, and the self-made man. The old agrarian ideal that sanctified work in the soil and the simple life was now combined with and supplanted by the Calvinist ethos that virtue was to be combined with success in business and the acquisition of material comforts.

NINETEENTH-CENTURY AMERICAN FARMING

In nineteenth-century America, before the Gold Rush, there was a Land Rush. Western public lands were opened to settlement while they were still under the control of the federal government. Federal law provided for a survey to divide western lands into township units and sections, with each section one square mile or 640 acres. Settlers who went west did not worry about the federal survey. Most could not secure legal title before they went west because in most cases they were not sure where they would settle. Most of the early settlers were squatters, as land surveys lagged behind settlement. (The squatter was the man who got there first.) In Illinois in 1838, about two-thirds of the population were squatters on land that technically belonged to the government. By a preemption act the government gave squatters the option to purchase the land they occupied at a price of $1.25 for a quarter-section (160 acres) whenever it was offered for sale by the government. Thus farming was the way of life of most people who spread across the young United States in the nineteenth century. In 1850, there were 1,500,000 farming units in the United States, three times more than existed in 1790. Farmers and farm laborers made up 60 percent of the labor force in 1860 and 52 percent in 1870.

During the nineteenth century farmers improved their crops through fertilization and improvement of seed, and improved their animals through proper breeding. Machines powered by horses and oxen were applied to every aspect of agriculture, from seeding and haying to plowing, harvesting, and threshing. No farm was self-sufficient. Tools and equipment had to be purchased and farmers bartered with their neighbors. Later, farmers purchased items that their wives and families wanted as their standard of living rose—furniture, mirrors, clothing, books, combs, jewelry, leather goods, fancy hats, and shoes. They exchanged labor for a barn or roof raising, and at harvest and plowing time. Collective labor also was resorted to as communities united to build, fix, and maintain local roads, drainage ditches, and fencing. Products from overseas were desired and purchased at the local general store—tea, coffee, sugar, molasses, spices.

Both urban and rural society in the nineteenth century were affected by the process of industrialization and market relations. There was a reciprocal relationship between industry and agriculture; factories supplied farm machinery that enhanced agricultural production, while farmers supplied industries with the raw materials that fed their machines. The processing of agricultural products was the first step for industrial development in the young republic, starting with textiles using the wool of sheep and the cotton of southern plantations. Shoemaking in New England used the hides of livestock. The early gristmills and sawmills that dotted streams and rivers throughout the American countryside were fed by farmers providing wheat to be processed into flour and logs to be cut into boards.

Improvements in animal husbandry and the selection of improved varieties of field crops changed the character of agriculture during the nineteenth century. The Hereford cow was a curiosity in 1850, but this hardy beef animal dominated the midwestern farms and ranches by 1900. At midcentury, Turkey Red wheat was unknown in the country, but by the end of the century it was the dominant variety grown in the winter wheat belt of the Central Plains. Every region generated its own lore about the best breeds of livestock and the best crops to grow.

There was no typical farm in nineteenth-century America. There were differences between easterners and westerners. The eastern farmer fenced with rails, the Kansan with wire; water supply was no problem for the New York farmer, but to the Kansan it was a life-and-death matter; western New Yorkers built log cabins, western Kansans built sod houses. Eastern farmers practiced diversification of crops, as agriculture in the East had been long established and the subsistence point of view was deeply entrenched. Most farms were small, the soil was of low fertility, and only those farms near urban markets moved to specialize in products such as milk, potatoes, and vegetables. In its earliest stages, agriculture in the West also focused on subsistence farming, growing wheat, corn, rye, barley, and potatoes, supplemented by hogs and cattle, fruit trees, and a garden patch. The soils of the West were more productive than those of the East, but great distances from markets was a serious obstacle to commercial farming. The transportation revolution between the 1830s and 1860s changed all this. There was a rapid shift to single-crop farming. This demanded crops that were high in value and not perishable. Thus, the principal crops were wheat and corn, both of which could always be sold no matter what the price.

There were also differences between northerners and southerners. Agriculture in the antebellum South concentrated the best land in the hands of large-scale, slave-owning staples planters, whereas in the North the pattern was one of small-scale independent farm owners. The rise of commercial and industrial cities in the North made it profitable for some farming regions to specialize in dairying, sheep raising, meat production, orchard crops, and garden vegetables. Northern agriculture was closely linked with canal and railroad construction, with urbanization and industrialization. In the South there was little urbanization, less railroad construction. However, some southern factories were built with a view of processing agricultural products—cotton for textile and tobacco for cigarettes and chewing.

Work Values of the Western Farmer

The possibility of entering farming as an occupation in the West was part of the thinking of many young men throughout the period of 1820–1870. In the earlier years there were few alternatives, since wage employment or apprentice training in nonfarm occupations was possible for a minority of the population. Half the population was involved in agriculture in 1870. Entering agriculture required appropriate mechanical skills, managerial capacities, some capital or credit, knowledge of crops and animals, and a willingness to work hard. For farmers who intended to stay on a particular piece of land, farming involved some kind of plan, whether explicit or not: (1) selection of crops to be produced and knowledge of prices of crops and costs to produce them, (2) methods of cultivation for each product, (3) what kind of animals to be raised, (4) a calendar of operation so that available labor was adequate to meet all requirements, and (5) a plan for use of the land. Prices quoted or received for products in the preceding year or two were the basic guides in determining a farm program. Most western farmers gave such questions little explicit thought or investigation. Adherence to a particular routine became common for a particular region, village, or town. Most farmers were unwilling to change techniques or shift from one crop to another. The large majority of farmers followed well-trodden paths and made no serious examination of alternatives. Deviations from the norm in a particular area were looked upon as foolhardy, courting failure, and a waste of effort.

The fact that western soils were covered with grasses rather than trees presented a significant difference from farming in the East. While preparation of grasslands for tilled crops required less labor and time for removing timber, grassland was more difficult to plough than soils newly cleared of timber. The virgin sod was tough and prairie soil breaking required three to eight yoke of oxen. It was common to hire the work out to specialists. Yields were small the first year and a fair return was not expected until the following season. The absence of timber was a disadvantage. Wood was needed for buildings, fencing, and fuel. An Illinois farmer commented that fencing in many places cost more than the land, and, not only that, fencing had to be bought for cash, while land could be bought on credit. Fences were one-third of the value of a prairie farm.

Another thing that was different about western farming was the space and sense of space. The vastness of the land and the endless distances affected the way of life, the culture, and the way people thought about the land and its use. Great availability of land and the scarcity of labor made for extensive agriculture in the Midwest, which was wasteful of the soil and placed a premium on machines to bring large tracts under cultivation. Already by the late 1850s, prairie farmers recognized that they had used the soil shamefully. One farmer commented: "It is true that us western farmers have been skimming God's heritage, taking the cream off, and leaving for parts unknown, until humanity has a heavy bill against us for wasting the vital energies of mother earth" (Sutherland, 1989:139).

His demand for expensive machinery, his expectation of higher standards of living, his tendency to go into debt to acquire acreage, created the urgent need for cash and tempted the farmer into capitalizing more and more of his single greatest asset—the unearned appreciation of the value of his land.

Immigrant farmers who sought land in the American West, yeomen with a background of genuine agrarian values, were bewildered at the ethos of American agriculture which made no provision for the future. In Europe, small farmers lived in villages, where generations of the same family were reared upon the same soil, and where careful cultivation and elimination of waste were necessary to support a growing population on a limited amount of land. Endless and patient work, including the labor of women and children, exploited land to a degree which Americans would not accept. "When the German comes in, the Yankee goes out," was a local proverb as Swedes, Bohemians, Germans, and other immigrants occupied the land in the West.

By 1851 Germans were becoming the nation's largest immigrant group and many were moving into agriculture. Germans went to Missouri, Texas, Wisconsin, and other midwestern states like Minnesota and Michigan. They settled on dispersed farmsteads rather than on the communal, open fields they had known in Europe. There was a contrast between Yankee and German farmers. The Yankee farmer was thought to lack sentimental attachment to his land and was ready to sell out at a profit and move on. He planted the same crop every year so that he wore out the soil. The German farmer was seen to have an intimate relationship to his land, with the deep desire to leave his offspring with a debt-free farm. He often retained the home place within his family which made possible his own retirement. With parental help a son could acquire a farm and be likely to remain in the township, which helped the parents who could turn to their children for comfort and support in old age. For most Germans, their work ethic was based on the planting of the perennial bond between family, land, and community in the midwestern heartland that spelled success in their farming endeavors.

Prospective settlers believed that the western agricultural frontier held unlimited opportunities for the person who would work hard. Americans always had a love affair with the land. The acquisition of 160 acres of land or more was the dream and ambition of thousands of young men and young women. Settlers wanted land on which to establish a home and earn a living. They hoped also to benefit from rising land values. Whatever their motives, their prime objective was to acquire land. It is clear that the hopes and dreams of many actually became reality. They may not have achieved all they wished for, but they made decent homes for themselves and their families. On the other hand, there were thousands whose expectations were unfulfilled and whose dreams were shattered by the realities of the prairie and the frontier.

BIBLIOGRAPHICAL ESSAY

An overview of American agriculture in the nineteenth century is provided by Steven Hahn and Jonathan Prude, *The Countryside in the Age of Capitalist Transformation: Essays in the Social History of Rural America* (Chapel Hill: University of North Carolina Press, 1985). The opening quote in this chapter is from this book (3). Hahn and Prude point out that in 1800, only 3 percent of inhabitants in the new United State lived in cities. The proportion of Americans living outside of cities was five out of six in 1860 and two out of three in 1900. Only in the 1880s did urbanization become a "controlling factor in national life," and not until 1920 did a majority of Americans begin living in urban areas. Thus, we can see how important the rural way of life was in the nineteenth century just in the matter of demographics. But it was more than population, as the country's culture and value system was enormously influenced by America's countryside and frontier throughout the century.

For a general review of Western farming in the nineteenth century, see Allan G. Bogue, Thomas D. Phillips, and James E. Wright, *The West of the American People* (Itasca, IL: F. E. Peacock Publishers, 1970). See particularly the essay in that collection by Allan G. Bogue, "Farming in the Prairie Peninsula, 1830–1890." For a short overview of American Agricultural History, see Vernon Carstensen, "An Overview of American Agricultural History," in *Farmers, Bureaucrats and Middlemen: Historical Perspectives on American Agriculture*, edited by Trudy Huskamp Peterson (Washington, DC: Howard University Press, 1980), 8–23. Also see the article by Earl O. Heady, "Agriculture in the United States," *Scientific American*, September, 1976. For a picture of farm life, especially along the frontier regions of Kentucky, Indiana and Illinois, see Carl Sandburg, *Lincoln: The Prairie Years* (Harcourt, Brace, 1926).

For a discussion of the relationship between rural and urban society in the nineteenth century and how it was affected by the industrial revolution and the consequent changes in the market, see Steven Hahn and Jonathan Prude, eds. *The Countryside.*

A case study of Sugar Creek, Illinois, was developed by John M. Faragher, "Open-Country Community: Sugar Creek, Illinois, 1820–1850," in Hahn and Prude, *The Countryside.* In this study Faragher provides a picture of subsistence agriculture in the community from its first settlement in 1817 until the coming of the railroad in 1850. Early settlers built cabins from squares of sod stacked like bricks and located them near water and timber land. Wheat and corn were planted along with vegetables. Livestock included oxen, horses, milk cows, beef cattle, hogs, poultry, and geese. Sheep, flax, or a cotton patch provided fiber for homespun clothing. Families made their own clothing, soap, candles, and maple sugar. Work was shared with neighbors at cabin raisings, haying, husking, butchering, harvesting, and threshing activities. There were exchanges of labor, products, and tools. The Sugar Creek community included a blacksmith, a wheelwright, a carpenter, a physician, and three millers. It consisted of small, self-sufficient farmers who farmed for the future, hoping to leave their offspring the fruits of their labor.

Claim Clubs and informal governments were set up during the early settlement of the West. A description of their functioning can be found in Daniel Boorstin, *The Americans: The National Experience* (New York: Vintage Books, 1965), 72–81. These claim clubs drafted constitutions and bylaws and settled disputes as there were no courts of law in the early days to protect their titles. They kept a register of land titles and in many ways acted as a government land office. In some places they became the whole government, punishing all crimes against person or property.

Settlers used different methods to transport themselves and their goods to the new land in the West. A man traveling only for curiosity used different means of transportation than men with families, goods, and furniture. There were inns of accommodation but if they were not available, people could sleep in wagons if they were covered with canvas. A wagon could travel a little short of twenty miles in one day. For a picture of these various means of travel, see Guy Stevens Callender, *Selections from the Economic History of the United States, 1765–1860* (New York: Ginn and Company, 1909), 617–621.

After the settler found a piece of land to occupy he would build a house and plant Indian corn. For a description of the kinds of houses built by the settlers, see the chapter on colonial construction, Carl W. Condit, *American Building* (Chicago: University of Chicago Press, 1982).

On farmer values and their outlook and way of life, see Richard Hofstadter, *The Age of Reform: From Bryan to F.D.R.* (New York: Alfred A. Knopf, 1955), 39–46; Daniel E. Sutherland, *The Expansion of Everyday Life, 1860–1876* (New York: Harper & Row, 1989), 136–139; Alexis de Tocqueville, *Democracy in America*, edited by J. P. Mayer (New York: Harper & Row, 1969), 554; Daniel Boorstin, *The Americans: The National Experience*, 71–80, 113–123. For the quote by the farmer on western farmers skimming God's heritage, see Sutherland, *The Expansion of Everyday Life*, 139.

On the possibilities of entering farming and all the requirements necessary for successful farming, including calculations about crops, labor, livestock, and machinery, as well as soils, prices, and farming methods, see Clarence H. Danhof, *Change in Agriculture: The Northern United States, 1820–1870* (Cambridge, MA: Harvard University Press, 1969), 73, 74, 123, 124, 131–135.

On the differences between farmers in the East and the West, and farmers in the North and South, see Allan G. Bogue, Thomas D. Phillips, and James E. Wright, *The West of the American People* (Itasca, IL: F. E. Peacock Publishers, 1970), 425–430; Harry N. Scheiber, Harold G. Vatter, and Harold U. Faulkner, *American Economic History*, 9th ed. (New York: Harper & Row, 1976), 135–138; Clarence H. Danhof, *Change in Agriculture*, 147–150.

On the mechanization of nineteenth-century agriculture, see Paul W. Gates, *The Farmer's Age: Agriculture, 1815–1860* (New York: Holt, Rinehart and Winston, 1960), 281–293; Clarence H. Danhof, *Change in Agriculture*, 185, 195–196, 198–199, 142–144.

On German farmers in the nineteenth century, see Kathleen Neils Conzen, "Peasant Pioneers, Generational Succession Among German Farmers in Frontier Minnesota," in *The Countryside*, edited by Steven Hahn and Jonathan Prude.

On the hardships of western farmers who failed, see Gilbert C. Fite, "Daydreams and Nightmares: The Late Nineteenth-Century Agricultural Frontiers," *The West of the American People*, edited by Allan G. Bogue, Thomas D. Phillips, and James E. Wright (Itasca, IL: F. E. Peacock Publishers, 1970).

During the nineteenth century the belief that farmers were engaged in productive labor and that agrarian beliefs were of superior virtue persisted in a country that was overwhelmingly rural. Agrarianism was strong in the agricultural press, landscape paintings, and writings of agricultural reformers. Farm journals mixed tributes to yeomen with advice on improving agriculture. Almanac writers and agricultural publishers insisted that farming was the most virtuous occupation, contrasting their life with that of the corruption of urban settings. The virtuous farmer was considered an independent soul without any master except the forces of nature. He was free to work and add value to the land and feed the country. Slothful behavior and careless farming were condemned. For a full discussion of the role of agriculture in the eighteen and nineteenth centuries, see Allan Kulikoff, *The Agrarian Oirgins of American Capitalism* (Charlottesville: University of Virginia Press, 1991). For a discussion of farmer values, see Chapter 3, 60–98.

Darrett B. Rutman, with Anita H. Rutman, wrote a book called *Small Worlds, Large Questions* (Charlottesville: University of Virginia Press, 1994). In the last essay in the book, "Community, A Sunny Little Dream," 287–304, Rutman explores the culture of the rural community, and along with it, the agrarian dream. The Rutmans state:

Sometime in the nineteenth and early twentieth centuries, at least in the Western world, the idea emerged that the small, intimate, face-to-face society somehow embodied all that was good in humankind, that it was a natural state in sharp contrast to the unnatural world of city, contract, bureaucracy, and technology that was rapidly developing. It underscores a tendency, certainly in Britain and America, to embrace the image of the small community as an antidote for all that is felt to be wrong in modern society: size, and with it complexity and impersonality; the rule of contract rather than trust, of law rather than culture; above all, the pursuit of individual comfort rather than taking comfort in the comfort of the group. (289)

The Rutmans link this small town life with "agricultural families faced with the same essential problem: how to extract from what land and skills they have the wherewithal to meet the family's needs and wants. . . . Life, in brief, was lived "face to face" in these small societies and on a scale easily described . . . as small, intimate, and essentially cooperative. Life was, moreover, lived slowly and in tune to its own cycles and seasons of the year" (293).

Another article that portrays the agrarian way of life and culture in nineteenth-century America is one by Jack Temple Kirby, "Rural Culture in the American Middle West: Jefferson to Jane Smiley," in *Agricultural History* 70, no. 4 (Fall 1996), 581–597. Kirby states that the moral aspect of rural culture is a trope of ancient origins. Simple assertions that farming is a superior way of life persist, but long ago evolved into elaborate moral philosophies or ideologies called agrarian (582). Kirby then traces the idea of farming and farmers as leading a superior way of life from Cato through the French Physiocrats to Thomas Jefferson. He discusses John Faragher's study of Sugar Creek, Illinois, a nineteenth-century farming community, and the influence of the German immigrants who settled in the Midwest. As discussed in the text, Kirby contrasts the attitudes of the German-American farmers who were community-rooted with that of the "Yankee" farmers who were less community-rooted and more likely to sell out and move on. Kirby points out that Germans brought to the Midwest their European experience of attachment to family and place, and a relentless determination to care for farmland and manage succession within families (590).

9

ARTISANS IN THE
NINETEENTH CENTURY

ETHIC OF INDEPENDENCE

By the middle of the nineteenth century, a work ethic pushed by manufacturers developed, based on the concept of the discipline of time. Its symbol was the milltower clock. This work ethic, powerfully argued for by the clergy and intellectuals, was nevertheless challenged by craftsmen and workers whose traditions clashed with factory discipline and the growing ethic of commercialism. The challenge was reflected in the persistence of work habits that frustrated and angered managers who could not understand the indifference of factory hands to steady work, being on time, and being at the workplace every day.

The nineteenth-century work force was a patchwork quilt of attitudes and cultures that varied according to skill level, ethnic background, religion, race, region, occupation, gender, and country of origin. There was no typical worker and no typical adjustment to factory discipline. It did not come easy to overcome traditional values of European peasants or the pride and independence of craftsmen. Small-town textile mills shut down when the circus came to town. Skilled craftsmen objected when factory gates were locked because it violated their view that they could come and go as free men. "Blue Monday" absenteeism, immigrant festivals, farm chores, and fishing jaunts that took priority over showing up for work were all evidence that nineteenth-century workers were not yet ready for the routine of an industrial society. Artisans did not want to give up time-honored work habits that they associated with the good and moral life. David Johnson, a shoemaker, recalled with pleasure the festivals, fairs, games, and excursions that were common rituals among Lynn, Massachusetts, cobblers. Samuel Gompers remembered with delight how New York cigarmakers paid a fellow craftsman to read a newspaper to them while they worked.

The functional autonomy of craftsmen in the nineteenth century was based on the superior knowledge that gave them a sense of independence. This applied to such active crafts as iron molders, glass blowers, coopers, paper machine tenders, locomotive engineers, mule spinners, boiler makers, pipe fitters, typographers, pottery jiggermen, coal miners, iron rollers, puddlers and heaters, shoe-stitching operators, machinists, and metal works fitters. These craftsmen exercised broad discretion over their own work as well as that of their helpers. They often hired and fired helpers and paid them out of their own earnings.

The work week of coopers (barrel makers) illustrates the work week of some nineteenth-century craftsmen. Coopers spent Monday sharpening tools, carrying in stock, and getting things in shape for the big day of work on Tuesday. "Blue Monday" was a tradition with coopers and was a lost day as far as production was concerned. But bright and early on Tuesday they would "give her hell" and would bang away for the rest of the week until Saturday, which was payday. Coopers lounged about on Saturday, another lost day to their employers. Early Saturday morning the brewery wagon would drive up to the shop and one of the coopers would invite the driver to bring in a barrel of beer. Groups would sit around upturned barrels and play poker, using rivets for chips, until they received their pay. Saturday night was a big night for the cooper. It was spent strolling around town, meeting friends at the saloon, and having a good time. The good time lasted into Sunday, so that by Monday, he was not in the best condition to settle down to work. Such traditions of work—in this case a four-day work week and a three-day weekend—did not sit well with manufacturers, temperance reformers, and clergy. To owners of competitive firms trying to increase efficiency and cut labor costs, behavior displayed by craftsmen like coopers proved the obstinacy of the craftsman and their resistance to management.

Other craftsmen also upheld venerable traditions of their trade and asserted their independence through the enforcement of the stint and working rules. For example, in the 1880s, the window-glass workers of Local Assembly 300 of the Knights of Labor had sixty-six rules for working. They specified that full crews had to be present at each pot setting, that skimming could only be done at the beginning of blowing, that blowers and gatherers should not work faster than at the rate of nine rollers per hour, and that the standard size of single strength rollers should be 40" x 58" to cut 38" x 56" glass. No work was to be performed on Thanksgiving Day, Christmas, Decoration Day, or Washington's Birthday. No blower, gatherer, or cutter could work between June 15 and September 15, that is, during the summer months when fires were to be banked. In 1884, the local assembly waged a long and successful strike to preserve its stint (quota) of forty-eight boxes of glass a week, a rule that its members considered the key to the dignity and welfare of the trade.

IMMIGRANTS AND TRADITIONAL WORK HABITS

Continual immigration during the nineteenth century, especially after the 1840s, was an important factor in continuities of traditional work habits, as immigrants brought a craft, peasant, and preindustrial culture with them to the United States. Seventy percent or more of the people in San Francisco, St. Louis, Cleveland, New

York, Detroit, Milwaukee, and Chicago were immigrants or children of immigrants in the last quarter of the nineteenth century. Strong family ties made possible the transmission of European work patterns to America. Common rituals and festivals bound immigrant communities together: Paterson, New Jersey, silk weavers had their Macclesfield wakes; Fall River, Massachusetts, cotton mill workers had their Ashton wakes; and British immigrants celebrated St. George's Day. Ethnic beliefs and common work habits sustained immigrant communities, but there were other cultural influences such as benevolent societies, holiday celebrations, friendly local politicians, libraries, participant sports, churches, saloons, beer gardens, concerts, and music halls. They all depended on the participation of artisans and laborers and they in turn influenced the outlook and habits of immigrant workers. Self-educated artisans particularly emerged as civic and community leaders among these immigrants. Skilled immigrant workers played important roles in successful manufacturing facilities in various cities. There were potters from Staffordshire, England, in Trenton, an important pottery center that was employing fifteen thousand workers in forty pottery works in the city by 1900. In Waterbury, Connecticut, which became the center of brass and brass manufactured products, skilled immigrant workers were brought over from Birmingham, England. The process whereby skilled European workers contributed to the transfer of technical knowledge and expertise from Europe to the United States continued through the end of the nineteenth century in iron and steel, locomotive production, farm machinery, textiles, metal trades, machine shops, printing, garment manufacture, brewing, tanning, flour milling, and other industries.

Population expansion was very important in the nineteenth century, serving as a market for the enormous growth and output of goods from American industry. This underscores the importance of immigration. With fertility declines in the nineteenth century, immigration represented the prime means for population growth, and immigrants in both the city and countryside served to boost demand for manufactured goods. They also provided labor for American industry. Economists have estimated that 50 percent of the increase in manufacture in the late nineteenth century can be attributed to greater numbers of workers—more people produce more products—with labor supply as important a growth factor as gains in productivity or capitalization. By 1900, more than 80 percent of America's industrial labor force were foreign-born workers and their children. These immigrants consisted disproportionately of males in their twenties and thirties, that is, of prime age for heavy, industrial work. Included in the contribution of immigrants must be added that of the Asians on the West Coast who worked in railroad construction and mining. The immigrants not only increased numbers, they brought critical knowledge and in many cases entrepreneurial skills, establishing small-batch, custom manufactories that added so much to the product mix of the country and its overall production.

PROTESTS TO NINETEENTH-CENTURY CHANGES

The reorganization of production in the shop widened the breach between masters and journeymen. The latter protested wage reductions, lengthening of the work day, decline of apprenticeship, general deskilling, and use of common day laborers for work. They formed nascent craft unions of journeymen that did not survive the major business collapses of the early nineteenth century. As business revived in the 1820s and 1830s, craftsmen again began to organize. In 1827, William Heighton, a shoemaker, founded the Mechanics Union of Trade Associations, the nation's first federated body of unions, and the *Mechanics' Free Press*, the nation's first labor newspaper. The association grew out of a strike by carpenters on behalf of the ten-hour day. Later, it led to the formation of the Working Men's Party of Philadelphia, the nation's first labor party. Workingmen's parties began to appear in a dozen states and many localities. Their programs included free, common school education, abolition of imprisonment for debt, legal protections for unions, abolition of prison labor, and payment of wages in hard currency rather than in scrip. The movement peaked early and by 1832 few of the local labor parties remained in operation. This did not end craft workers' protests. By 1836 central labor councils or federations were established in thirteen manufacturing centers from Boston to Washington, D.C., and west to Cincinnati. The most successful strike took place in Philadelphia in 1835, when about 20,000 workers walked off their jobs to achieve the ten-hour workday and succeeded in having their demands met by their respective employers. This was a high point, but by the end of the decade few traces of union effort or strength could be found. The economic crisis of 1837 decimated union organization as union members and others lost their jobs.

Protesting craftsmen of the 1820s and 1830s joined in the debate on the new American political economic order. They had immediate grievances and demands, such as the ten-hour workday, but the movement spoke to larger issues about the republic. Craftsmen acted more against the old regime of state privilege and empowerment of the merchant class than in favor of a specific future. They attacked vestiges of the old order such as debtors' prisons, elitism, monopoly power, and governmental favor, and they feared a new order of competitive, self-interested politics and rapacious economic activity. Journeymen imagined a self-regulated society of ultimately equal, hardworking people providing for each other's needs and respectful of each other's labors and rights to participation in the affairs of their communities. This mutualistic vision flowed from their craftshop experience and was the journeymen's particular input in the debates of early nineteenth-century America.

In the end, the journeymen failed to build a sustained working-class movement. There were divisions among workers by skill, gender, race, ethnicity, and experience. Economic depressions took their toll. Labor advocates challenged various inequities, but not property, wage labor, or market society as such. They valued craft labor and citizenship, but these were experiences open to skilled white men. Their vision did not speak to women, African-Americans, immigrants, common day laborers, and factory hands—groups whom the journeymen saw as strikebreakers and replacements, threats to their livelihoods, workplaces, and societal ideals. In boosting their cause the craftsmen of the shop delineated themselves from these other workers at the margins and in the process contributed to the racial, gender, and ethnic intraclass divisions of the day. This unwillingness of the craft activists to reach the diversifying work populace would blunt their own efforts.

CONCLUSION

The rise of factory production and the reduction of artisanal independence was not a uniform nor even a complete process in the nineteenth century. There were enormous variations in the organization of labor, the use of machinery, and the changing market structures among the industries of the nation, from the highly mechanized textile factories of New England, to the use of common labor to mine minerals and build railroad tracks in the West. The transition from the age of the artisan to the age of manufacturing and modern industry occurred over a protracted period of time that extended into the early twentieth century. The nineteenth century was still largely the century of the artisan in America along with the work ethic associated with craft and craftsmanship.

When the nineteenth century started the typical productive worker was the farmer and next was the artisan, who worked in a small workshop for a limited market. He made the entire product and sold it himself. By the end of the century, the nonfarm worker was increasingly a wage worker who worked on only one part of the product that he did not own and which was sold by his employer. What is significant is that even though the work environment changed drastically between 1800 and 1900, the work ethic—belief in hard work, belief that work was central to one's self-esteem and independence—continued to be a powerful part of American values.

The transformation from traditional craft methods to factory methods did not take place easily or peacefully. Craftsmen, artisans, and skilled workers fought and resisted the increased regimentation in the workplace. The central issue was the struggle between workers and management over control of work and working conditions. Control over one's work was part of the tradition of independence and self-reliance fostered by the American Revolution and its ideology. It was carried into the nineteenth century by the mechanics, artisans, and craftsmen active in the Revolution. Craftsmen did not easily let go of their traditions and their craft knowledge, which was still strong at the end of the nineteenth century. Thus, Taylorism, the scientific management movement designed to strip skilled workers of their superior knowledge and experience, was initiated to break down craft traditions and transfer control over their work from the skilled craftsman to the manager and foreman.

At the end of the nineteenth century there were still major industries where craft traditions prevailed—clothing, printing, construction, railroads, mining, metal trades, machine tools, carriage making, cigar making, and others. But the factory and the mill were the workshops of the future, and the craftsman was fighting a losing battle to retain his tradition of independence and control over his own work. Craftsmen founded the American Federation of Labor, a craft-oriented labor federation, in the hope that they could stave off the inevitable. However, today construction is the only major industry where skilled workers still control their own pace of work and in most cases, work with their own tools.

The craft tradition may be a thing of the past as far as the way work is organized in the 1990s, but its work ethic and its traditions are still an important part of America's heritage.

BIBLIOGRAPHICAL ESSAY

For a good introduction to the entire nineteenth century, the reader can consult Walter Licht, *Industrializing America: The Nineteenth Century* (Baltimore: Johns Hopkins Press, 1995). For a survey of the transformations of artisans into wage workers during the nineteenth century, see Bruce Laurie, *Artisans into Workers: Labor in Nineteenth-Century America* (New York: Hill and Wang, 1989). For a look at early industrialization and artisans and artisan reactions to early mechanization and industrialization, see Licht's book cited above, Chapters 2 and 3.

One of the best books on the nineteenth-century work ethic is that of Daniel T. Rodgers, *The Work Ethic in Industrial America* (Chicago: University of Chicago Press, 1974). Rodgers deals with the late nineteenth and early twentieth centuries. Basically, he deals with the ideology of the work ethic and shows how difficult it was to impose it upon the American working class, even though all the forces of the clergy and other intellectuals were used to espouse the importance of work values to society and culture.

Herbert Gutman was a pioneer in working class social and cultural history and his expertise was basically the nineteenth century. His pathbreaking article, "Work, Culture and Society in Industrializing America," *American Historical Review* 78, no. 3 (June 1973), 537–603, deals with the attempts of the new industrial management to impose discipline on the American work force and resistance to it by American workers. Gutman emphasized that immigrants brought a whole new cultural package with them when they came to the United States which they were not about to give it up easily. Thus, they maintained their festivals and religious celebrations and their community orientation and when this interfered with their work discipline there were struggles over this issue in the workplace. Gutman's views can also be found in a book of essays, *Work, Culture and Society in Industrializing America, 1815–1919* (New York: Alfred A. Knopf, 1976). Gutman was influenced and inspired by the work of E. P. Thompson, *The Making of the English Working Class* (New York: Vintage Books, 1963) and "Time, Work-Discipline, and Capitalism," *Past and Present*, no. 38 (December 1967), 56–97, in which Thompson spells out all the difficulties that capitalist management encountered when they tried to impose strict factory discipline on the English working class, which had been used to less formal discipline and modes of working during a preindustrial era.

A good case study of early industrialization and its effects on artisans is Cynthia J. Shelton, *The Mills of Manayunk: Industrialization and Social Conflict in the Philadelphia Region, 1787–1837* (Baltimore: Johns Hopkins University Press, 1986).

For a view of the struggles between skilled workers and artisans and other wage workers on control over work in the workplace, see David Montgomery, "Workers' Control of Machine Production in the Nineteenth Century," in *The Labor History Reader,* edited by Daniel J. Leab (Urbana: University of Illinois Press, 1985).

For additional material on worker struggles for control of their work in the nineteenth century, see David Montgomery, *Workers Control in America: Studies in the History of Work Technology and Labor Struggles* (New York: Cambridge University Press, 1979).

The description of the coopers work week was taken from Herbert Gutman, *Work, Culture and Society*, 37–38. On the "stint" of glassworkers, see Montgomery, "Workers' Control of Machine Production," 115–116. On immigrants and the work ethic, see Gutman, *Work, Culture and Society*, 44–46.

For a case study on Lynn shoemakers, see Alan Dawley, *Class and Community*: *The Industrial Revolution in Lynn* (Cambridge, MA: Harvard University Press, 1976). Paul G. Faler also deals with shoemakers in Lynn, Massachusetts. See his book, *Mechanics and*

Manufacturers in the Early Industrial Revolution: Lynn, Massachusetts, 1780–1860 (Albany: State University of New York Press, 1981). Also see article by Paul Faler, "Cultural Aspects of the Industrial Revolution: Lynn, Massachusetts, Shoemakers and Industrial Morality, 1826–1860," in *American Workingclass Culture: Explorations in American Labor and Social History*, edited by Milton Cantor (Westport, CT: Greenwood Press, 1979).

On worker attitudes toward the value of their own labor and their view that they were the creators of wealth in society, see Maurice F. Neufeld, "Realms of Thought and Organized Labor in the Age of Jackson," *Labor History* 10, no. 1 (Winter 1969), 5–43. Also see Paul Faler on the same subject, "Cultural Aspects of the Industrial Revolution," 185–188.

A case study of Newark, New Jersey, one of the important industrial centers in the nineteenth century, can be found in Susan E. Hirsch, *Roots of the American Working Class: The Industrialization of Crafts in Newark, 1800–1860* (Philadelphia: University of Pennsylvania Press, 1978). The material on the transformation of artisans into wage workers in the city is dealt with at length in this book, along with the ideological and theoretical aspects of the changes. Newark evolved from a preindustrial town into an industrial city in less than forty years–1820 to 1860. By 1860 Newark was a major industrial city, with 74 percent of its labor force employed in manufacturing. It ranked sixth in the nation in the value of its manufactured products. Its crafts included blacksmithy, carpentry, hat making, jewelry making, leather making, shoemaking, saddle making, and trunk making. Each craft differed in the extent of its mechanization. In 1826 these eight crafts comprised 52 percent of all Newarkers at work. By 1860 they were down to 38 percent. Although industrialization proceeded unevenly in the different crafts, it undermined household production, traditional skills, work rhythms, and old relationships between master and journeyman. The factory system fostered a split between work and life by separating production from the home. In the sphere of the family, journeymen could combine the values of their artisanal, ethnic, and religious heritage. Wives and children were isolated from the world of work when it was removed from the home. Few journeymen were able to rise to self-employment and most remained employees. Craftsmen who did become employers, joined the merchants and professionals, while journeymen and apprentices aligned themselves with wage workers. Crafts in Newark declined as an important status attribute, while the wealthy became more influential, favoring the employer over the employee. On immigrant and ethnic groups in Newark's work force, see Hirsch, *Roots of the American Working Class*, 48–49; 78–79, 103. On craft unions in Newark, see Hirsch, 130–135.

On the transformation of artisans into factory artisans in Cincinnati, see Steven J. Ross, *Workers on the Edge: Work, Leisure and Politics in Industrializing Cincinnati, 1788–1890* (New York: Columbia University Press, 1985).

A picture of the railroads and the railroad crafts in the nineteenth century can be found in Walter Licht, *Working for the Railroad: The Organization of Work in the Nineteenth Century* (Princeton, NJ: Princeton University Press, 1983). Daniel Boorstin also discusses the significance of the railroads in the nineteenth century, *The Americans: The National Experience* (New York: Vintage Books, 1965), 102, 168. There is also a discussion of railroad workers and the railroads in Daniel E. Sutherland, *The Expansion of Everyday Life, 1860–1876* (New York: Harper & Row, 1989), 180–182. For a discussion of the role of railroads and the industrializing trends of the nineteenth century, see Walter Licht, *Industrializing America*, 82–86. On the role of George Westinghouse and the development of the automatic air brake in the railroad industry, see the article by Curt Wohleber, "St. George Westinghouse," *Invention and Technology* 12, no. 3 (Winter 1997), 28–42. For a picture of strikes among the railroad craft workers, see Howard Zinn, *A People's History of the United States* (New York: Harper, 1990), 230, 240–246, 254, 263–264, 272–275.

10

FACTORIES IN THE NINETEENTH CENTURY

After the Revolutionary War, the young nation was a country of small farmers, artisans, small shopkeepers, servants, laborers, slaves, merchants, seamen, cartmen, carpenters, blacksmith, and all the petty trades that distinguish and represent a preindustrial society. A hundred years later, by the 1880s, the United States was on its way to becoming the leading industrial producer on earth. Other than farmers, most gainfully employed persons at the time were wage earners. After the Civil War, the factory and the mill, along with the farm, came to be the dominant means for the organization of work and the creation of products.

THE FACTORY SYSTEM

A mill or factory was a single building or collection of buildings that contained power-driven machinery and tools for the manufacture of products. It was a place for storing raw materials and finished products, and for placing machines, materials, and workers in such a way as to create a continuous flow of production.

The emergence of the factory system was not automatic. A number of problems had to be solved. These included (1) a source of power to run the machines, (2) machines to be built and acquired, (3) a means to accumulate the capital to build the factories, purchase machines, and hire workers, (4) a source of labor supply, and (5) new methods of labor control appropriate to the new factory system.

Locating a source of power was solved by building factories near falling streams or rivers. New England was blessed with many rivers and streams and thus the infant textile industry was located there. Acquiring machines was a problem because England, which manufactured such machines, prohibited the export of the machines or any drawings of them. Samuel Slater solved that problem because he had worked in England and had seen machines built and was able to re-create some of them from memory in the United States. He came to this country, built the machines, and went into business with American business-men who had the capital to build the factories and hire the labor. Merchants assembled capital, setting up partnerships and corporations under new laws of incorporation in New England.

Finding an adequate labor supply was difficult, especially since early factories were located away from population centers and in rural areas where there were streams. With so many opportunities for self-employment in the early years of the nineteenth century, it was difficult to find men willing to work for wages. Some could be found but it was not enough and thus, employers turned to recruiting women and children. Samuel Slater, in addition to hiring individuals, employed whole families. Other entrepreneurs, such as those in Lowell, Massachusetts, recruited women from farm families in the countryside.

Another problem was how to impose a factory discipline upon workers who cherished their freedom and independence. Many associated factory work with wage slavery. Males especially opposed such work believing that it robbed them of freedom of movement, independence, and self-respect. Throughout the nine-teenth century, manufacturers faced the problem of getting workers to shed their traditional modes of working and accept the routines and disciplines of factory work.

The technical and operative elements of a factory involved a coordinated plan designed to make it an efficient producing organization. What distinguished the factory was the organizing principles by which owners organized its labor process. Owners hired wage workers to carry out production under supervised discipline that regulated the pace of the work. In the early days, many of the shops were small enough for the owners to do their own supervision. This changed when the scale of operations expanded in the 1830s and 1840s and hundreds and even thousands worked in factories. The work habits, aspirations, and behavior of the men and women new to factory life, many of them from craft and farm backgrounds, did not accord with the aspirations and expectations of early factory and mill owners. Workers often frustrated cost-conscious manufacturers by not showing up on time, by leaving before their contracts expired, by taking off for certain holidays, and by taking time out to tend to farm duties. Over the course of the nineteenth century and into the twentieth century, owners were able to rationalize and organize production under one roof and on a large scale and to put into place a system of worker discipline that enabled them to plan their production and output and to control their costs. This was not accomplished, however, without many struggles, trials and errors, many businesses going bankrupt, and many changes due to economic cycles, changing technology, and business competition.

THE FACTORY AND THE AMERICAN WORK ETHIC

Mill owners and factory owners espoused their version of the work ethic that required diligent attention to work, discipline in the workplace, and being on time every day. Industrial workers of the nineteenth century had their own reaction to factories and the industrial system of work. Industrial workers themselves or through their spokesmen asserted the dignity of labor and the worth of those who soiled their hands with honest labor. They resisted the new work disciplines of the factory masters, a resistance that expressed itself in workers reporting irregularly for work, moving constantly from job to job, or engaging in slowdowns, work restrictions, and strikes.

One of the big issues that divided the work ethic of owners from the work ethic of industrial workers was the length of the workday. Workers hoped for a workday that would permit them some measure of leisure so they could devote themselves to their families, have time for self-education, and enjoy some measure of leisure. They did not want work to completely absorb their lives. Factory owners on the other hand stressed the sunup-to-sundown workday and in the early nineteenth century worked their factory hands twelve to fourteen hours a day. The campaign for shorter hours began early in the nineteenth century with the appearance of the first workingmen's organizations. By the 1840s and 1850s the demand for the ten-hour day was taking hold in the textile mills of New England. After the Civil War the National Labor Union, the Knights of Labor, and the American Federation of Labor all made the eight-hour workday a central plank in their programs. On May 1, 1886, a massive eight-hour demonstration took place throughout the country, followed by workers flocking into labor unions with hopes for a shorter working day. Shorter hours was seen by workers as a means of spreading the work being relentlessly wiped out by machinery and employing the unemployed. While many arguments were advanced for reducing the hours of work, from time for self-education to having time to spend with one's family, the basic appeal to the hard-pressed worker subjected to the toil of factory work was the simple one of relief from toil. Workers could still believe in the work ethic that encompassed the dignity and honesty of labor and yet campaign for shorter hours without compromising their dedication to honest work as the pathway for the good life.

A second issue involving the clash of values between owners and workers was the question of workplace discipline. Factory owners had to engage in a long, persistent campaign of using fines, dismissals, firings, and other punishments to quell the traditional work habits of immigrants, farm hands, and craftsmen who found their way into the new factories of the nineteenth century. For many workers in the nineteenth century, adjustment to the employers' demand for regular, clock-disciplined work never came at all. A sizable portion of nineteenth-century American workers never converted to the creed of day-in and day-out labor. Irregular work patterns were particularly common among piecework trades where work itself was often irregular and a day's lost pay might be partially made up by harder work the next day. In the anthracite coalfields immigrant holidays persisted well into the twentieth century. However, by the turn of the century factory management had succeeded in exacting more regular attendance at work than existed in the shops and mills of the early nineteenth century.

Another aspect of worker opposition to employer values was the quit rate among factory workers. The average mill girl in Lowell in the mid-1840s had been on the job a year or less. Half the work force of the Lyman Mills in Holyoke, Massachusetts, in 1860 were short-term workers. A fifth of the men at the Pullman plant in

1894 had less than a year's tenure. Employers had to hold back wages or face the prospect of finding their hands gone in the morning. Turnover was higher in the good years when jobs were plentiful than in the depression years when those who had jobs worked hard and tried to hold on to their employment. Thus, some aspect of the turnover rates had nothing to do with resistance to factory discipline but was a function of the economic cycle. Turnover rose in the spring and fell in the winter. Many left to find better opportunities or because they simply decided to leave town. The nineteenth-century work force was generally restless and mobile, as workers shuttled from job to job.

Even those nineteenth-century industrial workers who showed up at the factories regularly and on time did not necessarily accept the new factory discipline and its work ethos. Many workers were able to maintain their own work norms and work customs that undercut the formal factory rules and expectations of factory owners. Some skilled workers such as glassblowers, potters, iron molders, iron puddlers and iron rollers openly regulated their workday's output through the "stint," an informal quota that all workers were expected to adhere to. In the building trades, the production quota was a long-time tradition and still exists among construction workers in twentieth-century America. Throughout American factories of the nineteenth century, workers established informal rules in both union and nonunion factories to enforce production quotas. Where workers could not control the factory pace because of the efforts of their employers or because their own informal enforcement was not strong enough, they could at least turn their resentments against the exceptionally fast worker who could be showered with epithets or socially ostracized. Workers in many nineteenth-century factories, especially where there were skilled workers, resented management attempts to place them under constant observation and supervision. It threatened their autonomy, their sense of self, and it truly threatened to make them into wage slaves. Working without time for rest or talk or a moment's loafing was no longer hard work, it was considered downright slavery. Craftsmen like machinists always had time to talk, to rest while their automatic lathes were running and they objected to attempts to account for every minute of their time.

To be sure, there were many workers who accepted the work ethic of hard, untiring labor as necessary for the good of the economy and for the well-being of the individual. Many workers saw hard, diligent work as the means to get ahead in the world and they complained about fellow-workers who were lazy and indigent. There was a middle group, neither adhering to the values of their employers nor the solidarity of those who resisted factory discipline, but who were success-driven workers who believed in discipline, sobriety, ambition, and diligence as the means to bettering one's life.

The question of how the European immigrant affected the work ethic is a complex one. Some European-born workers came to America from agricultural labor and never made the adjustment to the new expectations of the factories. A sizable number simply left and returned home. Others, clinging to the ways of work they had known and the unsteady rhythms of agricultural labor with its holidays and festivals, added to the turbulence of American factories. Still other immigrants brought with them ambition and faith in toil itself.

Many, if not most, immigrants to industrial America after 1850 were not uprooted but ambitious emigrants caught in the European social turbulence of the second half of the nineteenth century. The attractive wages and the chance to work one's way up through the social ranks dominated the vision of America among young, ambitious Europeans. Most emigrants not only were ambitious but they brought a belief in the value of work. Peasant work ideals were strong and the willingness to work ran deep among Europeans coming to America. What happened to them depended on the state of the American economy. If times were bad and if the emigrant came without family or friends they might find themselves caught in the pain of unemployment and a round of temporary jobs. Thus, the factories of the last quarter of nineteenth-century America were filled with a complex mixture of work ethics—men reared in the American work ethic, immigrants wrenched from traditional patterns, and workers willing to accept long hours and factory discipline. Resistance to factory regimens existed among industrial workers of all kinds, including immigrants and the native born. Absenteeism, mobility, and worker slowdowns were the most obvious manifestations of worker values in conflict with that of employers and management officials.

Throughout the factories, industrial workers chafed at their jobs and dreamed of a shorter working day and more leisure and engaged their employers in long and bitter disputes over working conditions. Workers rallied to the ideas and speeches of labor leaders like William Sylvis, Terence Powderly, and Eugene Debs who spoke about the dignity of labor and the worth of those who did the real work of society. While they were pushed to the wall and made to feel inferior to the men of wealth and those of the middle-class, praise of work was a useful and essential message for working people as it gave them a sense of status and self-respect. They listened with great interest to Terence Powderly, the leader of the Knights of Labor, whose message was to bring a sense of pride to the labor movement and a deep sensitivity to the dignity of labor. This message was also taken up by socialist Eugene Debs, who told his followers that workers were the only class essential to society, as they were the producers and builders and the creators of civilization. The fervent praise of work was mixed with the praise of leisure as socialists and radicals sought to work for a future society in which work would be reduced to a minimum number of hours, and in which working men would have the leisure to frequent libraries, art galleries, gymnasiums, and music concerts. The socialist paradise envisioned a future when work would be minimized and would be freely chosen.

Thus, the reactions of American factory workers was a mixed one. They chafed at the rigid discipline that factory owners wished to put into place, while asserting the dignity of labor. They asserted their pride in their work while at the same time complaining about the monotony of work. They resented accusations of soldiering (taking time off at work) from Taylor and others, but at the same time imposed their own informal quota and stints on what they were willing to give to their employers. Workers in the nineteenth century asserted the moral centrality of work but resisted the interpretation of the work ethic which employers and owners tried to impose upon them in the form of strict control over the work process.

CONCLUSION

Despite divisions and discontinuities, a certain logic united the history of American workers during the first century after the American Revolution. In 1776, American leaders proclaimed a set of natural rights to equality and personal autonomy. Over the next hundred years, various groups of Americans were swept up into the regimen of wage labor and factory work—Yankee farm women, displaced farmers, Irish and German immigrants, southern freedmen, deskilled artisans. They became aware of the disparity between the new wage system and America's promise of social and political progress. Not all workers came to the same conclusions about how best to better their lot, and a significant portion of American workers reconciled themselves to a subsidiary position in status and income in the new industrial system. Other American wage workers, in organized and informal groups, sought to combat the decline of independence and freedom promised by the revolution as they saw their lives in factories subjected to authoritarian and dictatorial rule. For many workers in nineteenth-century industrial America, adjustment to the employers' demand for regular, clock-disciplined work was resisted for a long time. High absenteeism, mobility, and quotas existed in virtually all factory payroll records before the turn of the century.

The 1880s and the 1890s were characterized by great upheavals and labor strife. It was a period of widespread and massive challenge to the emerging and consolidating industrial, capitalist social order. Wage workers embarked on a series of strikes, particularly in the steel, railroad, and mining industries. Farmers organized the Populist Movement that challenged the two-party system. Earlier in the century there was a labor demand for the ten-hour day, but later the agitation for the eight-hour day was launched with massive demonstrations of nearly a quarter million people in 1886. Reform movements of all kinds emerged, including women's voting rights, temperance, prison reform, child labor laws, and industrial safety. But the challenges to the growing industrial order were beaten back by the start of the twentieth century. A powerful industrial and commercial capitalist class was plainly in control of manufacturing, banking, and the transportation system of the country. From that position they were able to dominate the two political parties, the newspapers, the courts, and social institutions that enabled them to guide American society so as to make it function in accordance with most of the principles of the new industrial order.

BIBLIOGRAPHICAL ESSAY

For a good introduction to the relationship between work and time in the early factory organizations of the United States, see David Brody, 1993, "Time and Work During Early American Industrialism," in *Labor's Cause: Main Themes on the History of the American Worker* (New York: Oxford University Press, 1993). Besides discussing the importance of time, Brody makes a number of important points regarding early factory organization. Citing Barbara Tucker, *Samuel Slater and the Origins of the American Textile Industry, 1790–1860* (Ithaca, NY: Cornell University Press, 1984), Brody comments that the family system in the Slater mills was a concession to traditional ways, a means of recruiting factory labor without endangering patriarchy and solidarity. Brody also remarks that outside of textiles, industrial production got started with no technological breakthrough comparable to the power loom (23). Citing a Ph.D. dissertation (40–41, n. 84), Brody points to the interaction in early factory organization between capital and household labor, particularly the reliance on outwork production (23–24). Except in certain industries like tanning, paper making, and iron making, the average factory norm was twelve hours on average over the year. But the early factory did not necessarily demand more intensive work than the farm or the artisan shop. The notion of an industrial discipline was slow to take hold. Workers did not immediately lose their agrarian ties and moved regularly out of the mills during harvest time or at the call of family responsibility (24–25).

There has been a great deal of attention given to the early New England textile mills, where historians have studied the beginnings of American industrialization and the introduction of the factory system in cities such as Lowell, Massachusetts. However, there were mills established in rural and country settings. Among the earliest of these mills were those established by Samuel Slater in the Slater and Merino villages. These were the settings where entire families were hired to make up the labor force. For a review of the social system in these country mills, see Jonathan Prude, "The Social System of Early New England Textile Mills: A Case Study, 1812–40," in *Working-Class America: Essays on Labor, Community and American Society*, edited by Michael H. Frisch and Daniel J. Walkowitz (Urbana: University of Illinois Press 1983), 1–36.

One of the major theoreticians on the effects of factory organization in the nineteenth century on American workers and their work ethic was Herbert Gutman. Two works in particular should be consulted: "Work, Culture and Society in Industrializing America, 1815–1919," *American Historical Review* 78, no. 3 (June 1973), 537–603; and *Work, Culture and Society in Industrializing America: Essays in American Working-Class and Social History* (New York: Alfred A. Knopf, 1976).

A good survey of the industrialization process and the introduction of the factory system can be found in the book by David. M. Gordon, Richard Edwards, and Michael Reich, *Segmented Work, Divided Workers: The Historical Transformation of Labor in the United States* (Cambridge: Cambridge University Press, 1983). The reader should look at Chapter 3, "Initial Proletarianization: 1820s to 1890s," in which the authors outline the process of the growth of the factory system and the trends which made wage labor the normal condition of workers in the United States.

For a picture of the early textile industry, there are the works of Thomas Dublin, as follows: *Women at Work: The Transformation of Work and Community in Lowell, Massachusetts, 1826–1860* (New York: Columbia University Press, 1979); *Farm to Factory: Women's Letters, 1830–1860* (New York: Columbia University Press, 1981); and *Lowell: The Story of an Industrial City* (Washington, DC: U.S. Department of the Interior, 1992). On the reactions of New England textile workers to their work and their conditions of work, there is an original work by someone who was a worker in the mills, Lucy Larcom, *A New England Girlhood* (Gloucester, MA: Peter Smith, 1973 [orig. 1889]). For a modern work which is a review of worker attitudes and reactions to mechanization and industrialization in the textile mills, see David A. Zonderman, *Aspirations and Anxieties: New England Workers and the Mechanized Factory System, 1815–1850* (New York: Oxford University Press, 1992).

For a view of industrialization and mechanization in the shoe industry in Lynn, Massachusetts, see Alan Dawley, *Class and Community: The Industrial Revolution in Lynn* (Cambridge, MA: Harvard University Press, 1976). Also on the shoe industry in Lynn, see Paul G. Faler, "Cultural Aspects of the Industrial Revolution: Lynn, Massachusetts, Shoemakers and Industrial Morality, 1826–1860," in *American Workingclass Culture: Explorations in American Labor and Social History*, edited by Milton Cantor (Westport, CT.: Greenwood Press, 1979); and *Mechanics and Manufacturers in the Early Industrial Revolution Lynn, Massachusetts, 1780–1860* (Albany: State University of New York Press, 1981).

On the subject of the mobility and transiency of workers during the nineteenth century, see Stephan Thernstrom, "Urbanization, Migration and Social Mobility in Late Nineteenth-Century America," in *Towards a New Past: Dissenting Essays in American History*, edited by Barton J. Bernstein (New York: Pantheon Books, 1968). Also see Thernstrom's *Poverty and Progress: Social Mobility in a Nineteenth-Century City* (New York: Athenaeum, 1971).

One of the important innovations in factory production during the nineteenth century was the system of interchangeable parts. It divided the manufacture of a complicated machine into the separate manufacture of each of its component pieces. Each piece could then be made independently and in large quantities by workers who lacked the skills to make the whole machine. The numerous copies of each part would be so nearly alike that any one would serve in any machine. If one piece broke, another of its type could be substituted without shaping or fitting. The modern mass production assembly line is based on this principle. For a discussion of interchangeable parts, see Daniel J. Boorstin, *The Americans: The National Experience* (New York: Vintage Books, 1965), 32–33; and the article by Robert B. Gordon, "Who Turned the Mechanical Ideal into Mechanical Reality?" *Technology and Culture* 29, no. 4 (October 1988), 744–778.

For a review of industrial expansion and the growth of the factory system, see Walter Licht, *Industrializing America: The Nineteenth Century* (Baltimore: Johns Hopkins University Press, 1995), 103–117. In addition to that material, on factory expansion in Philadelphia in the textile industry, see Cynthia J. Shelton, *The Mills of Manayunk: Industrialization and Social Conflict in the Philadelphia Region, 1787–1837* (Baltimore: Johns Hopkins University Press, 1986). Shelton discusses the conflicts between the immigrant handloom weaver and the Philadelphia capitalist who began to invest capital in spinning frames and power looms and in mills located on the newly constructed canal on the Schuylkill River for the utilization of water power. For a discussion of industrialization in Paterson, New Jersey, with its silk manufacturing, textile machinery, locomotive factories, and plants manufacturing steam engines, see Herbert Gutman, *Work, Culture and Society in Industrializing America: Essays in American Working-Class and Social History* (New York: Alfred A. Knopf, 1976), 216–219, 234–240. For a discussion of industrialization in the city of Troy, New York, with its vigorous iron industry, see Daniel J. Walkowitz, "Statistics and the Writing of Working-class Culture: A Statistical Portrait of the Iron Workers in Troy, New York, 1860–1880," in *American Workingclass Culture*, edited by Milton Cantor.

The pin industry has always been a popular industry with which to explain the philosophy of factory manufacture because of the incongruity between the size of a pin and the amount of labor, capital, and technology that goes into making it. The Howe Manufacturing Company was one of the largest pin manufacturers in the United States. The Howe factories were highly mechanized with only a few skilled men overseeing the operation of the pinmaking machines which for the most part ran without much human intervention. For a discussion of factories and technology associated with pin manufacturing, see Steven Lubar, "Culture and Technological Design in the 19th-Century Pin Industry: John Howe and the

Howe Manufacturing Company," in *Technology and Culture* 18, no. 2 (April 1987), 253–282.

The iron and steel industry was an important one for factory organization and the use of wage labor in the industrialization process of the nineteenth century. For a discussion of the late nineteenth-century American iron and steel industry see the following works: Samuel Eliot Morison, *The Oxford History of the American People, Vol. 3: 1869–1963* (New York: Mentor, 1972), 72 ff.; Daniel E. Sutherland, *The Expansion of Everyday Life, 1860–1876* (New York: Harper & Row, 1989), 174–176; Michael Nuwer, "From Batch to Flow: Production Technology and Work-Force Skills in the Steel Industry, 1880–1920," in *Technology and Culture* 29, no. 4 (October 1988), 808–838. For an additional description of how steel was produced in the nineteenth century, see William Serrin, *Homestead: The Glory and Tragedy of an American Steel Town* (New York: Random House, 1992), 56–58. David Jardini, in his article "From Iron to Steel: The Recasting of the Jones and Laughlins Workforce between 1885 and 1896," provides an insight into the changing technology in the iron and steel industry in the late nineteenth century. His article appeared in *Technology and Culture* 36, no. 2 (April 1995), 271–301. Jardini deals with the change from puddling furnaces to Bessemer furnaces, as the industry changed from wrought iron to steel. There was a tremendous increase in output and productivity as well as a change in skill level, as Bessemer technology required almost half the skill levels required of the older puddling furnace technology. Many of the puddlers in the older technology were contract workers, being paid by the ton and hiring their own assistants. With the new technology fewer men were required per output of steel and the output per man increased tremendously, thus reducing the wages bill per ton of steel for the employers. Jardini argues that despite the reduction of skill levels with the Bessemer process of producing steel, it did not eliminate worker bargaining leverage, as far as Jones and Laughlin was concerned. Industrial capitalists in the steel industry were able to control the course of innovation but they did not exorcise workers' control from the shop floor. Jardini concludes: "While the productivity advantages of Bessemer steelmaking were clear to industrialists, the implications of the new technology for labor relations were ambiguous at best and presented a balance of new opportunities checked by increased vulnerabilities" (301).

The section in the text entitled, "The Factory and the American Work Ethic," is based on Daniel T. Rodgers, "Sons of Toil: Industrial Workers and Their Labor," in *The Work Ethic in Industrial America, 1850–1920* (Chicago: University of Chicago Press, 1974).

For surveys of workers in the nineteenth century, two works are important. The first is Bruce Laurie, *Artisans into Workers: Labor in Nineteenth-Century America* (New York: Hill and Wang, 1989). The second is Sean Wilentz, "The Rise of the American Working Class, 1776–1877, A Survey," in *Perspectives on American Labor History*, edited by J. Carroll Moody and Alice Keller-Harris (Dekalb: Northern Illinois University Press, 1989).

For a good introduction to early industrialization from 1800 to 1860, see Brian Greenberg, *Worker and Community* (Albany: State University of New York Press, 1985), 9–14. Another good introduction to work and the growing industrialization of the North prior to the Civil War is provided by Bruce Levine, *Half Slave and Half Free: The Roots of Civil War* (New York: Hill and Wang, 1992); see Chapter 2, "Each Person Works for Himself: The Ideal and Reality of Free Labor," 46–70.

11

LABORERS AND MANUAL WORKERS
IN THE NINETEENTH CENTURY

This chapter deals with laborers and manual workers who did not fit into the categories of farmers, factory workers, or artisans. Many were wage workers and others were independent, like gold miners. There were also cowboys, hardrock miners, canal builders, and men who laid track for railroads and had nothing to offer for their wages other than their physical strength and determination.

Common laborers were highly exploited, worked for low wages, and were socially fragmented. As a result their work culture reflected alienation and insecurity. Their struggles in the workplace were often uncoordinated efforts to secure and maintain their employment. Powerlessness and dislocation for the most part dominated their lifestyles. But they were also carefree and adventurous. Mark Twain's description of riverboat laborers captures the character of the men who performed the hard labor on canals and railroads, in mines, on docks loading ships, and in the mountains seeking beaver pelts:

> [River-boat commerce] gave employment to hordes of rough and hardy men, rude, uneducated, brave, suffering terrific hardships with sailor-like stoicism; heavy drinkers, coarse frolickers . . . heavy fighters, reckless fellows, every one, elephantinely jolly, foul-witted, profane; prodigal of their money, bankrupt at the end of the trip, fond of barbaric finery, prodigious braggarts; yet in the main, honest, trustworthy, faithful to promises and duty, and often picturesquely magnanimous. (Twain, 1982:238)

CANAL DIGGERS

Men who dug canals during the 1820s and 1830s, were among the unskilled, roughneck outcasts. Canal diggers were young, male, mostly Irish immigrants searching for security in a new land, bartering their working power for subsistence in a frequent unfriendly labor market. They were immigrants from a disrupted peasant economy and they lacked community structures in America. Their only resource was their brute physical power. Their public presence was rough hewn and their message was not harmony with employers or even with themselves, but rather a physical expression of conflicting interests. Feeling excluded from society, canallers reinforced the barrier by assaulting it. At work or in their shanties they created a distinctive life-style that set them apart from most of society. Their fierce competition and their drinking and brawling threatened whatever solidarity they promoted among themselves. Their culture was a mixture of weakness and strength, uncertainty and integrity.

Canal building peaked in the 1820s and 1830s, with 3,326 miles finished by 1840. Approximately 35,000 men worked on canals by 1840. When the depression of 1837 lifted in the mid-1840s, the competition of railroads and lack of canal investment sounded the virtual death knell for artificial water transportation. Canal construction was performed by independent builders who put up the initial capital, mobilized the work force, and had contracts to complete a section of the canal. The contractor often provided food and shelter for his workers while working alongside them. Men carried out the work using traditional tools—shovels, picks, wheelbarrows, and carts. Canallers toiled under a harsh labor regimen for twelve to fifteen hours a day in all kinds of weather. They suffered many health-threatening illnesses, including malaria, yellow fever, and cholera, as well as work-related injuries. The work was physically demanding, ill-paid, and dangerous.

Work on canals included clearing and excavation of earth and rock, masonry quarrying, erection of weirs and bridges, and building of rubble embankments and dams. Contractors recruited drivers with teams of oxen and horses from nearby villages and settlements. The first task was the removal of brush and trees. Workers hauled away large trees by using oxen, while they removed stumps by undermining or blasting them. Canal cuts and the building of embankments necessitated the removal of large volumes of earth and rock. This involved pick and shovel work, the strong point of the Irish. Canallers removed loads from the bottom of the canal with barrow runs composed of planks laid up the sides of the embankment that served as runways. The strongest men pulling loads ran up the planks aided by ropes attached to the laborer's belt at one end and around a pulley at the other end on top of the embankment.

Most canal workers moved into construction from farming. Alienated from land and loved ones in America, they had no support groups to ameliorate their hardships. Instead of a village, they lived in temporary shanty camps, all-male barracks, or in family huts on the work site or in nearby towns. They moved frequently, rarely staying in one place long enough to leave a trace of their presence. They had to fight over limited jobs. Their situation made for a rough and tough worker culture during the main canal era. Experiencing the same conditions and sharing a similar ethnic background, canallers developed a rough camaraderie reinforced by male bonding. The dangerous nature of their work shaped a work ethic of physical prowess, virility, nonchalance to risks, and drinking and fighting as the main measures of a man's worth. Emphasizing their strength and endurance, typical male values, was a way for canallers to define themselves. By working hard and laughing in the face of danger, canallers were engaging in self-exploitation, simultaneously pushing themselves to prove their own worth and enriching the contractor.

COWBOYS

Cowboys in the nineteenth century can be culturally defined as manual workers. Cowboy work included cattle drives, branding, castrating bulls, roundups, and maintenance of the herd. In all their tales, songs, and books, cowboys represented themselves as engaging in some form of labor.

Cowboying involved mastering certain skills. The cowboy was a good horseman, a windmill mechanic, a fence builder, a roper, an amateur veterinarian, and a brander. Ranchers owned the land, livestock, equipment, and houses; the cowboy owned a horse, a saddle, and some personal possessions. Cowboys were mostly bachelors because ranches lacked facilities for keeping families. They lived with danger, risking their lives roping a bull, fighting a prairie fire, chasing a runaway herd of cattle, working in blizzards, trying to cross swollen rivers, or being killed by Native Americans or other cowboys. They retained a strong tradition of storytelling. They also had a sense of humor that they used as a buffer between themselves and a world that included the wrath of nature, animals that would not respond, and employers who exploited them and mercilessly punished those who crossed them. A cowboy lived with animals and came to respect them, especially his horse for its athletic ability and its vision, sure feet, intelligence, and courage. Cowboys spent much time with animals, helping them come into the world and standing by them when they left the world. The cowboy myth, for better or worse, is part of the American belief in individualism, courage, hard work, and independence.

In the nineteenth century, ranchers hired mainly unmarried cowboys, as married men required higher wages to support families and had divided loyalties between employers and families. Bachelors could subsist on lower wages, live on ranches, and share cramped quarters in bunkhouses. They were always there when the cattlemen needed them. Working on predominantly male ranches, or being away on all-male cattle drives, cowboys almost never met women, except on paydays when they went to town, got drunk, and met prostitutes, or when they entered cowtowns at the end of cattle drives. Cowboys were forced to remain unmarried or risk being fired for moving to town, getting married, and fathering offspring.

Beef on the hoof was its own transportation system and rewards were rich when steers could be bought for $3 or $4 a head in Texas and sold for $35 or $40 a head up North. To deliver a big herd of three thousand cattle from Texas to Wyoming or Kansas required as much skill as moving an ocean liner across the Atlantic. Men had to be stationed at the head and tail of the herd and along the sides. Men on the sides made the herd go fast or slow by changing the width of the herd which could be fifty to seventy feet. Communication on the trail, where the rumble of hoofs smothered words, was by hand signals mostly borrowed from the Plains Indians. The greatest peril was the stampede, terrifying when three thousand head of cattle suddenly became a thundering mass. To stop it, cowboys had to steer the cattle into a circle that kept pressing inward until it became so compact that it ground to a halt. Failure to do that could result in cattle flying out like sparks and, if at night, disappearing into the darkness. Cowboys found themselves riding blind through the night, unable to see the prairie-dog holes, the gullies, and the precipices that even in daylight would be treacherous. A thundering herd could generate so much heat that they scorched the faces of the men riding alongside. There were few occupations as risky as herd droving. One single misstep or wrong move and the drover could lose his entire herd.

At the end of the nineteenth century the cowboy's unemployment rate increased. Cattlemen's need for employees abated with the smaller herd size and new methods of fencing and transportation. In the 1890s, economically pressed cattlemen cut expenses by building fenced-off enclosures, shipping their stock over railway lines, and firing cowboys. Unable to find work, cowboys sometimes resorted to cutting fences and rustling. Stealing, rebranding, and selling the cattle they stole allowed cowboys to support themselves using skills they acquired as workers on the unfenced frontier. Caught by cattlemen's livestock detectives, rustlers were tried and convicted and served time in prison.

Some cowboys resorted to strikes to improve their wages and conditions of work. Some tried to become independent ranchers. All attempts to challenge the Cattlemen's Association's dominance over the economic and political structure of western cattle country proved futile. Still, the cowboy left a tradition and folklore that celebrated his fierce independence, his endurance, his dedication to his work, and his belief in justice and individualism.

MINERS

In the last quarter of the nineteenth century, 150,000 miners worked at the extraction of coal, lead, copper, gold, and silver. Cornish and Irish workers each made up a third of the hard-rock miners in the camps. Hard-rock miners in the smaller operations used hand tools—hammers, picks, shovels, and hand-drills. In company-owned deep mines, miners descended in cages operated by steam winches. Each man carried his lunch pail, an allotment of candles, a candle holder or lantern, and a box of matches. Miners spent the day drilling, blasting, and shoveling rock. The least skilled shoveled rock and pushed ore cars. Miners used hand drills until 1872, when the compressed-air drill was introduced.

The hard-rock miner gained recognition by his work, his physical skill, his technical knowledge, and his coolheadedness and courage. Miners usually worked a shift of from eight to ten hours. Starting the day he reported to the shift boss and descended the shaft on a five-foot-by-five-foot platform or cage crowded with a dozen men. When he reached his working level he picked up his candles, drill, hammer, pick, and shovel and went to the area assigned to him. Candles were attached to his cap or mounted on steel holders driven into a crack in the rock. Miners worked in pairs. One wielded an eight-pound hammer while the other twisted a one-inch drill. With each blow the miner made a hissing noise to warn his partner that the hammer was coming, the hiss also serving to vent his concentrated energies. It required strong nerves to stand and let a big hammer whiz by the miner's ear, especially since the drill head was a hard target to hit in the faint light of a couple of tallow candles. Periodically the pair stopped to clean out the hole and change places. Mine owners introduced machine drills, powered by compressed air, in the Comstock mines in the early 1870s. The drill bit was attached to a reciprocating piston driven by compressed air. An air compressor located on the surface provided the air piped to the drills in the mine and also served to ventilate the working area and power small hoists, pumps, and blowers.

After miners drilled the hole to sufficient depth, it was cleaned and loaded with explosives. In small mines holes were fired at any time. In larger mines blasting took place between shifts or during meal breaks to allow time for the smoke and dust to clear before work resumed. When smoke and dust cleared, the shoveler, or mucker, removed the rock. The mucker was often an apprentice who served a dozen miners and had to load about sixteen one-ton ore cars during his shift. Most miners and muckers in western mines worked for wages of $3 to $5 a day. Some hired on as contract miners, so much per running foot of tunnel or drift. Besides miners and muckers there were carmen who moved the ore out, timbermen who braced the roof, engineers and mechanics operating and maintaining boilers, hoists, air compressors, pumps, and other machinery. There were also blacksmiths to reforge dull drills and picks, and messengers to carry tools, orders, water, and ice to the miners. Men on each level were supervised by a foreman.

One of every thirty western miners was disabled every year. One of every eighty was killed. The hard-rock miner could expect to be either temporarily or permanently disabled in one or more accidents during his lifetime. He had an even chance of being killed before he retired. The hard-rock miner could be blown to bits in an explosion, drowned in a sump, suffocated and incinerated in a fire, scalded by hot water, crushed by falling rocks or cave-ins, caught in machinery, ground under the wheels of an ore car, have his head split open with an ax or pick, his neck broken by being pulled up into the hoist frame, or his whole body smashed by falling down a shaft.

COMMON LABORERS

The organization of work in the second half of the nineteenth century included the common laborer everywhere. Laborers included every category from the shovelers that Frederick Taylor, the founder of scientific management, found at Bethlehem Steel to the tens of thousands of workers who laid railroad tracks and built bridges, roads, and dams. It also included the hundreds of thousands of men who manned the country's vast transportation network, all sorts of dray, hack, stage, cab, coach, and omnibus drivers who hauled freight or transported people. Horse-drawn trolleys were a major mode of urban transportation and employed lots of people, including drivers who came in from the farm and had no trade. Women and children were also among the laborers, women as servants and children employed in all kinds of odd jobs. The common laborer might work six months in a steel mill and then move on to help build a railroad. The common laborer worked wherever his or her physical strength was in demand. According to the United States Bureau of the Census, taking into account miners, homeworkers, farm laborers, and all other categories of common labor, laborers were the largest single group among working people at the end of the nineteenth century.

For all intents and purposes laborers' work was pure toil and the wages for this toil was subsistence wages. They remained a constant in a world of fast changes. Between 1877 and 1910 the wages were usually somewhere between $10 or $11 a week, or about $1.50 to $1.75 per day. On docks and in construction, common labor hourly rates were higher, but given the seasonal nature of the work, the overall result was the same. Nor was the $10 per week a guaranteed income. Given the business cycle, accidents, and sickness, the laborer who had a steady job was lucky.

Two developments at the turn of the century profoundly changed the world of the laborer: scientific management and new immigration from Southern and Eastern Europe. Scientific management transformed laborers into machine hands; immigration from Southern and Eastern Europe provided a cheap supply of common laborers. Unskilled immigrant labor continued to come in increasing numbers during the last part of the nineteenth century and beyond, with capitalists dependent upon the use of this constant influx of foreign labor in their planning and business practices.

Common laborers were widespread in the last quarter of the nineteenth century, in the construction of new steam and electric railways, the digging and enlarging of waterways, the development of water supply and sewer systems in towns, the maintenance of railroads, in the lumbering industry, in the ice harvest, in canneries, and in the grain and berry fields. Thus, laborers did not disappear with "progress." Some of them became unskilled factory workers, others continued the old, pure physical toil. Many moved back and forth between the old and new forms of work. Together with other men and women in factories, farms, and workshops, they were reshaping the American working class.

The work ethic of the common laborer was an ethic of survival and an ethic of hard toil. Laborers had nothing to offer but physical labor and endurance and they had to accept intermittent employment and unending exploitation as members of a large reserve of workers. There were always more common laborers than demand for them. In the nineteenth century, the work ethic of the common laborer was outside the recruiting drives of unions, since up to the Civil War there were no unions willing to recruit the laborers. After the Civil War, the Knights of Labor did take in laborers, but that organization was limited and short-lived. Common laborers found themselves part of a multi-ethnic environment competing for jobs on their own, relying on their own resources and their own wits. Their plight forced on them a work ethic of constant struggle and hard toil. For males it was an ethic of display of physical strength and endurance and acceptance of existence on the margins of society. For females it was acceptance of wage scales inferior to males and of employment in menial positions. Through it all, however, the common laborer, by virtue of his and her work, and the necessity of such work for the building of America, was able to maintain his and her sense of worth through the exercise of essential labor.

BIBLIOGRAPHICAL ESSAY

For an overview of common laborers in the late nineteenth century, see Andrea Graziosi, "Common Laborers, Unskilled Workers: 1880–1915," *Labor History* 11, no. 4 (Fall 1981), 512–544. Another description of common laborers is provided by Peter Way in the introduction to his study of canal construction laborers, "Evil Humors and Ardent Spirits: The Rough Culture of Canal Construction Laborers," *Journal of American History* 79, no. 4 (March 1993), 1400–1401.

The quote from Mark Twain on river-boat laborers is from his *Mississippi Writings* (New York: Literary Classics of the United States, 1982), 238. For a description of wage-earning laborers, see David Montgomery, *Citizen Workers: The Experience of Workers in the United States with Democracy and the Free Market during the Nineteenth Century* (New York: Cambridge University Press, 1993), 14, where he quotes from the Reverend Joseph Tuckerman, who in 1829 wrote an "Essay on the Wages Paid to Females for their Labour." Tuckerman states:

> The classes are very numerous, of those who are wholly dependent upon wages.... This large division includes shop, market and other porters; carmen; those who are employed in lading, and unlading vessels; wood-sawyers; hod-carriers; house servants; those employed by mechanics in a single branch of the business; and multitudes, who are men and women of any work, occasionally required in families, as washing, scouring, etc; or on the wharves, or in the streets of the city.

One group of workers who did not fit into other categories of workers, and one not dealt with in the text because of space constraints, were fur trappers. They worked in danger like miners. They were independent outdoorsmen like cowboys. They had the fierce combativeness of the roughneck laborers. And they used skills the equal of any man. They were hard-drinking, courageous men who created a culture that lasted till mid-century and made fortunes for others like the Hudson Bay Company and the Rocky Mountain Fur Company. They were a tiny minority but they left a rich heritage of folklore and some of them, like Jim Bridger and Kit Carson, became the stuff of legends. Their exploits were heroic and they served a market that linked the ways of tribal Indians to the tastes of wealthy Europeans. They were special, even unique, and they deserve an honored place in the history of laboring men in the nineteenth century. One of the best and most complete descriptions of fur trappers is in Bernard DeVoto, *Across the Wide Missouri* (Boston: Houghton Mifflin, 1947). Other studies of fur trappers can be found in Allan G. Bogue, Thomas D. Phillips, and James E. Wright, eds., *The West of the American People* (Itasca, IL: F. E. Peacock Publishers, 1970), particularly the essay by Ray H. Mattison, "The Upper Missouri Fur Trade: Its Methods of Operation"; and the essay by William H. Goetzmann, "The Mountain Man as Jacksonian Man."

A nineteenth-century people whose work will not be dealt with because of space constraints were the Native Americans. On Native Americans in the nineteenth century, see Samuel Eliot Morison, *The Oxford History of the American People, Vol. II* (New York: Mentor, 1972), 187–195, 299. Also see D. E. Brown, *Bury My Heart at Wounded Knee: An Indian History of the American West* (New York: Holt, Rinehart and Winston, 1971). For a history of the strife between Native Americans and white invaders of the West, see Richard H. Dillon, *North American Indian Wars* (Greenwich, CT: Brompton Books, 1993), 73–251. On the removal of Native Americans west of the Mississippi following the election of Andrew Jackson, see James Kirby Martin, Randy Robert, Steven Mintz, Linda O. McMurry, and James H. Jones, *America and Its People* (New York: HarperCollins, 1989), 278–279.

For a case-study of a nineteenth-century Native-American culture at work, see E. Adamson Hoebel, *The Cheyennes: Indians of the Great Plains* (New York: Holt, Rinehart and Winston, 1960).

Europeans were not successful in coercing or enslaving Native American labor in most parts of the country. In California, however, the story was different. From the 1770s to the 1850s, the scarcity of alternative sources of labor and the geographic isolation of California limited the number of Hispanic, European, and American settlers until the gold rush. Thus, the Spanish, through their missions and through a system of debt peonage and vagrancy laws, were able to tie Indians to the land and involve them in work on the missions. Approximately sixty thousand Indians worked in the missions and were the main labor force in California up to the 1850s. The Spanish were able to impose a work ethic and discipline on their Indian work force who became highly productive workers, toiling in all facets of the diverse mission agriculture economy. They also worked as nonagricultural laborers and even as artisans. The missions became the centerpiece of the California economy, providing food and other commodities to the population. For a picture of this social situation see Douglas Monroy, "Brutal Appetites: The Social Relations of the California Mission," in *Working People of California*, edited by Daniel Cornford (Berkeley: University of California Press, 1995), 29–56.

The section in the text on the work culture of canal diggers is largely based on Peter Way, "Evil Humors and Ardent Spirits: The Rough Culture of Canal Construction Laborers," *Journal of American History* 79, no. 4 (March 1993), 1397–1428. Also see William N. T. Wylie, "Poverty, Distress, and Disease, Labour and Construction of the Rideau Canal, 1826–1832," in *Labour/Le Travailleur* 11 (Spring 1983), 7–29.

For cowboys in the nineteenth century, consult John R. Erikson, "The Cowboy," in *Ranching Traditions: Legacy of the American West*, edited by Alan Axelrod (New York: Cross River Press, 1989). In the same collection by Alan Axelrod, see the essay by David Dary, "How It all Began." Jack Weston discusses cowboy culture and its work ethic in *The Real American Cowboy* (New York: New Amsterdam Books, 1985). The work culture of American cowboys is analyzed in Blake Allmendinger, *The Cowboy: Representations of Labor in an American Work Culture* (New York: Oxford University Press, 1992). For a description of cattle runs from Texas to Wyoming and Kansas, see Daniel J. Boorstin, *The Americans: The Democratic Experience* (New York: Vintage Books, 1974), 11–13.

On the California gold rush and the work of placer mining, see Charles Howard Shinn, "California's Golden Prime of Forty-Nine," in *The West of the American People*, edited by Allan G. Bogue, Thomas D. Phillips, and James E. Wright. An excellent description of the placer miner, how he worked and how he saw the world can be found in Jack London's short story, "All Gold Canyon," in Jack London, *Novels and Stories* (New York: The Library of America, 1982), 777–796.

For hard-rock miners of the West, see the excellent study by Richard E. Lingenfelter, *The Hardrock Miners: A History of the Mining Labor Movement in the American West, 1863–1893* (Berkeley: University of California Press, 1974). For a further discussion of miners and their work see Daniel E. Sutherland, *The Expansion of Everyday Life, 1860–1876* (New York: Harper & Row, 1989), 171–174.

On unskilled immigrant labor, see David M. Gordon, Richard Edwards, Michael Reich, *Segmented Work, Divided Workers: The Historical Transformation of Labor in the United States* (Cambridge: Cambridge University Press, 1982), 73–77.

12

SLAVERY AND BLACKS
IN THE NINETEENTH CENTURY

Any analysis of African-Americans in the nineteenth century must deal mainly with slavery. That was the condition of the great majority of blacks until the Civil War, and slavery cast its long shadow over blacks until the end of the nineteenth century and into the twentieth. The slave system was mainly a southern plantation system, producing commercial crops for a domestic and world market. The main crops were cotton, tobacco, rice, sugar, and hemp. Slaves who produced these commodities were themselves commodities, a fact that differentiated them from all other workers. Blacks made up one-third of the South's population at the time of the Civil War—4 million out of 12 million. There were about 1.25 million white households in the South, of which about one-fourth owned slaves. The majority of southerners were family farmers, even those who owned one to five slaves. Only 8,000 southern households owned more than fifty slaves, the number required for a large plantation. A majority of blacks worked in agriculture, with most in cotton cultivation. Only 20 percent were involved in growing tobacco, rice, sugar, and hemp. In short, southern commercial agriculture in the nineteenth century was a cotton culture sustained by slave labor.

The lives of slaves were affected day in and day out by the basic reality that they were not their own masters. If a slave's workload was reasonable, or if slaves were allowed to till their own plots and sell their own products, it remained so only at the master's discretion, not because the slave decided such matters. If slaves married or visited family and friends on other plantations, it was only with the permission of his master. If slaves married they remained together only so long as their master did not separate them through sale. In every act, every expression or gesture, slaves had to consider the consequences of their masters' response. In that sense the line between freedom and slavery penetrated every corner of a slave's life. It was absolute and overwhelming. Even the most poverty-stricken white living in the worst hovel never asked to be a slave.

Slavery was foremost a system to manage and control labor.

Slaves worked. When, where, and especially how they worked determined, in large measure the course of their lives. So central was labor in the slaves' experience that it has often been taken for granted.... The struggle over the slaves' labor informed all other conflicts between master and slave, and understanding that contest opens the way to a full comprehension of slave society.... Work informed the culture slaves created, providing the ideological and material basis for their most precious institutions and beliefs. The character of the slaves' work, moreover, influenced the hopes and aspirations they carried into freedom, giving direction to the postemancipation struggle for equality. The legacy of slavery cannot be understood without a full appreciation of the way in which slaves worked. (Berlin and Morgan, 1993:1–3)

Slavery was a system based on force. Slaves did not have the liberty to be idle, to choose their jobs, or to determine the allocation of their work. The essence of slavery was the master's power over the slave's life. For slaves there was always the threat of punishment, of sale away from one's family, of whippings. In the minds of everyone, white and black, the lash stood as an ever present reminder of where authority lay. While the periodic shock of family breakup or a brutal whipping was unsettling, it was the relentless, perpetual intrusion of the master's power over the daily existence of slaves that demonstrated the denial of their freedom.

WORK ROUTINES

The work routines of slaves depended on a large variety of factors—the season, the crop, the size of the master's holdings, the historical period, the area, the master's economic condition, the economic cycle. Slaves were employed differently on the frontier than in the older settled regions. While the typical white slave owner possessed fewer than five slaves, the typical rural slave lived on a large plantation. Over half resided on plantations of more than twenty bondsmen. Thus, most slaves lived in close proximity to numerous other slaves. This was culturally significant since being with other blacks enabled slaves to find companionship and marriage partners that made life more bearable. Black religious and musical expression, black family life, and folklore were all the richer as a result of slaves being able to congregate and create their communities in their quarters on the large plantation.

Slaves sometimes took pride in their work and performed at levels of competence and efficiency that pleased their masters. Some bondsmen found a portion of self-respect in the skill with which they conducted their work. On smaller farms, slaves worked alongside masters and personal relationships often transcended color. On the largest plantations, professional overseers operated the plantation for the owner, with field slaves seldom having contact with white masters. On large plantations, slaves usually worked in gangs under the direction of a slave driver.

This lessened the chance for individual initiative, but it added to the sense of group solidarity. Working together, slaves could slow down the work pace more effectively and with less danger of personal blame than could individual workers. Through give and take, slaves and their masters acquired a mutual understanding of how much work was to be done in a normal day. Slaves considered excess work a severe infringement on the limited time reserved for themselves. Planters came to realize that they were supervising other humans who could, and did, retaliate in numerous ways against treatment judged too harsh. The conflict between master and slave took place over the organization of work, the pace of work, and the division of labor. The weapons used by workers included feigning ignorance, slowing the line, maiming animals, disappearing at critical times, and as a last resort confronting their superiors with violence.

On small farms there was little specialization for slave men and women. A slave woman gave domestic service, but in times of harvest she would shift her work to the fields. A slave man would do whatever had to be done. On plantations with more than twenty slaves there emerged a degree of labor specialization, the most basic being that of house slaves and field slaves. Besides common field labor on a large plantation there were skilled craftsmen—carpenters, masons, blacksmiths, cooks, teamsters, livestock handlers, and so on. There were also positions of authority, namely black drivers who were basically foremen directing the work. On the three thousand grand plantations there was also a large retinue of house servants—laundresses, nursemaids, butlers, valets, cooks, and house cleaners.

A large proportion of cotton-field workers wielded the hoe, chopping grass away from cotton plants. Such routine labor required some skill for a hoe swung an inch too far would snip the cotton stalk. The experienced hand with a clean stroke could cultivate the soil and cut the grass, which if left alone, would take over a cotton field. The plow gang kept the middle of the rows clean of grass, and the thin layer of free dirt thrown up by the plow covered up, killed, and retarded the growth of grass along the edge of the rows. Choppers worked to keep the cotton "out of grass," a constant battle especially during a wet period. Plowing required much skill and strength. The plow would dig alternately deep, then shallow and wobble across the field, leaving a crooked furrow. Adept plowmen could plow even, straight furrows, with fresh-turned dirt and arrowlike rows, a testament to their skill. Slaves did take pride in a job well done, in a crop safely gathered, in a furrow plowed straight and true, or a fence neatly mended. Their pride was in their own achievement and did not imply a surrender to values imposed by the master. If they were efficient workers within the system of slave-master paternalism, they were also effective workers of the system and they knew how to work it for their own ends.

The number and variety of jobs to be done on a plantation were almost endless. In addition to working on crops, slaves worked to clear land, cut firewood, shear sheep, husk corn, repair barns and fences, shovel manure, dig ditches, and so on, as circumstances and time permitted. On rainy days, women worked at a loom or a spinning wheel rather than laboring in the fields. On large plantations, slave blacksmiths kept horses shod and tools sharpened and repaired. They also made hinges, nails, and other metal products. Slaves worked as carpenters and cabinet-makers, as gardeners, stablemen, and dairymen; they operated cotton gins and cotton presses; they boiled sugar on sugar plantations; they ran mills to grind wheat and corn; they husked rice; and they made clothing. On cattle ranches in Texas, slave cowboys branded and rounded up cattle.

Working hours were long, traditionally from sunup to sundown. The peak demand for labor came at the end of the season, at cotton-picking time, when every available hand was needed in the fields. The productivity of the cotton plantation was limited by the task of picking. The South had the capacity to grow more cotton than it could pick. Until that problem was solved there was little incentive to mechanize or modernize the earlier stages of cotton cultivation.

SLAVERY AND WORK INCENTIVES

The low-incentive labor system of slavery gave slaves few reasons to overexert themselves when working in their masters' fields. Slaves realized they had to work at a moderate pace for their own physical self-preservation. They did accept responsibility to work at a level that eventually came to be accepted by slave and master alike. There was a perpetual war of the wills, with masters' cajoling, threatening, and whipping on occasion, while slaves worked at a deliberate pace. Slaves practiced minor sabotage like breaking tools, "accidentally" plowing up crops, or "carelessly" letting the teams get out of the barn. When a master or overseer tried to force slaves to work harder, they might slow their pace or feign illness. On any plantation at any given time there were always slaves laid up for sickness, real and pretended. Thomas Chaplin, a St. Helena planter, vowed not to let any slave shirk from work with sham sickness. He would force them out. But his resolve would slacken, and if a man or woman worked hard and took a day in the sickhouse for no perceptible cause, he would look the other way. Some workers would show up for work and withhold their minds. Chaplin might tell hands to hoe and instead they would haul. They would cover grass with dirt when he wanted them to chop it out. He would send for fence rails and they would bring poles. Chaplin was at a loss how to respond. What should he do when the hands worked hard, but not at the tasks he assigned?

Most intelligent planters understood that slaves would have something to lose and would be easier to manage, if owners introduced some incentives into a system that was based on force. Thus, permitting the slaves' independent economy was one means of tying them to the plantation. Slaves were allowed to cultivate plots in their own quarters and even keep livestock sometimes for their own use. They were in some cases permitted to sell products either to their masters or to others. Although force was the basis of the slave system it had distinct limits. Slaves had too many annoying means at their disposal to take revenge on their masters. In an effort to discredit a bad overseer, slaves on an Alabama plantation got together to cover up the weeds in the cotton field instead of chopping them out, hoping to lose the crop and see the overseer fired. One master told his diary, "I give up; they will have their time out." Another in Mississippi enjoined his overseer to give his slaves all they needed to eat, "lest they steal." Frederick Douglass argued that slaves had the right to steal since the morality of a free society had no application to a slave society, and as freedom of choice is the essence of accountability, to make a man a slave was to rob him of choice.

RUNAWAYS

When slaves felt unjustly treated they ran away. Runaways were a chronic problem for southern planters. Usually when the runaway returned he would receive a whipping or some other punishment, but occasionally owners disregarded the infraction. Running away was an accepted method for angered slaves to work out their feelings in a safe form. It relieved tensions, allowed resentments to cool, and reduced the possibility that suppressed rage might build to explosive levels. The separation of slave families caused many bondsmen to leave their plantations in an effort to reunite with loved ones. Slaves who ran off usually did not run far or stay away long. Some ran to the woods and marshes to avoid punishment, others because they were tired or fed up. One runaway, a man whom Thomas Chaplin had previously owned, accosted him from across a fence and asked him to buy him back. Chaplin declined, but did not try to catch the fellow or report him to the patrol. From the master's viewpoint the chief danger of runaways was that they demoralized others. Once a slave was out for two or three weeks, his master placed a notice in the newspapers offering a reward for his or her return. Sweet must have been the knowledge to a runaway field hand that he was depriving his master of a week's hard work. Overt rebellion existed, but it was for the few. For the majority a well-timed lie, a petty theft, or feigned illness seemed the appropriate defense. One folk tale told about an old slave who never worked because he convinced his master he was a cripple. When the master found out and prepared to whip the old man, the magic of a black "doctor" intervened and none of the licks touched him and he had his freedom.

THE CIVIL WAR

The Civil War gave the answer as to how contented the slaves were with the institution of slavery. Approximately 100,000 ex-slaves fought as soldiers for the Union cause, and perhaps 500,000 or more fled their plantations and sought aid from Union armies. Many slaves were cautious and waited for the right moment to flee and seek freedom. Most chose freedom when the opportunity allowed. Along the battle routes slave owners fled from Union troops and took their slaves with them. Bondsmen overwhelmingly chose liberty, not loyalty to masters, when presented with a genuine option for freedom. Few things disconcerted slave owners more than their slaves forsaking them and fleeing to the Union armies. Often it was not the field hands who left first, but the house servants who the whites trusted most. Whites were thunderstruck, frustrated, and angry at the supposed ingratitude of their runaways. No other event showed how little whites really understood the blacks among them. Lincoln's Emancipation Proclamation of January 1, 1863, declared that freed slaves would be received into the armed service of the United

States. Thereafter black soldiers became commonplace, eventually numbering 178,895, of whom 133,000 came from former slave states.

SHARECROPPING

After the Civil War, though much had changed, whites still owned the land and blacks had only their labor to offer. Whites needed black labor as badly as blacks needed white-owned land, and gradually mutual accommodations were worked out that resulted in a system of agriculture called sharecropping. The majority of former slaves—freedmen—remained in rural areas. Hundreds of northern schoolteachers came to the South and found black adults and children eager to learn. Black emancipation was a great revolution but much remained unchanged. The climate and soil were the same and cotton was still the great money crop. Power was still in the hands of whites, politically and economically. Blacks wanted to live apart from landowners, on separate land where they could grow crops as independent family units. Freedmen preferred payment in the form of a share of the crop rather than receiving a wage from landowners. Planters did not have the cash to pay wages and they too welcomed the sharecropping system. Sharecropping gave ex-slaves control over their work schedules and privacy in their home life. Material income of blacks increased about one-third as a result of emancipation. What they valued most was control over their own lives, work, consumption, and time.

By 1880, about one-fifth of black farmers in the South owned their land, a miraculous accomplishment, though their farms averaged half the size of white-owned farms. Most blacks were sharecroppers. They were in no position to provide themselves with draft animals, provisions, and implements. For food and clothing, sharecroppers had to find suppliers who would extend credit, with the balance due when the cotton was picked. Thousands of small country stores mushroomed across the South in the years following the Civil War. Merchants charged the sharecroppers prices that included interest rates averaging 60 percent, as sharecroppers had no alternative suppliers. Large northern wholesale houses supplied the local stores on credit and charged high interest rates because of the risks involved. Sharecroppers found that their one-half of the cotton crop would not cover their debt at the local store. At the end of the year, after the landowner took his share and the storekeeper settled up his account, the sharecropper family had no choice but to ask for credit for another year. But another year of work and another middling crop left them deeper in debt.

The tragedy of slavery is that it prepared neither blacks nor whites for a changing economic system. No one escaped poverty, racism, and the hopelessness of the postwar South. There was protest near the end of the nineteenth century, a farmers' rebellion that included southern blacks and held the promise of biracial political cooperation. However, the primacy of cotton did not wane until the twentieth century when the boll weevil, farm mechanization, the automobile, paved roads, and World War II finally forced the South out of its one-crop economy, labor-intensive farming, rural isolation, and paucity of capital. Not until nearly a century after the Civil War did southern blacks begin to move beyond racism and poverty and into freedom. Not until then did the South lift itself into the national pattern of industrialization, large commercial cities, and a standard of living enjoyed by the rest of the United States.

CONCLUSION

The master-slave relationship was contradictory as it simultaneously denied and recognized the will of the slave. The master owned the slave and all the slave produced, but was also responsible for the care of the slave. The slave's will was denied in his or her forcible enslavement and in the exercise of the master's power. At the same time, the slave had to be treated as human, whose mind and will were recognized. Slaves possessed the capacity for thought and rational action that distinguishes humans from other animals, which made them superior to and irreplaceable by livestock. Slaves could be taught the production process, given verbal instruction, and could carry out orders under the threat of punishment or the promise of reward. Slaves could be trained as skilled craftsmen. However, the slave's productive capacities could be developed only if he or she was taught language, taught about production processes, and taught the constellation of social relationships in which he or she was to participate. The will of the slave had to be recognized along with his or her ability for self-conscious action. Yet this capacity of the slave for action was also a capacity for conscious resistance. Slaves could have the motivation to work or to resist. This human capacity gave slaves a will that would inevitably conflict with that of their masters.

In the final analysis, the institution of slavery created an attitude of dependency. The real wrong in slavery did not affect the body as much as it was a curse to the soul and mind of the slave. The aim of the master was to keep down every principle of manhood and growth. This held true for good and bad planters alike, and was the condition of slavery itself.

The study of slavery illuminates how a resilient people can survive an institution designed to retain them in a perpetual state of dependence. Slaves endured and understood that slavery was a wretched institution whether they were beaten and abused every day or not. The study of slavery is a study of how the spirit of freedom, which is of the mind as well as of the body, can never be extinguished because it is the study, in essence, of human beings. Though slaves remained subordinate until slavery's grip was broken, they were not impotent. Employing their numbers and their knowledge, they struggled to shape their own world. Notions of freedom, forged in the crucible of slavery, informed the aspirations of black people once slavery ended. With emancipation former slaves made it clear that they wanted, above all, access to land and resources so they could work for themselves in family and communal groups.

BIBLIOGRAPHICAL ESSAY

For a fine analysis and discussion of slavery and work, see Ira Berlin and Philip D. Morgan, *Cultivation and Culture: Labor and the Shaping of Slave Life in the Americas*

(Charlottesville: University of Virginia Press, 1993), 1–45. Many ideas in this chapter are based on this volume, especially the Berlin and Morgan introduction.

For an overview of the South, the slave system, and the work of slaves, see James West Davidson, William E. Gienapp, Christine Leigh Heyrman, Mark H. Lytle, and Michael B. Stoff, *Nation of Nations* (New York: Alfred A. Knopf, 1991), 450–485.

For an excellent study of the social system of slavery and the role of black men and women under that system, see John B. Boles, *Black Southerners, 1619–1869* (Lexington: University Press of Kentucky, 1983). For a discussion of the work routines of slaves, see Boles, 82–84. Another study of the slave system within the southern context is provided by James Oakes, *Slavery and Freedom: An Interpretation of the Old South* (New York: Alfred A. Knopf, 1990).

For a discussion of the economic efficiency of the southern plantation system for cotton, see Oakes, *Slavery and Freedom*, 143–44. Also Gavin Wright, *Political Economy of the Cotton South: Households, Markets and Wealth in the Nineteenth Century* (New York: W. W. Norton, 1978), 90–97.

For a poignant description of the struggles between master and slave and the unsuccessful attempt to break the spirit of a slave, see Chapters 15–17 on the struggles between Douglass and Covey in Frederick Douglass's *Autobiography: My Bondage and My Freedom* (New York: Library of America, 1994), 258–287.

Bruce Levine provides an analysis of the causes of the Civil War by describing the nature of American society, both North and South, in the 1850s. He provides a valuable review of the southern plantation system and the slave system which supported it. See Bruce Levine, *Half Slave and Half Free: The Roots of Civil War* (New York: Hill and Wang, 1992), 3–45, 95–120. Levine presents a number of insights and valuable data in Chapter 1, "Our Laborers Are Our Property." He points out that the typical slave owner, who comprised about 65 percent of slave owners, had five to six slaves and worked in the fields alongside his slaves. The next group of slave owners had between 15 to 50 slaves and comprised 25 percent of slave owners. At the very top of the slaveholding pyramid stood the planter aristocracy, owning at least 100 slaves and they comprised 10 percent of slave owners. Ten percent of all enslaved blacks in the South worked in industry and 6 percent of southern blacks (262,000) were free, mostly living in the upper South, Louisiana, and the Carolinas (22–23). Levine stresses that the slave system was based on force and he quotes from Judge Thomas Ruffin that the system of slavery had as its end the profit of the master and that obedience from slaves was based on "uncontrolled authority over the body" of the slaves (33). Levine quotes Solomon Northup, a slave who was later freed and wrote about his experiences, and Dr. John Wesley Monette, a proslavery writer, to the effect that slaves were whipped if the quota of cotton picked did not measure up to the quota established by their overseers (34–35). Levine summarizes the status of nonslaveholding white farmers, who were made up of two main groups. Those who lived near large plantations and were dependent upon the large planters to gin, transport, and market their cotton, and those who lived outside the plantation districts in the southern hill country and concentrated on growing subsistence crops, notably corn, and consuming what they themselves could produce with their own hands (38). Referring to the backwardness of the South, as compared with the North in industrial power, Levine states that 60 percent of the North's labor force was working outside agriculture by the Civil War, while only 16 percent of the South's labor force was similarly occupied (41). Finally, commenting on the independent economic pursuits of slaves, Levine stresses how much the slave owners resisted it, because, as Olmsted observed, it gave the slaves "too much liberty and [they] were acquiring bad habits" (43). A picture and description of white slave owners can be found in Peter J. Parish, *Slavery, History and Historians* (New York:

Harper & Row, 1989), 27–29; also in Bruce Levine, *Half Slave and Half Free*, 95–104; and see Davidson et al., *Nation of Nations*, 460–469, on the same subject.

On the work routines of slaves, see Boles, *Black Southerners*, 78–79, 107–111, 112–115; and Charles Joyner, *Down by the Riverside: A South Carolina Slave Community* (Urbana: University of Illinois Press, 1984), 57–59. In addition see Parish, *Slavery, History and Historians*, 30–31, 48; and Wright, *Political Economy*, 64–74.

For slave drivers, see William L. Van Deburg, *The Slave Drivers: Black Agricultural Labor Supervisors in the Antebellum South* (Westport, CT: Greenwood Press, 1979). In addition see Willie Lee Rose, *Slavery and Freedom*, edited by William W. Freehling (New York: Oxford University Press, 1982), 65; Theodore Rosengarten, *Tombee: Portrait of a Cotton Planter, Journal of Thomas B. Chaplin, 1822–1890* (New York: William Morrow, 1986), 162.

On the task system and the gang system employed by different plantations in different areas and for different crops, see the following: Berlin and Morgan, *Cultivation and Culture*: 14–16; Rosengarten, *Tombee*, 80; Robert Fogel, *Without Consent or Contract: The Rise and Fall of American Slavery* (New York: W. W. Norton, 1989), 27–28; Drew Gilpin Faust, *James Henry Hammon and the Old South: A Design for Mastery* (Baton Rouge: Louisiana State University Press, 74–75, 92. Also see Philip D. Morgan, "Work and Culture: The Task System and the World of Lowcountry Blacks, 1700 to 1880," *William and Mary Quarterly* 39, no. 4 (October 1982), 563–599.

Part of the testimony of Solomon Northup and John Wesley Monette referred to by Bruce Levine in n. 7 on the slavery system can be found in *A Documentary History of Slavery in North America*, edited by Willie Lee Rose (New York: Oxford University Press, 1976).

Figures on the labor participation rate of slaves can be found in Fogel, *Without Consent or Contract*, 52–55; and in Parish, *Slavery, History and Historians*, 41.

On methods employed by slaves to thwart the will of their masters, see Rosengarten, *Tombee*, 157–158; and Boles, *Black Southerners*, 178. Regarding stealing by slaves, see Rose, *Slavery and Freedom*, 32; and Frederick Douglass, *Autobiography*, 553–554. For a discussion of slave runaways, see Boles, *Black Southerners*, 176–179; Rosengarten, *Tombee*, 159; and Rose, *Slavery and Freedom*, 69.

A major contribution to the study of industrial slavery is Charles Dew's book on slave labor at Buffalo Forge. Buffalo Forge was an extensive iron-making and farming enterprise near Lexington in the Valley of Virginia. During antebellum years, almost every job, skilled and unskilled, was performed by slave labor. Records of the lives of these workers have survived and Charles Dew has reconstructed the stories of slaves and masters in their economic roles. See Charles B. Dew, *Bond of Iron: Master and Slave at Buffalo Forge* (New York: W. W. Norton, 1994). On industrial slavery also see Ronald L. Lewis, *Coal, Iron and Slaves: Industrial Slavery in Maryland and Virginia, 1715–1865* (Westport, CT: Greenwood 1979). For additional information on industrial slaves in the iron industry, see Charles B. Dew, "Disciplining Slave Ironworkers in the Antebellum South: Coercion, Conciliation and Accommodation," *American Historical Review* no. 79 (April 1974). For an analysis of the separation of black and white workers in the tobacco and textile factories of the antebellum South, see Dolores Janiewski, "Southern Honor, Southern Dishonor: Managerial Ideology and the Construction of Gender, Race and Class Relations in Southern Industry," in *Work Engendered*, edited by Ava Baron (Ithaca, NY: Cornell University Press, 1991), 75–77.

For an overview of black workers, see Philip S. Foner and Ronald L. Lewis, *Black Workers: A Documentary History from Colonial Times To The Present* (Philadelphia: Temple University Press, 1989), 61–123. On the status and experiences of slaves in southern cities, see Frederick Douglass, *Autobiography*, 887; Parish, *Slavery, History and Historians*, 98–101; Boles, *Black Southerners*, 129–130, 137–139.

The social organization of slaves within their own quarters was an important part of their maintaining their own culture, including the sustenance of their families, their music, their religion, their songs, and stories. On this subject, see John W. Blassingame, *The Slave Community: Plantation Life in the Antebellum South* (New York: Oxford University Press, 1972), 105–107, 271–272; also see Davidson et al., *Nation of Nations*, 474–481.

On the master-slave relationship, see Julie A. Matthaei, *An Economic History of Women in America: Women's Work, the Sexual Division of Labor, and the Development of Capitalism* (New York: Schocken Books, 1982), 76–79. For the reaction of slaves during the Civil War, see Boles, *Black Southerners*, 183–193. For the post–Civil War period and the development of the sharecropping system, see Boles, *Black Southerners*, 199–204, 207–209, 209–213. For a picture of the daily life of a sharecropper, see Davidson et al., *Nation of Nations*, 622–623.

On the slave economy, see the following essays in Ira Berlin and Philip D. Morgan, *Cultivation and Culture* (Charlottesville: University Press of Virginia, 1993): Joseph P. Reidy, "Obligation and Right: Patterns of Labor, Subsistence and Exchange in the Cotton Belt of Georgia, 1790–1860"; John Campbell, "As 'A Kind of Freeman'? Slaves' Market-Related Activities in the South Carolina Up Country, 1800–1860"; and Roderick A. McDonald, "Independent Economic Production by Slaves on Antebellum Louisiana Sugar Plantations."

On the Reconstruction period following the Civil War, Eric Foner's defining and influential book *Reconstruction: America's Unfinished Revolution, 1863–1877* (New York: Harper and Row, 1988) is a must.

13

WOMEN IN THE NINETEENTH CENTURY

Women in the nineteenth century occupied many positions between the two poles of traditional and modern culture, pushed and pulled according to changing demands of family, community, and self. Women experienced these pushes and pulls in the nineteenth century as the cultural system of America deposited many injustices upon their backs. She was a half-person in the courts and a nonentity at the ballot box. If she worked outside the home she earned half a man's wages and if she toiled at housework and child rearing she earned nothing at all. She was barred from most men's work and was hobbled by a culture that constrained her with conventional codes of behavior and propriety based on male dominance.

A thicket of social and biological arguments emerged in the nineteenth century to justify women's exclusion from paid work and their relegation to a separate sphere. American ideology spawned a series of cultural expectations that discouraged women from seeking paid work—arguments about women's natural inferiority, lack of physical stamina, and delicate sensibilities. Many nineteenth-century Americans viewed female participation in the work force as a temporary stage to be superseded, upon marriage, by the practice of homemaking. However, women who worked viewed their work ethic as providing them with a public identity of their own and a sense of their own worth. By the end of the nineteenth century American women, especially those from the middle class, were simmering with discontent as reflected in the rise of their organizations and the volumes of public speeches and printed words that flooded the American cultural scene.

Women's work took place in the household and revolved around the family. When they ventured forth out of the family, as they did in the New England textile factories, it was for a short period and they returned to their families to marry and settle on farms. In the course of the nineteenth century, however, women began to join the work force outside the home in larger numbers. This forced them to face the problem of how to reconcile their primary responsibilities to the household with their new role in the public sphere. By 1850, women worked in more than 200 occupations, with a total of 181,000 employed in manufacturing. The major occupations of women wage workers in that year were domestic service—330,000; clothing—62,000; cotton textiles—59,000; wool textiles—19,000; shoes—33,000; hats—8,000; and teaching—55,000. Apart from teaching, all of the above categories were traditionally thought of as women's work.

FEMALE OCCUPATIONS

Domestic Service

By 1870, nearly two million women filled hundreds of occupations, from domestic service and sewing to less feminine pursuits as teamsters, bridge keepers, and undertakers. Domestic service claimed half of all female workers. The average maid received $2 a week, plus room and board. Good cooks commanded as much as $10 a week, while scullery maids often settled for $1. Immigrant domestics were roughly a third of all servants. Live-in domestics were expected to be at work or on call before the family arose from bed and after it went to sleep. By 1900, 60.5 percent of Irish-born wage-earning women in the United States were servants. Black women were also recruited as domestics by employment agents who traveled South and offered them transportation and jobs. Black women constituted about a fourth of the servant population in 1900.

Sewing Trades

The sewing trades were second to domestic service for female employment, providing work for nearly 100,000 seamstresses, tailoresses, and shirt, cuff, and collar makers. Most sewing women were paid by the piece, either working in their homes or in large mass-producing warehouses. Many women worked in sewing lofts, laboring from 7 A.M. to 6 P.M. Some took work home to sew for another two to four hours after supper. Most shops were unhealthy, with inadequate ventilation or heat, poor toilet facilities, and poor drinking water. Needlewomen earned $2 to $6 a week, their jobs were seasonal and few worked more than six months a year.

Most women's clothing could not be purchased ready-made until the end of the nineteenth century. Poor people made their own clothing during the nineteenth and well into the twentieth century. However, by the end of the nineteenth century, the sewing machine had come into general use and large numbers of men and women began to be employed in tenement shops, where merchants farmed out bundles of cloth to contractors who hired operators to manufacture clothing. These tenement shops, or sweatshops, were places where women worked for piece rates, laboring nonstop for fourteen hours. The Maryland Bureau of Statistics reported that the price paid for a complete lace dress was 50 cents, for making a skirt from 17 to 19 cents. The New York State Bureau of Labor Statistics reported that women in the clothing industry generally earned from $3 to $6 a week. Small shops in tenements proliferated after the Civil War. By 1900, they paralleled but did not replace home work in the garment industry, which remained an important source of income for women.

Clerical Work

Clerical work provided new job opportunities for women in the period following the Civil War, when paperwork mushroomed in government and business. Women were viewed as better suited than men for two skilled jobs—stenographer and typist—and they were hired for less wages than men. The typewriter facilitated the emerging dominance of women in clerical work. Early machines were slow, expensive, and undependable, but government, legal, and business offices were employing type girls by the mid-1870s. Women rushed to fill openings created by expanding business and the use of typewriters. As there were few job opportunities for women in the professions other than nursing and teaching, literate women turned to office work. Office work was clean, quiet, and less strenuous than factory work and socially more acceptable. The vast majority of early office workers were native-born, middle-class white women with a high school education. It was rare for an immigrant, a black woman, or a Jew to get a white-collar position. Most were young and single, and many were daughters of professionals. They sought work to supplement family incomes, though in some cases they needed to support themselves. Office workers were paid weekly; work was steady and layoffs infrequent. On the other hand, salaries were low and the need to dress well was an added cost. There were just 19,000 women office workers of all kinds in 1870. By 1900 there were 503,000. In the District of Columbia, women federal clerks found the average annual salary of $900 very appealing compared with teachers' salaries of $400 to $800 per year. Women office workers faced stiff opposition as they entered a male-dominated world. Citizens worried about the moral effect of men and women working together, about adulterous affairs, and about women deserting their responsibilities as mothers and housekeepers. Whatever their motivations for working, few female office workers could expect to become office executives. A talented woman might be promoted to a low-level managerial post, such as supervisor of a typing pool or head of a bookkeeping department, but she could never expect to become a junior executive. Ironically, the typewriter both eased the entry of women into the formerly masculine office and enslaved them to a subservient status in the office once they entered.

Nursing

Nursing schools were established in the last third of the nineteenth century, the first at Bellevue Hospital in New York in 1873. It attracted middle-class women interested in service work. The hospital became the locale for momentous events in the life cycle—birth, sickness, and death—events that had previously taken place at home. Childbirth now took place in delivery rooms, while mothers recuperated in maternity wards and their infants spent their first days in nurseries. The very ill were treated in the hospital and many of the terminally ill spent their final hours in hospital beds. Innovations in anesthesia, antiseptic principles, and knowledge of germ theory transformed surgical practices within hospitals. By the turn of the century, x-rays, clinical hospital laboratories, twenty-four hour nursing, and house staffs led to an increased demand for registered and practical nurses.

Few of the 40,000 nurses and midwives counted in the 1890 census had formal professional training. Nursing education was still largely on-the-job training in hospitals, with second-year students teaching the incoming first-year group. Working conditions and wages were poor but did include room and board. However, dormitories were crowded and cold and food was very poor. Nurses averaged $1 a week to start and gradually moved up to $4 a week after two years of training. Even supervisors earned no more than $500 a year. Only private-duty graduate nurses earned high wages, perhaps $15 a week. While this was good money at the time, nurses had to work seven days a week to earn it. Nursing as a professional occupation did not become a reality until twentieth-century developments transformed nursing education and led to the creation of professional nurses' associations.

Teaching

Women entered teaching in substantial numbers as early as the 1830s. As opportunities increased and women attended school, this became the profession of choice for middle-class women. The supply of teachers was plentiful and school boards were happy to hire them for one-half to one-third of what they paid men. Women came to outnumber men almost three to one and by the end of the nineteenth century half a million taught school, many of them in one-room schoolhouses. Most women teachers were young and single and in many cases, marriage meant an automatic bar to teaching for a woman. Few completed college and many had only eight years of formal schooling. Not until 1907 did the first state, Indiana, insist that its licensed teachers had to complete high school. In 1898, the New York State Legislature set $600 a year as the scale for women teachers, when the scale for men was $900 a year. It was not until 1912 that equal pay for men and women was instituted for high school teachers in New York. Most male teachers were employed on the high school level, while almost the entire elementary school staff was female. School superintendents and principals were almost entirely male. One of their biggest battles was over the right of women to keep their teaching jobs when they were married, which they finally won by World War I.

Textile Workers

There was a mass movement of women into textile mills so that by 1860 more than 60,000 women were employed in the cotton textile industry in New England. Before the Civil War, Lowell was the largest textile center based on capital invested, workers employed, and cloth produced. Mill owners in New England acted jointly in establishing wage rates, hours, and production methods, but they all watched innovation and technological development in Lowell. Lowell started as a town of

2,500 in 1826 and by 1850 had grown to 33,000. At that date Lowell was the leading textile center in the nation and second largest city in Massachusetts.

Mill women made Lowell a cultural center. Many of the women, most of whom were under thirty, found the energy at the end of the long workday to organize and attend lectures, forums, language classes, sewing groups, and improvement circles. Out of one of these circles grew the *Lowell Offering*, the first journal written by and for mill women. Owners financed the journal, seeing it as a useful vehicle for counteracting community prejudice against women in mills. The women who wrote for the journal found it an outlet for their talents and a vindication of their roles as millworkers. They portrayed themselves in a dignified light, and they believed that through their work they achieved social status.

By the late 1840s, the exodus of New England farm women from the mills began. Some went home to marry, some to teach in New England towns or in the West, and some sought work in other occupations in offices or stores. As they left immigrants took their places, particularly the Irish fleeing from the potato famine in their homeland. The Irish were later followed by French Canadian and Eastern European women. By the end of the nineteenth century, Lowell was a city of ethnic diversity in its neighborhoods and in its work force.

Women in Agriculture

The Midwest became the nation's bread basket. The general division of work by gender on the midwestern farm in 1850 was quite clear. Men performed the plowing, planting, and harvesting work. Their other work included upkeep of tools, implements, and wagons, fencing, chopping wood and storing it, caring for draft animals, maintenance of the barn, ditching and trenching, laying down straw and hay, and hauling manure. Men also hunted to supplement the family diet with protein.

Women were in charge of the garden that supplied the family with fresh vegetables, as well as the henhouse and the dairy. Women milked cows first thing in the morning and last thing at night. Manufacture of butter and cheese was also a central task for females on the farm, tasks that were a matter of pride among farm women. There were areas of work that overlapped. Women helped men slaughter and dress hogs, prepare hams for curing, and make cider. All of the orchard work was a joint project. Women often assisted in the cornfield, following their husband's plowing with a bag of seed corn. And men helped seed the vegetable garden.

Farm wives fitted and cut cloth for their own slip-on dresses as well as those of their daughters. They made their sons' and husbands' pants and shirts. Sewing as a feminine skill was a domestic necessity but it could become an art form when practiced and refined. Coverlets, cross-stitched samplers, and elaborate patch-work or appliqué front pieces for quilts were expressions of creative outlets for women. One farm woman remarked, "I would have lost my mind if I had not had my quilts to do." On a more mundane level of women's work, clothes had to be washed. By all accounts Monday was the universal washday. Many women made their own soap, using hardwood ashes over which they poured water. They collected the lye that they later boiled with fat. If everything went well, the soap would come after long, hot hours of stirring. Then they poured the hot soap into molds or tubs and stored it. Soapmaking was an all-day job done only two or three times a year.

Women on farms also exchanged goods and services outside the family. Products of the dairy, henhouse, garden, and loom were often exchanged for other family necessities. Flour, glass, dyes, crockery, coffee, tea, store cloth, metal utensils, and sugar were bought from the local merchant with products produced by women on the farm—butter, cheese, eggs, vegetables, homespun, and whiskey. Commodity exchange in corn and grain surpluses were most frequently male economic pursuits used for paying off the farm mortgage, speculating in new land, and for farm equipment. Men's products were for sale, women's products were for barter. In the nineteenth century, it was still the men who controlled the farm property. Iowa did not grant women title to their own earnings until 1886 and control of their own property until 1897.

Farm women played a crucial role in their rural communities. By virtue of their presence in the community, women became bulwarks in its daily affairs, helping to preserve its customs. Through visiting and conversation they kept abreast of what was going on with neighbors and kin, and once alerted to problems, performed many acts of kindness. When relatives or neighbors became ill and could not work, local women voluntarily stepped in to care for them and their children. When a family did not have enough to eat, neighboring women took them food and shared what they had. When someone died, they prepared them for burial, kept vigil, and provided the grieving family with baked goods and other necessities. These and other neighborly acts fostered a sense of closeness and strengthened common bonds among farm families in the rural communities and small towns of the nineteenth century.

CONCLUSION

In spite of the broad range of experiences of women in the nineteenth century as part of the shift from a household economy to a nascent industrial economy, domesticity persisted along with the separation of men and women into two separate spheres. Domestic ideology, in particular the values of motherhood and the emphasis on women's moral responsibilities to their families, was central to the worldview of a majority of nineteenth-century women. Domesticity was never a theory of idleness, except perhaps for upper-class women. It always underscored the importance of work. The labor of farm women was indispensable to the success of the family farm. The work of married women in cities was often the margin between subsistence and starvation for working-class families. A virtuous woman used her work and her talents to establish and maintain a proper home, a sphere that would provide a refuge for her husband and a school of virtue for her children. To be successful she had to be resourceful, dynamic, and skillful. Teaching was appealing to women in the nineteenth century because it combined aspects of domestic ideology with autonomy and advancement. For scores of overworked and underpaid women in domestic work, sales, and factory work, marriage and raising a family still represented a genuine hope for a better life.

During the last quarter of the nineteenth century, American middle-class women debated their status and what could be done to improve their self-esteem. Debates and discussions took place in the pages of women's magazines, in forums and lectures, in women's organizations, and in books and periodicals. Almost all commentators expressed dissatisfaction with the life of a leisured lady released from work through the hiring of servants, and divorced from the public side of life through a concentration on social events, fancy dress, and the affectations of manners. One school, led by Catherine Beecher, sister of Harriet Beecher Stowe, pressed women to become active homemakers, efficient in all the arts of cooking, making clothes, and household management. Beecher stressed the creativity and importance of homemaking and child rearing. Another school of thought, advanced by Charlotte Gilman, stated the belief that without work outside the home, women would forever remain subordinate and dependent. According to Gilman, paid work was the path to self-esteem and social status as it projected women into the public sphere where service to the larger community was recognized as necessary for recognition and individual self-esteem. While middle-class women may have had some choice regarding home or work, black women, poor women, and new immigrants were never included in the cult of domesticity that theoretically assigned white women of the middle and upper classes a life of efficiency within the home. Women of color and women of the working class were always expected to work if possible and to accept inferior wages and treatment. Farm women always worked in the fields and barns as well as in the farmhouse, plying all kinds of useful skills.

Without the contribution of women, both in the home and in the mill, the transition from an agricultural to an industrial society in the nineteenth century would not have been possible. Not only were women the first mill workers on a large scale in the textile factories of New England, but they played a large role in the clothing industry, in education, in office work, in manufacturing, and in the early trade unions. In addition, they were consumers and users of products in the home; products that represented an important demand for the nascent United States industries. Finally, women and their work were crucial for the operation and success of American agriculture in the nineteenth century; an agriculture that proved to be the most advanced and most productive in the world.

BIBLIOGRAPHICAL ESSAY

Julie A. Matthaei has been the source of many ideas in this chapter. See her *An Economic History of Women in America: Women's Work, the Sexual Division of Labor, and the Development of Capitalism* (New York: Schocken Books, 1982). See Part II, "Women's Work and the Sexual Division of Labor under the Cult of Domesticity," 101–232.

I have also used women's views of the work ethic in the late nineteenth century as presented by Daniel T. Rodgers, Chapter 7, "Idle Womanhood: Feminist Versions of the

Work Ethic," in *The Work Ethic in Industrial America, 1850–1920* (Chicago: University of Chicago Press 1974).

On domestic ideology of women in the American West in the nineteenth century, see Robert I. Griswold, "Anglo Women and Domestic Ideology in the American West in the Nineteenth and Early Twentieth Centuries," in *Western Women: Their Land, Their Lives,* edited by Lillian Schlissel, Vicki L. Ruiz, and Janice Monk (Albuquerque: University of New Mexico Press, 1988).

For an introduction to women's work in a historical perspective, containing a representative series of essays, see Carol Groneman and Mary Beth Norton, *To Toil the Livelong Day: America's Women at Work, 1780–1980* (Ithaca, NY: Cornell University Press, 1987). For the nineteenth century, see Parts I and II.

An excellent, well-researched and detailed review of women at work in American history is provided by Alice Kessler-Harris, *Women Have Always Worked: A Historical Overview* (New York: McGraw-Hill, 1981).

For a review of women in American society, see William H. Chafe, "Women and American Society," in *Making America: The Society and Culture of the United States* (Chapel Hill: University of North Carolina Press, 1992), 327–340.

Kenneth Lipartito, "When Women Were Switches: Technology, Work and Gender in the Telephone Industry," *American Historical Review* 99, no. 4 (October 1994), 1074–1111, deals with women's work in the telephone industry during its early days and why women were sought out by the telephone company for this kind of work.

For a discussion of female opportunities for employment and for women's labor and its importance on the farm, see Kessler-Harris, *Women Have Always Worked,* 14–15; Julie Matthaei, 1982, *Economic History of Women,* 153–156; and Nancy Grey Osterud, "She Helped Me Hay It as Good as a Man," in *To Toil the Livelong Day,* edited by Carol Groneman and Mary Beth Norton, 90, 91–94.

On the technology of cooking and women's work associated with cooking, see Jack Larkin, *The Reshaping of Everyday Life, 1790–1840* (New York: Harper Perennial, 1988), 51–52; Siegfried Giedion, *Mechanization Takes Command* (New York: W. W. Norton, 1948), 534–536; and Daniel E. Sutherland, *The Expansion of Everyday Life, 1860–1876* (New York: Harper & Row, 1989), 62–64. Regarding the problem of washing and cleaning and getting a supply of water, see Sutherland, 65–66.

For a survey of female occupations, see Sutherland, *Expansion of Everyday Life,* 163–167; also see Thomas J. Schlereth, *Victorian America: Transformations in Everyday Life, 1876–1915* (New York: Harper, 1991), 71–74. In addition see Rodgers, "Idle Womanhood," 204. On percentages of women in the various general categories of employment, see Kessler-Harris, *Women Have Always Worked,* 63–65, 70, 80.

A review of clerical work and the job opportunities that were opened up for women in the late nineteenth century can be found in Barbara Mayer Wertheimer, *We Were There: The Story of Working Women in America* (New York: Pantheon Books, 1977), 97, 168–169. Also see Sutherland, *Expansion of Everyday Life,* 205–207; and Schlereth, *Victorian America,* 67–69. For a discussion of women in the nursing profession in the nineteenth century, see Schlereth, 286–287; and Wertheimer, *We Were There,* 243. On the teaching professional and the female role in it, see Wertheimer, 246–247.

There is a large literature on women in the early textile mills in the nineteenth century. Thomas Dublin has written a classic work on the subject, *Women at Work: The Transformation of Work and Community in Lowell, Massachusetts, 1826–1860* (New York: Columbia University Press, 1979). David A. Zonderman examines the attitudes and aspirations of female mill workers in New England in his excellent study, *Aspirations and Anxieties: New*

England Workers and the Mechanized Factory System, 1815–1850 (New York: Oxford University Press, 1992). Zonderman not only deals with the various motivations of young women working in the textile mills, but also their attitudes toward the factory and the machines that were part of their working environment.

For women in the clothing industry and the sweatshops, see Louis Levine, "The Women Garment Workers," in *America's Working Women*, edited by Rosalyn Baxandall, Linda Gordon, and Susan Reverby (New York: Random House, 1976). Also see Kessler-Harris, *Women Have Always Worked*, 87. For women in the shoemaking industry, see Wertheimer, 1977, *We Were There*, 85–86, 169–171. For women in the detachable collar and cuff starching and washing industry in Troy, New York, see Wertheimer, 171–173.

For women in the trade union movement in the nineteenth century, see Philip Foner, *Women and the American Labor Movement* (New York: Free Press, 1982), 1–184; also Wertheimer, *We Were There*, 190–191, 97, 168–169, 195–197, 204–205.

Nineteenth-century American farm women were crucial to the successful pursuit of farming in the United States. For women in farming see John M. Faragher, "History From the Inside-Out: Writing the History of Women in Rural America," *American Quarterly* 33, no. 5 (Winter 1981), 537–557. Also see Faragher's article, "Open-Country Community: Sugar Creek, Illinois, 1820–1850," in *The Countryside in the Age of Capitalist Transformation: Essays in the Social History of Rural America*, edited by Steven Hahn and Jonathan Prude (Chapel Hill: University of North Carolina Press, 1985). See also Faragher's book, *Women and Men on the Overland Trail* (New Haven: Yale University Press, 1979).

For a compelling report on women's participation and work during the great migration to Oregon and California, see Lillian Schlissel, *Women's Diaries of the Westward Journey* (New York: Schocken Books, 1992). Also consult Amy Kesselman, "Diaries and Reminiscences of Women on the Oregon Trail: A Study in Consciousness," in *America's Working Women*, compiled and edited by Rosalyn Baxandall, Linda Gordon, and Susan Reverby (New York: Random House, 1976).

One group of women not dealt with at length in this chapter is that of southern women in the nineteenth century, both white and black. For a well-written and thoroughly researched study of white and black women in the antebellum south see Elizabeth Fox-Genovese, Within the Plantation Household: Black and White Women of the Old South (Chapel Hill: University of North Carolina Press, 1988). Fox-Genovese points out that the persistence in the South of the household as the dominant unit of production and reproduction differentiated it from the North, where the household was undergoing a reconversion into a home where it was ascribed to the female sphere. The practical importance of the household in southern society reinforced gender constraints by ascribing all women to the domination of the male heads of households and to the company of the women of their own households. The experience of black slave women, however, differed radically from that of all white women, for they belonged to households that were not governed by their own husbands, brothers, and fathers. Fox-Genovese makes an important point regarding the relation between the experiences that unite women as members of a gender and those that divide them as members of specific communities, classes, and races. She emphasizes that class and race, as well as wealth, region, and historical periods are central rather than incidental to women's identities and behavior and to their sense of themselves as women (38–39). She therefore cautions against generalizing from the experience of women of one region that obscures differences based on class and race. Fox-Genovese states: "All women, like all men, are a product of social relations defined to include gender, class, nationality, and race. Their innermost identities, their ideals for themselves, and their views of the world all derive from their sense of themselves as women in relation to men and other women—their sense of themselves as the female members of specific societies" (42–43).

Part III

THE TWENTIETH CENTURY

14

THE AMERICAN WORK ETHIC
IN THE TWENTIETH CENTURY

From 1900 to 1970, American work was propelled by a society that generated dramatic increases in goods through mass production and mechanization of the labor process. In manufacturing, the work process was characterized by the factory system, nonhuman forms of energy, automatic and high-speed machinery, standardization of parts, repetitive and precise work tasks, and the intensive subdivision of labor. In agriculture, expansion of productivity resulted from the use of machinery, irrigation, fertilizers, and scientific knowledge applied to soils, plants, and animals. The growth in the American economy during this seventy-year period averaged 3.5 percent per year and the growth in productivity averaged 2 percent per worker, per year. Since the 1970s, the United States has become an information and communication society, with armies of computer operators storing and transmitting information required by national and international enterprises. Computers and microprocessors in manufacturing work have become tools used to design, plan, manage, and carry out work tasks. The consequence of the change to a computer- and information-dominated society is that work and the work ethic is being redefined as the twentieth century comes to a close. Workers desiring good jobs require better education and need to be more flexible and prepared to change jobs as rapidly as changing markets for goods and labor change. In industries using new technologies the work environment is in constant change due to new products. Companies with fast technological changes tend to employ workers with higher levels of education, the kind of workers who have more flexibility and the capacity for further learning.

During the twenty years from 1970 to 1990, the rate of growth of the economy slowed to an average of 2.5 percent per year, and the rate of productivity fell off to only 1 percent or less. The result has been a crisis in the economy and society and increasing fear in the workplace for jobs and security. What has happened is that the vast, efficient American marketplace is no longer the province of Americans alone. Since the 1970s, American businesses and their workers have faced intense competition from new mass producers overseas. Another factor responsible for our slow growth rate is that conventional mass production and distribution and their advantages are now in retreat because of flexible production and fragmenting markets. These facts have resulted in reduced utilization of capital and higher costs for mass producers of autos and steel, which need high volume to stay competitive. Finally, in the face of rising competition, uncertainty, and failing returns, American business has reduced its capital investment. The result has been fewer jobs in high-wage manufacturing industries. As the rate of capital investment fell, productivity growth slowed and as productivity slowed, business cut even more jobs and held down wages. This has been manifest in the wave of "downsizing" that has seized the American economy and put fear and insecurity into the families of the vast majority of American workers. This chapter examines the broad flow of events that have influenced work and the work ethic in twentieth-century America.

Appelbaum and Batt state the following:

> Academic researchers have attributed the rapid growth of the industrialized economies in the period from (approximately) 1945 to 1970 to the cumulative gains in productivity and growth in output inherent in a socioeconomic system based on mass production. That system relied on a set of interrelated characteristics: dedicated technology; Taylorist work organization; the sharing of performance gains between workers and firms; consumption growth based on the rise of real wages; and investment dynamics based on the accelerator principle, which relates expansion of capital stock to the rate of growth of consumption demand and to internal cash flow, whereby improvements in technology are embodied in later vintages of capital. The conditions for this "virtuous circle" of growth are captured in the Kaldor-Verdoorn law . . . which is summarized in the following two statements:
>
> Mass production based on the application of Taylorist work organization yielded economies of scale and a reduction in unit labor costs, allowing productivity to increase when output increased and plants operated at close to full-capacity utilization. Thus, strong demand growth favored growth in productivity.
>
> Unions in these mass-production industries bargained for real wage increases in line with average gains in productivity in the economy as a whole. At the same time oligopolistic price behavior (mark-up pricing by firms largely insulated from international competition) meant that profits grew in line with productivity while the relative price of standardized, mass-produced products fell. The result was that rising real wages and falling relative prices supported the growth of consumption. (1994:14–15)

These increases in consumption demand (via the accelerator), coupled with the stable share of profit in output, fueled investment in newer vintages of capital (yielding higher labor productivity). This sharing of productivity gains between workers, firms, and consumers meant that productivity growth favored demand growth.

Many workers outside primary manufacturing firms and labor markets did not share fully in the benefits of growth. The application of Taylorist principles in service industries such as insurance, for example, allowed firms to cut costs and increase volume and profits, but low unionization rates meant that firms were not compelled to share these gains with front-line workers. Nevertheless, wages grew outside the unionized sector as well. A rising standard of living for workers and a growing middle class contributed to the growth in mass consumption that justified mass production and made it profitable. If private sources of demand growth faltered, monetary and fiscal policies to jump-start the domestic economy and stimulate demand growth would soon restore the virtuous circle of growth.

Traditionally, workers through their trade union organizations have campaigned for shorter hours both to relieve the burden of excessive hours of work when they had to endure ten- and twelve-hour days, and to provide themselves with enough leisure hours away from work to devote themselves to their families and friends. The ten-hour-per-day movement and later the eight-hour-per-day movement of the nineteenth and early twentieth centuries resulted in established patterns of work beyond which workers were to be compensated with overtime pay. In 1938, with the Fair Labor Standards Act, the eight-hour, forty-hour week was established, beyond which workers were to be compensated with overtime pay. This provision was most enforced where there were union contracts. Unions and management could establish their own standards for a fair day's work and some unions, like electricians in New York City, established a thirty-five hour week. However, in recent years, the traditional stance of unions in campaigning for a shorter work week has been on hold. At a time when such a movement would have a beneficial effect on the work force in helping to spread the work at a time when corporations are downsizing, unions seem to have given up any drive for a shorter work week. The facts are that Americans workers have opted for more hours at work and less hours of leisure. Juliet B. Schor has documented that Americans workers in 1989 spent the amazing equivalent of four weeks more a year on the job than they had two decades earlier (Schor, 1991).

THE JOB MARKET

Increasing affluence in America has not triggered a mass exodus from the workplace for the simple reason that only a small layer of the 130 million people in the work force are truly affluent. Between 1900 and 1960, labor force participation rate rose from 50.2 percent to 59.4 percent. This percentage is a ratio of those in the work force as compared with the civilian noninstitutional population 16 years of age and over. Despite the talk of the demise of the work ethic, more Americans are working as a percentage of the population in 1994 than ever before. Between 1960 and 1994, the labor participation rate rose from 59.4 percent to 66.6 percent. However, this percentage reflects the fact that the labor participation rate of women has risen so much that it has offset a fall in the labor participation rate of men. The male participation rate has fallen from 83.3 percent in 1960 to 75.1 percent in 1994, while the female participation rate has risen from 37.7 percent in 1960 to 58.8 percent in 1994. The fall in the male participation rate reflects the fact that many males are retiring at an earlier age. In 1994, only 2.9 percent of the labor force were 65 years of age or older. In 1990, for the first time, working wives in America outnumbered wives who do not work. The rapid movement of women into the work force stems mainly from their economic needs. However, it is also attributable to their need for the sense of identity and self-esteem that derives from work. In addition, structural changes in the economy has increased the demand for female work in the service, health, and office work sectors.

The labor market in the late twentieth century is characterized by two distinct segments. The first, that can be designated the primary job market, offers good wages and working conditions, as well as job security and prospects for advancement. The other, the secondary job market, provides low-paying jobs with poor working conditions and no security or benefits. Workers trapped in secondary markets are forced to accept unstable employment with little chance for advancement. Education and advanced training are the keys to entry into the primary job market. In the 1990s, as a result of corporate downsizing, there is insecurity throughout the labor market in both the primary and secondary sectors, as white-collar workers and middle management are now experiencing the insecurity that formerly plagued blue-collar workers only.

The job market in 1990 is considerably different from what it was in 1950. The percentage of workers producing goods fell from 42 percent of the work force in 1950, to 33 percent in 1980, to only 25 percent in 1990. At the same time, the proportion of the labor force in service and white-collar jobs increased to 75 percent by the 1990s. Only 12.5 percent of the American work force is self-employed, compared to 21.5 percent in 1910. Public school teachers outnumber production workers in the steel, chemical, oil, rubber, plastic, and paper industries combined. There are more secretaries than auto workers. The office is replacing the factory as the primary workplace. Service workers as well as government employees each outnumber factory workers. Agriculture, which accounted for 40 percent of the work force in 1900, account for just 3 percent today. Manufacturing is no longer the generator of jobs it once was. The service sector accounted for 84 percent of all jobs created between 1950 and 1980. Large corporations have streamlined their work force and are contracting out jobs and services they formerly performed themselves to small businesses. The shift toward service employment is in many ways the result of rising affluence and technological advances. Only an affluent society could afford the luxury of freeing so many of its workers from the production of goods to provide services that were not even contemplated in 1900. The hottest job prospects for the future with regard to income and benefits are health care specialists, computer and electronic engineers, scientists, systems analysts, human services workers, management, and professional workers.

HISTORY OF AMERICAN TWENTIETH-CENTURY WORK FORCE

Between 1900 and 1930, partially the result of the ideas and programs of Taylorism, there was a homogenization of the American labor force as craft skills were broken down and laboring skills were graded up. The result was the creation of a work force suited to mass production, that is, a mass of semiskilled operatives in auto and textile factories, in steel mills, in electrical equipment plants, and in all kinds of manufacturing facilities. Management could train workers in just weeks, or at most a few months, for most of these jobs, and they were easily replaced. At the Ford Motor Company, from 1910 to 1917, the number of semiskilled operators rose from 30 percent to 62 percent. Plant size increased enormously in the major industries such as auto, steel, farm equipment, electrical equipment, meat packing, and communications, with some plants containing 20,000 or 60,000 workers in a single complex. Plants of this size required a tremendous expansion of management authority, an enlargement of hierarchy and bureaucracy, and an increased role for the foreman on the shop floor. The number of foremen increased from 90,000 in 1900 to 296,000 in 1920, an increase of 300 percent, while manufacturing employment rose by 90 percent. One observer called this period the "foreman's empire." The declining skill requirements of most operative jobs and the easy substitutability of factory workers for one another removed inducements for workers to remain long on the job and turnover rates rose drastically, exceeding 100 percent in many instances.

During the 1930s, the period of the Great Depression, unemployment and low wages were the major concerns of American workers. Insecurity of employment was rampant as large companies cut back their work force and many small companies went out of business. At the time there was no unemployment insurance or social security or welfare, and families without a breadwinner used up their meager resources and sought relief from families or the government. The New Deal put millions of men to work through various public works programs under the Works Progress Administration (WPA), the Public Works Administration (PWA), and the Civil Works Administration (CWA), generating some 30,000 individual projects and putting some seven to nine million men to work. When World War II came and the economy heated up and twelve million men were drafted into the armed services, the situation changed for the American working man and woman. There was a labor shortage and everyone could find work, including many women who entered the work force for the first time. Wages improved and with limitations on what one could buy, families began to save, which provided the basis for the ability of Americans to buy the goods that would pour out of American factories in the postwar period.

The United States came out of World War II with a robust economy. Americans as workers and as consumers would enter a period of some twenty-five years in which real gains would be made in their standard of living and their opportunities for steady, meaningful employment. In postwar America a steady job was on the minds of workers and their families. The postwar relationship between large corporations and workers rested on a quid pro quo. In one direction, workers ceded to corporate management unbridled discretion to organize production. In the other direction, corporations bought worker cooperation by promising to raise real wages, provide employment security, and improve working conditions. At the same time, government sought to solidify the relationship by regulating union-management relations and by providing a social welfare program to provide a safety net for working people. Workers in basic industries such as auto, steel, rubber, electrical machinery, textiles, machine-tools, farm machinery, appliances, transportation, and so forth could look forward to long-term employment at the end of which they could retire with funds from their union pensions and government old-age benefits. They could also afford to send their children to school in the hope that through a college education their children would move up the social ladder and be better off than their parents. This optimism that things were getting better and would continue to do so seemed to be working through the 1950s and the 1960s.

Post–World War II capitalism in America generated two kinds of jobs. The core of the economy—big firms, government bureaucracy, and the military—expanded in the quarter-century after the war. Corporations were making profits, governments hired more teachers and policemen, and unions improved many formerly unstable jobs. Jobs in this sector, both white collar and blue collar, provided relatively well-paid, virtually lifetime employment. However, millions of jobholders shared none of these benefits. Farm laborers, cabdrivers, cannery workers, retail and office clerks, typists, domestics, and others were poorly paid and lacked security. They were part of the secondary labor market, essential to the economy, but segregated from the core economy. Most of these workers came from "marginal" groups such as racial minorities, teenagers, and women.

In the postwar years there were three major changes in the labor market. First, there was the flight from agriculture and the rise in service, sales, and clerical work and the increasing employment of women. The country's postwar agricultural population fell from one in five to one in twenty. A second great change in the American work force after the war was the rapid rise in the number of jobs in government, services, and retail trade. Between 1950 and 1970, 9 million jobs opened up for secondary-school teachers, hospital support staff, and local government office workers. The growing demand for consumer goods spurred the creation of new department stores and supermarkets, staffed by 3 million additional employees. Meanwhile, new white-collar jobs were created in almost every large corporation. Millions more found jobs in planning, advertising, sales, and public relations. Finance, real estate, and insurance companies added 4 million new workers from 1950 to 1970. In 1956, for the first time in United States history, white-collar workers outnumbered blue-collar workers. Professional managerial, clerical, and sales workers, who composed less than a third of the work force in 1940, swelled to almost half by 1970. Meanwhile, blue-collar employment declined to 35 percent of the work force by 1970. Although blue-collar workers were a declining proportion of the work force in the 1950s and 1960s, they actually increased in numbers from 22 million to 26 million between 1950 to 1970. The third great change in the American work force was the influx of 10 million women. In 1950, a total of 31 percent of all women were employed; in 1970, 41 percent worked outside the home. Unlike women workers during World War II who found jobs in industry, those in the postwar work force were largely confined to so-called female jobs. Ninety-five percent of all women worked in just four job categories: light manufacturing, retail trade, clerical work, health, and education. Within these categories, high-status work was usually male, low-status work, female. In 1960, for example, high-school principals were 90 percent male; while elementary-school teachers were 85 percent female. Job segregation helped keep women's work low paid and dead end.

By the 1970s the rapid progress of the fifties and sixties slowed for the majority of American workers and was reversed for many of them. The average wage of the 80 percent of workers who were not managerial fell over the twenty-year period between 1970 and 1990, probably the longest decline in America since the industrial revolution. The standard of living fell, stagnated, or grew very slowly for most Americans even though they worked longer and harder. Workers at all levels felt insecure in their place in society and were not optimistic about the future, as revealed by many polls taken between 1990 and 1996. As material expectations were disappointed, working Americans were now involved in a zero-sum situation in which the benefits for some led to losses for others.

Despite the presumption that too many Americans are not working hard enough, Americans in fact responded to their changing economic fortunes by working much harder. The average full-time male employee now works about a week and a half longer a year than in 1973, the first extended increase in hours worked in this century. Seven million workers hold at least two jobs, the highest proportion in fifty years. The number of two-worker families rose by more than 10 percent in the 1980s. In 1993, only 34.6 percent of those aged 25 to 29 owned a home as compared with 43.6 percent in 1973. Because of the loss of good jobs and changing corporate practices, only about 45 percent of all male workers participated in a private pension plan in 1992 compared with about 54 percent in the late 1970s.

Workers today, in 1998, no longer enjoy any of the conditions that were once the basis of their cooperation and loyalty to corporate America. Real wages have stagnated, unemployment is a threat to all workers and there is no longer any security for core industry workers who suffered layoffs in the recession of 1989–1993. Corporations have accelerated their relocation of plants and are expanding their operations overseas. There has been an intensification of drives against unions that are being asked for "give backs," that is, giving up gains on wages and benefits under the threat of plant closings. Security for core workers is out the window as large corporations downsize and embark on massive layoffs, both of production workers as well as of middle management and technical personnel. Almost everyone has relatives or knows someone who has been laid off. Everywhere—in the press, among intellectuals, in speeches of politicians, among economists, and among social scientists of every stripe and persuasion—the American work ethic is being examined, questioned, and reformulated. Where is it all leading, everyone is asking, and few, if any, are sure.

AMERICAN WORK ETHIC: TWENTIETH-CENTURY PERSPECTIVE

There is a belief that the work ethic is fading, that work plays less of a central role in American lives today, and that it is no longer viewed as an end in itself. As we look at the twentieth century, we see that profound changes have taken place in the way work is viewed, pointing to significant departures from past patterns of work and attitudes toward work.

The work ethic has been affected by two opposing trends. On the one hand, we see more and more Americans, specifically older Americans, 55 years and older, dropping out of the work force. A large proportion of these choose to stop working, opting for the leisure of retirement. Many others are coerced into retirement, being unable to continue working, or having lost their jobs and being unable to find work because of age, illness, or disability. Those who stop working can do so because of the support they receive from the federal government's social security and Medicare programs, plus their union or company pension plans, plus whatever resources they accumulated in the form of a paid-off home, savings accounts, and insurance policies. The other trend is an increased participation in work on the part of women and longer working hours by the entire work force. This latter trend is related to necessity, the reality that more than one wage earner is required for the family to earn enough to meet their necessities.

Still, although most people must face the necessity of work to earn a livelihood, almost everyone recognizes that work is not all there is to life. There has been a tremendous growth in leisure activities and industries. Americans are involved in a wide range of leisure pursuits including gardening (practiced by some 90 million people), camping, boating, picnicking, walking, bicycling, hunting, traveling, vacationing, visiting historic and scenic places, mountain climbing, skiing, craft pursuits, hobbies, artistic pursuits, and so on. Leisure industries are an important, integral part of our economy. Leisure hours are spent socially with family, friends, and neighbors, in community affairs, in political activities, and in charitable work. Still, one's work and income have a large influence on the kind of leisure one can enjoy. Thus, work and leisure are inextricably linked. Furthermore, leisure is becoming available to more Americans and is no longer the privilege only of the wealthy.

With the increase in leisure activities in the United States there has developed a leisure ethic alongside the work ethic. It has not yet translated itself into the demand for shorter hours. However, historically, the working population has demanded shorter hours based on the belief that those who work should have time for themselves, meaning time when they can be free to do what they wish, when they can engage in the spontaneous, self-actualizing aspects of life that begins after work. Thus, in addition to the work ethic and leisure ethic there is also a life ethic, one that seeks more free time away from work so that one may enjoy "life." Workers have also traditionally demanded shorter hours so they could have time for self-education. Today, in modern America, there is the notion that education should be a life-long process, and we see many older Americans going back to school and taking classes in continuing education programs. Finally, with the growth in service and caring occupations we find an increasing proportion of our work force involved in taking care of others—the elderly, children, the disabled and handicapped, the homeless, the needy. Thus, along with the work ethic there is growing in America a leisure ethic, a life ethic, an education ethic, and a caring ethic, all of which can combine to make life richer and more fulfilling. Nevertheless, the enrichment of life still depends on the prosperity of the country, which in turn is based on the work habits and performance of Americans in the workplace.

I have used the work ethic concept in many contexts within this book, as a general term that implies that its meaning and content apply across the vast, complex terrain that comprise our work force. While this is sometimes a convenient way to discuss the ideology of work and the work ethic, it is important to recognize that different occupations have different cultures, different modes of carrying out work, and different ideologies. Workplaces and occupational groups generate collectively held beliefs that impel members to act in certain ways. The so-called work ethic is really composed of many work ethics that vary with occupation, workplace, industrial organization, enterprises, corporations, government workplaces, and institutions.

BIBLIOGRAPHICAL ESSAY

For a short history of the American economy that influenced some of the ideas in this chapter, see Jeffrey Madrick's excellent study, *The End of Affluence: The Causes and Consequences of America's Economic Dilemma* (New York: Random House, 1995), 3–92. This book not only contains a concise analysis of why the United States now faces an uncertain future regarding its social and economic structure, but it contains material that is of value to historians of business and the consequences for working people. It is also extremely well-documented and provides excellent sources for further study.

In order to understand the issues and strategies involved in the use of flexible production to meet foreign competition and to respond to a changing and fragmented marketplace based on fluid consumer demand, it is useful to see how this is applied in a specific industry. For a study of this process as it has taken place in the clothing industry, see the fine study by Ian M. Taplin, "Flexible Production, Rigid Jobs: Lessons From The Clothing Industry," *Work and Occupations* 22, no. 4 (November 1995), 412–438. What Taplin discusses is that, with the changing marketplace in the United States, firms have attempted to substitute economies of scope for economies of scale, to lessen their reliance on large numbers of unskilled or semiskilled workers, and to better coordinate production so that supply matches demand variability. Taplin deals with the technological issues, especially those in the clothing industry. He also points out that firms in the clothing industry have not done away with traditional methods of production, but have combined new technology and new ways of organizing workers with older techniques. In other words, mass production and flexible specialization are not opposite paradigms since there is ample evidence that the two coexist under capitalism. Further, flexible production does not always lead to job enrichment, as he plainly shows in the case of the clothing industry. Taplin provides the reader with details on management strategies from five different types of plants in North Carolina, which is the leading state in the production of men's and boy's shirts, in terms of employment and number of establishments.

A fine summary of the relationship between the mass-production industry, mass consumption and benefits to working people can be found in a book by Eileen Appelbaum and Rosemary Batt, *The New American Workplace: Transforming Work Systems in the United States* (Ithaca, NY: ILR Press, Cornell University, 1994), 14–15.

Research on the increase in hours in the current American workplace is contained in Juliet B. Schor's *The Overworked American: The Unexpected Decline of Leisure* (New York: Basic Books, 1991).

For documentation on the increase of women in the labor force, see "Rethinking Work," *Business Week*, October 17, 1994, 74–105. There is also an analysis of the female labor-participation rate in Sar A. Levitan and Clifford M. Johnson, "The Survival of Work," in *The Work Ethic—A Critical Analysis* (Madison, WI: Industrial Relations Research Association, 1983), 1–8. On the changes in the work tasks associated with changes in the composition of the labor force from 1950 to 1990, see Robert F. Szafran, "The Effect of Occupational Growth on Labor Force Task Characteristics," *Work and Occupations* 23, no. 1 (February 1996), 54–86. Szafran discusses in detail the concepts of substantial complexity, gross and fine motor skills, and social interaction skills. Current labor-participation rates can be found in the *Statistical Abstract of the United States* (Washington, DC: Bureau of the Census, 1995), 399–402.

A valuable work on the segmented labor force and the concept of the primary and secondary labor markets is that of David M. Gordon, Richard Edwards, and Michael Reich, *Segmented Work, Divided Workers: The Historical Transformation of Labor in the United States* (Cambridge: Cambridge University Press, 1982). The authors show how in the initial period of Taylorism (early twentieth century) there was a homogenization of labor in the industrialized factories, but by mid-twentieth century there began to develop a primary and secondary labor market, with high wages, job security, and benefits characterizing the former and low wages, unstable employment, and no benefits characterizing the latter. Today, in 1996, there is insecurity of employment everywhere in the United States labor market as major corporations downsize, contract work out, and hire temporary and part-time workers to lower labor costs. On this see *The New York Times* series of articles, "The Downsizing of America," March 3 to March 9, 1996. For a survey of the distribution of jobs by industry and for a projection of the hottest jobs in the future, see "Jobs in America," *Fortune* , July 12, 1993, 33–64.

On the plight of the United States steel industry, consult Paul A. Tiffany, *The Decline of American Steel: How Management, Labor and Government Went Wrong* (New York: Oxford University Press, 1988); also see Richard Preston, *American Steel* (New York: Prentice-Hall Press, 1991). Richard Preston not only analyzes the American steel industry, but he discusses the new technology of minimills and continuous casting, using the Nucor Corporation as his case study. Preston, through his study of Nucor, presents alternatives to traditional work processes in steel, especially the team approach and the reliance on shop-floor, decentralized decision making.

During the period of the expansion of mass production methods in manufacturing there was a sizable increase in the numbers and powers of foremen within the system of centralized and hierarchical control of the workplace. The period was termed the "foreman's empire" by Daniel Nelson. For a discussion of this phenomena within the framework of the factory system, see Daniel Nelson, *Managers and Workers: Origins of the New Factory System in the United States* (Madison: University of Wisconsin Press, 1975). On the centralization of control with the factory system and mass-production methods, see Richard Edwards, *Contested Terrain: The Transformation of the Workplace in the Twentieth Century* (New York: Basic Books, 1979), 72–89.

For labor turnover rates, that increased during the period of centralized control and mass production, see Harry Braverman, *Labor and Monopoly Capital: The Degradation of Work in the Twentieth Century* (New York: Monthly Review Press, 1974), 124–137, 149–151; and Gordon, Edwards, and Reich, *Segmented Work, Divided Workers*, 148–153.

On the labor movement in the first three decades of the twentieth century, see Gordon, Edwards, and Reich, *Segmented Work, Divided Workers*, and Richard H. Zieger, *American Workers, American Unions, 1920–1985* (Baltimore: Johns Hopkins Press, 1986), 6–10. Also Joshua Freeman et al., Chapters 4, 5, 6, in *Who Built America: Working People and the Nation's Economy, Politics, Culture and Society.* Vol. 2 (New York: Pantheon Books, 1992).

The period of the 1930s was a very difficult one for working people, suffering from vast unemployment and struggling to makes ends meet. However, it was also a heady period for the trade union movement which scored historic victories and witnessed the birth of the C.I.O. and labor legislation at the federal level that recognized at last basic workers' rights such as the right to organize, gain union recognition, and establish certain democratic grievance procedures in the workplace. Despite the decline of union power in recent years and a declining percentage of workers in unions, these gains in the 1930s have never been lost. For a picture of the union movement during the 1930s, see Zieger, *American Workers*, Chapter 2, "The Rebirth of the Unions, 1933–1939." Also see Gordon, Edwards, and Reich, *Segmented Work, Divided Workers*, 176–182 for this same period. Freeman et al., *Who Built America*, contains a full account of this period, with all its social and economic aspects, as well as the union movement, in Chapter 8, "Labor Democratizes America," 373–423. Freeman et al. conclude their chapter, as follows:

> The dramatic gains of the New Deal era would have been unimaginable had not workers themselves arisen in a storm of angry protest to organize new industrial unions. . . . By challenging big business's political and economic domination, workers extended the formal democracy of America's political system into their workplaces and communities. For the next forty years, in many industrial communities throughout America, in places such as Johnstown, Flint, and Chicago, working people exercised real power in their local governments and cultural institutions. (422)

John Galbraith has provided a theoretical analysis of the role of unions in an industrialized society in *The New Industrial State* (Boston: Houghton, Mifflin, 1985), 270–291. For an analysis of labor unions and the New Deal and the passage of the Wagner Labor Relations Act, see Stanley Vittoz, *New Deal Labor Policy and the American Industrial Economy* (Chapel Hill: University of North Carolina Press, 1987). Vittoz demonstrates that labor and its political allies, armed with the purchasing power theory of the time, took initiative for proposing new laws and policies. Reforms were possible because portions of the business community believed that government-enforced labor standards could serve their own competitive interests.

For a review of the trade union movement since World War II, see Zieger, *American Workers*, Chapters 4, 5 6, which deal with the post–World War II strength of the unions, which reached its zenith in the 1960s and then began to decline. Zieger describes the reasons for the decline that includes the changing composition of the labor force and the decline of the mass-production industries, as well as the globalization of the world economy and the flight of American corporations to low-wage, nonunionized areas of the country and overseas. William Issel, *Social Change in the United States, 1945–1983* (New York: Shocken Books, 1987), also provides a description of post–World War II changes and how it affected work in his chapter, "The Changing Nature of Work," 55–69.

On the importance of the relationships on the shop floor and its significance for workers who need to assert some rights and some margins for democracy in the workplace, see David Brody, *In Labor's Cause: Main Themes on the History of the American Worker* (New York: Oxford University Press, 1993). Brody points out that industrial workers in all societies hold notions of what is right and honorable at the workplace. Brody also states that out of the struggle for industrial unionism there emerged a strongly rooted system of workplace representation based on shop-floor rights, a grievance procedure, and workplace contractualism that gave workers certain basic human rights. These rights have been further articulated with the recent various experiments by corporations extending worker participation in decision making and decentralized work teams.

For a thorough analysis and review of the various experiments to transform the American workplace through the institution of various plans to increase worker participation, see Eileen Appelbaum and Rosemary Batt, *The New American Workplace*. Appelbaum and Batt point out that various movements have been tried, starting with the humanization of work in the 1960s, to job satisfaction in the 1970s, to quality circles in the 1980s. The quality circles were a fad, but have since been discredited in most U.S. applications as not sustainable and providing limited results. Appelbaum and Batt have concluded that most changes which have been tried are marginal, involving few employees, and have not changed the work system or the power structure of American corporations in any fundamental way (70). While the majority of workplace experiments have taken place in manufacturing firms, service industries and public sector organizations have also attempted to eliminate management layers, cut costs, and improve productivity by redesigning jobs and introducing employee involvement and team techniques. Appelbaum and Batt point out that even the best-practice cases tend to be at the level of one plant or one work site and are not diffused throughout entire organizations. What is more significant, especially during this period of corporate downsizing, is that in only a few cases reviewed by Appelbaum and Batt were there commitments to employment security as an explicit part of work reform (72).

An equally pessimistic view about the effectiveness of changes in the workplace is contained in an essay by Rosabeth Moss Kanter, "The New Work Force Meets the Changing Workplace," in *The Nature of Work*, edited by Kai Erikson and Steven P. Vallas (New Haven: Yale University Press, 1990), 279–303. Kanter argues that the shift to a more participative role of workers is not compatible with the command orientation and bureaucratic-hierarchical methods of today's organizations. Kanter explains the problems in the following passage:

> I have identified three principal strains. First is the shift from status to contribution as a basis for pay, as the new workplace attempts to improve performance and allow initiative to be expressed. Second, entrepreneurial management modes that take advantage of employee initiatives are incompatible with the command orientation and bureaucratic-hierarchical trappings of organizations. Third, the thrust of the new workplace is toward greater employee participation and making earnings dependent on initiative. Great participation could so increase the time demands of work that those shouldering the burden of out-of-work responsibilities (primarily women) could be excluded at the time that the rhetoric offers them equal opportunity. All three strains represent the major tensions that organizations, particularly large corporations, need to manage as we enter the last decade of the century. The cracks in the old system are showing. What will happen is still to be determined. We may see conservative keepers of the old way attempt to patch the cracks and fortify the walls against the new challenges, thereby shoring up an obsolescent system. Or we may witness the gradual crumbing of the traditional hierarchy and the reshaping of the work-family nexus. (300–301)

For a review of growth rates in the post–World War II period, 1947 to 1990, see the *New York Review of Books* 41, no. 17 (1996), 16.

On the problem of labor and its declining political clout, see Sidney Lens, "Labor and Capital Today and Tomorrow," in *Working for Democracy: American Workers from the*

Revolution to the Present, edited by Paul Buhle and Alan Dawley (Urbana: University of Illinois Press, 1985). For an assessment of the decline of trade unions and its causes, as well as prospects for the future, see Daniel B. Cornfield, "Union Decline and the Political Demands of Organized Labor," *Work and Occupations* 16, no. 3 (August 1989), 292–322.

On the extensive use of temporary and part-time labor, see Lance Morrow, "The Temping of America," *Time*, March 29, 1993, 40–47; also *Forbes Magazine*, Technical Supplement (Chicago, IL: Forbes ASAP, 1994); Cornfield, "Union Decline," 315, 318, also discusses the issue of the contingent work force.

On the ethnic dimension of the American work force, see Thomas Sowell, *Ethnic America: A History* (New York: Basic Books, 1981), 58–59, 122, 141–142. Also see John Bodnar, *Workers' World: Kinship, Community and Protest in an Industrial Society, 1900–1940* (Baltimore: Johns Hopkins University Press, 1982), 170–171, 173.

The question of technology, deskilling, and the nature of work in the twentieth century has been the subject of much research and debate. Besides Braverman, "Labor and Monopoly Capitalism," there have been many studies. For a summary of many of the issues see Steven P. Vallas, "The Concept of Skill: A Critical Review," *Work and Occupations* 17, no. 4 (November 1990), 379–398. Also see Larry Hirschhorn, *Beyond Mechanization: Work and Technology in a Postindustrial Age* (Cambridge, MA: MIT Press, 1984).

On the work ethic in the workplace of the future, see Arthur G. Wirth, *Education and Work for the Year 2000: Choices We Face* (San Francisco: Jossey-Bass Publishers, 1992). Also see Ross Bishop, "Computer Integrated Manufacturing: The Human Factors," in *The World of Work*, edited by Howard F. Didsbury, Jr. (Bethesda, MD: World Future Society, 1983), 61–83. For an interesting twist on the way we think about employment and leisure, see the article by Robert Theobald, "Toward Full Unemployment," in *The World of Work*, edited by Howard F. Didsbury, Jr. (Bethesda, MD: World Future Society, 1983), 49–60.

William Form provides an excellent summary and survey of the working class, its trade unions, and the labor movement in relation to politics in the United States in the twentieth century, especially during the period from the New Deal to the present. See his essay, "Organized Labor and Welfare State," in *The Nature of Work*, edited by Kai Erikson and Steven Peter Vallas (New Haven: Yale University Press, 1990), 319–342. Form argues that the power and influence of the trade union movement reached its peak in 1945, when it had organized 36 percent of nonagricultural workers in the country. Since then it has declined because of the changing composition of the work force, legislative actions by Congress against the labor movement, and its own ineffectiveness in dealing with the new social and economic environment. Organized labor was a double beneficiary of the original welfare state created by the New Deal in the 1930s. It received government protection to organize and increase earnings through collective bargaining and it received social insurance benefits extended to all citizens. However, organized labor did not unite with groups during the new welfare state created in the 1960s which sought to benefit the disadvantaged—blacks, Hispanics, and new immigrants—which now compose 20 percent of the labor force and over one-third of all manual and service workers. While the labor movement did support the consumer lobbies, the Civil Rights Act of 1964, the War on Poverty in 1964, the creation of the Department of Housing and Urban Development, and the 1965 Medicare-Medicaid Act, it did not unite with or establish ties with the constituencies that were supposed to be the beneficiaries of those acts. Labor union members even opposed entry of blacks into certain unions, especially in the building trades. The labor movement supported the establishment of the Occupational Safety and Health Administration (OSHA) in 1970, but it has not pressed to enforce the act in small, marginal enterprises that employ the bulk of the working poor. Form states that unless and until the labor movement spends its funds to organize minorities and women in the nonunion service sectors of the economy and until it learns to unite with the new consumer-oriented lobbies, it will continue to decline in political influence and in the way it is viewed by the general public.

Both Fred J. Best and Herbert J. Gans have postulated the possibility that in the future there will not be enough jobs to provide employment for all those who wish to work. See their two essays in *The Nature of Work*, edited by Kai Erikson and Steven Peter Vallas. Fred Best's essay is called "Work Sharing: An Underused Policy for Combating Unemployment?" 235–257. Herbert Gans's essay is called "Planning for Work Sharing: The Promise and Problems of Egalitarian Work Time Reduction," 258–276. Best points out that when unemployment rates are high many persons advocate a reduction of work time as a means of combating joblessness by spreading employment among larger numbers. Herbert Gans argues that while official public figures at the present time indicate that unemployment is low, between 5 and 8 percent, the actual percentage is higher since those who have stopped looking for work because of the futility of their search have dropped out of the labor force. There are also many who would enter the work force if economic conditions warranted it and in fact, who need to enter the labor force to make ends meet financially. The real unemployment rate is probably twice as high as the official rate. Gans states that while work sharing is not now on the political agenda in the United States, it has been tried in Europe in countries such as Germany, France, Holland, and Belgium. There is much research needed to evaluate the results, but Gans calculated that for every reduction in work time there is a 40 percent benefit either in new jobs or jobs not eliminated. Gans further points out that such programs are effective when governments initiate the changes and make it attractive for private enterprise through taxing and other policies. While work sharing may not be on the agenda in the United States at the present time, if unemployment rates ever reach double-digit proportions and our society can no longer fulfill its obligation to provide work for those who want and need it, then many schemes may be tried, including work sharing, in order to meet the crisis.

For an excellent review of the concepts and the details of occupational subcultures and how they function with their own ethics of work, see Harrison M. Trice, *Occupational Subcultures in the Workplace* (Ithaca, NY: ILR Press, 1993).

The conceptualization of the work ethic in modern society was formulated by Max Weber at the turn of the twentieth century and has been the subject of commentary and a vast literature since the publication of his essay, *The Protestant Ethic and the Rise of Capitalism* (London: Allen & Unwin, 1930). For a discussion of the Weberian thesis and some of the commentary associated with it, see Herbert Applebaum, *The Concept of Work: Ancient, Medieval and Modern* (Albany: State University of New York Press, 1992), 321–337, 582–583. On the controversy that still rages over the Weberian thesis, see Luciano Pellicani, "On the Genesis of Capitalism," *Telos* 74 (Winter 1988), 43–64; and "Weber and the Myth of Calvinism," *Telos* 75 (Summer 1988), 57–86. On the Weberian thesis, see Guy Oakes, "Four Questions Concerning the Protestant Ethic," *Telos* 51 (Fall 1981), 77–85. Also see David C. McClelland, *The Achieving Society* (New York: D. Van Nostrand, 1961). Again, on the same subject, see S. N. Eisenstadt, *The Protestant Ethic and Modernization* (New York: Basic Books, 1968). A fine study of the work ethic which also contains a discussion of the Weberian thesis is P. D. Anthony, *The Ideology of Work* (London: Tavistock, 1977). Edmund F. Byrne, *Work, Inc.* (Philadelphia: Temple University Press, 1990), provides a complex, insightful study of the work ethic worthy of its nuances and complexity, particularly in Chapters 2, 3, 4, and 5. As Byrne puts it, "[t]he work ethic is, in other words, a simplistic rationale for extremely complex human behavior" (45), and he goes on to demonstrate why. Finally, there is an excellent volume on the work ethic edited by Levitan and Johnson, titled *The Work Ethic*. For a picture of the work ethic in modern, late twentieth-century American society, there is no other single work that provides such a rounded picture of a very complex concept.

15

FACTORIES IN THE TWENTIETH CENTURY

In twentieth-century America, factory and machine production dominate the way work is organized for making goods, both semifinished and finished products. The factory brought into being a new workplace ethic. In a sense, the factory has become the metaphor for an industrial society, just as the computer is a metaphor for the postindustrial, information society. As the mill and the factory replaced the workshop, the underlying logic of work motivation changed, not just in the factory, but in the entire culture. A work ethic is only as effective as it is incorporated by workers and then reinforced by the family, the political system, the education system, and the mass media. A certain work ethic becomes motivational to workers when it reflects sentiments and meanings strongly held by the society.

With the coming of the large-scale twentieth-century factory there was a need to get workers to accept centralization and collective behavior in the workplace. Factory production required synchronized production in a shared work space. A single craftsman can only do one thing at one time and in one place. In the factory, many workers can do many things in many places at the same time. In order to accomplish this goal workers must be forced to follow certain rules—no spontaneous, unpurposeful actions; no wandering from one's work station; no gazing out the window; no absenteeism; and no lateness. Those who resist such rules are resisting the factory work ethic and there is much evidence that such resistance was widespread throughout the twentieth century.

The automobile industry provides a classic example for the study of factory organization in the twentieth century. In large part, the twentieth century in America might be called the century of the automobile, representing as it does mass-production and assembly-line organization of work. The automobile changed the culture of America, criss-crossing it with roads, creating the need for bridges, tunnels and cloverleafs, and as an unintended consequence, led to the clogging of cities and the smogging of the atmosphere. In the 1950s and 1960s, one out of six or seven jobs in the United States was directly or indirectly attributable to the auto industry. The automobile industry came to symbolize the new industrial order, growing from an industry producing luxury vehicles for the wealthy to an industry making a mass-produced good for a mass-consuming public. The auto assembly line defined modern industry and its practices well into the last quarter of the twentieth century. The automobile factory, with its planning and design, represented the direction of modern industry, both in building style and production methods. It reflected the recognition of factory design as a means to facilitate the perfection of assembly-line production and as a way to better manage workers. It led to the stage of industrialization during which the experience of work in the factory was completely different from life outside the factory. The factory, with its special purpose machines, division of labor, moving assembly line, and mechanized handling, left the worker with few of the freedoms he enjoyed outside the factory.

The traditional craftsman ethic died slowly and workers took a long time to adapt to the new factory ethic. When Ford introduced his new assembly line methods in 1913, workers deserted him in droves. To add 100 men to his factory, he had to hire 963. Employers and workers had to develop and accept a new concept of work motivation, one that emphasized extrinsic benefits rather than intrinsic benefits or pleasures from work. These benefits included steady employment, higher wages, vacations, health care coverage, and pensions. Workers generally gave up hope of intrinsic satisfaction from factory work since the routinization and subdivision of work tasks rendered factory work monotonous and meaningless for most workers. Workers therefore set their sights on pleasures outside the workplace that were obtainable with good wages.

Another aspect of the ethic of factory work was the standardization of workers. If parts were to be standardized and interchangeable, so were workers. Their work was to be simplified by Taylorism and Fordism so they could easily be exchanged for one another. Using time-motion studies, management trained each individual to perform the same task in exactly the same way as every other worker performing that task. Employers viewed workers as mechanical units. Siegfried Gideion (1948:99) explained that "Taylorism demands of the mass of workers, not initiative but automatization. Human movements become levers in the machine."

FACTORY ORGANIZATION OF WORK

What are the elements that make up the factory organization of work? First, factory production permits the coordination of different aspects of work within one building or complex of buildings. Prior to the use of the factory system, materials had to move into and out of different workshops and various work tasks were subdivided between different work establishments. With the gathering of workers under one roof it was possible to coordinate work to make it a continuous process without the delays of moving raw materials and semifinished products from one workplace to another. Later, during the first two decades of the twentieth century, the use of conveyor belt systems in auto plants allowed workers to remain at their work stations while parts and semifinished products were brought to their work stations. This further sped up the work process, smoothed it out, and made it more efficient.

A second aspect of factory work is that it eliminates outside diversion from the work process. Work carried on in the workshop or in the home subjects the work process to outside interruptions, as craftsmen take time off to fulfill family obligations or engage in diversionary activity like visiting neighbors or going fishing. Any passerby could enter a workshop and interrupt the work by engaging the craftsman in conversation or by asking to be shown a sample of the product being worked on. Bringing workers into factories and controlling entry and exit allowed employers to keep workers at their tasks and prevent interferences from the larger community.

A third aspect of factory organization is the control that it permits over the quality of production. Each step in the work process can be subjected to inspection and inferior workmanship and defective materials can be intercepted and discarded. Raw materials can be ordered with detailed specifications and accepted or rejected before they enter the factory.

Fourth, factory organization permits supervision over the entire labor process. Entrepreneurs can use supervisors, managers, and foremen to enforce work rules. The factory system allowed owners to subdivide the work and break the monopoly on the organization of work formerly enjoyed by craftsmen in the prefactory workshop. What was previously under the control of craftsmen was transferred to planning and engineering departments in factory offices and to foremen on the factory floor.

Finally, the factory system led to the introduction of machine technology based on nonhuman sources of energy to run the machines. Factories can house large machines driven by water, steam, and electrical power. Machine technology meant fast and more precise production and the transfer of human skills to automatic machines. Use of machines influenced employer decisions, since owners making large investments in machines wanted to keep them running continuously if machines were to be used profitably. Entrepreneurs therefore had to develop a labor process without interruptions, loss of time, or waiting for parts. The automobile assembly line and the automated factory using robots are prototypes of modern technology seeking to eliminate production stoppages. Factory work permitted synchronization of work tasks that increased predictability and control of the work process.

THE FACTORY OF THE FUTURE

The high-tech factory represents a manufacturing system that promises to supersede present factory production. It is not yet a complete reality, but it is coming and it is gaining momentum. In the old industrial system, an army of people performed boring and repetitive jobs. The production line was an unforgiving taskmaster to which workers had to adapt. In the high-tech factory, a sophisticated computer system controls manufacturing equipment and machines that take over many routine functions, thus freeing workers to make decisions.

Product design is based on computer-aided design (CAD), replacing the need for endless rows of draftsmen. The computer makes detailed drawings, debugs designs, and offers alternate suggestions. In automobile design, it can perform stress and reliability tests, try out various parts and innovations, and look at various shapes and interiors, thus minimizing design problems and lead time. Computer-aided manufacture (CAM) is the application of computer technology to the manufacture of products based on intelligent machines and robots. General Motors has developed robots for assembly, loading and unloading, and other tasks. GM came to realize that new technology pays off when coupled with changes on the factory floor that give workers more say. New technology may change jobs and eliminate some jobs, but it will not eliminate the need for human beings. Computers are fast, but stupid. Human beings are slow, but brilliant. The combination of the two is unbeatable.

In the high-tech factory machines perform work formerly done by people. Machines move and whir and products move through the assembly process as if orchestrated by magic. The manufacturing process is organized around cells of general-purpose machines. Reprogrammable general-purpose equipment performs a wide range of functions and is itself produced at lower costs that in turn reduce batch break-even costs. In 1980, 60 percent of U.S. manufacturing was in batches too small for mass production. This has allowed many new companies to compete with established firms committed to old technologies, old production systems, and old management theories. People and robots perform very different functions. In the traditional factory, workers performed the mindless, repetitive line work. Robotics and new production methods have eliminated the need for people to function like machines. In the high-tech factory, workers control production systems using their heads instead of their hands. Production is decentralized, with operating and planning decisions made on the shop floor. Workers perform an array of servicing, monitoring, and planning that keeps the pace of the factory running smoothly. Stress is high as an error means wasted product and expensive downtime. Each cell has a host of support people. Skilled trades are employed in maintaining machines, modifying the lines, and installing new equipment. There are many data entry people, systems analysts, schedulers, computer technicians of all kinds, planners, and coordinators. They are not blue-collar nor are they management; they have been dubbed gray-collar workers. Robotic technology and computer-integrated machines have downtime that is a 20 percent improvement over human labor, as robots do not get bored, take vacations, or require coffee breaks, and they are not sensitive to heat and noise. They can be easily reprogrammed so a line can be "retooled" quickly. Quality control is high because the machine can monitor itself. It can tell if it is nearing tolerance limits and will either self-correct or notify the operator.

One question is when will the new workplace come into being? The answer is that it already has, a little bit every day. But it is not happening as fast as many have predicted. It will be an evolutionary process during which both the workplace and the work ethic will be transformed. The second question is how will the new workplace impact workers and their work ethic?

The Future Factory and the Work Ethic

Computer technology is already impacting the workplace. Initially it has taken over a certain number of dangerous and unpleasant jobs like spray-booth painting, underwater tasks, or work at heights. As the technology improves robots will assume more mindless and repetitive tasks. The transfer of work from man to machine is what the industrial revolution was about. The transfer of intelligence to machine will redefine the concept of work. Work in the future will have little resemblance to the sweat-and muscle-jobs of the past. The United States will move from being a nation of tool workers to a nation of knowledge workers. In the production of machine tools, for example, once requiring high-grade human skills, humans now monitor and feed information into automatic machinery programmed for the output of certain types of tools.

Skills needed require analytic and logical ability rather than workplace-acquired experience. In the electronics industry, components once produced mainly by semiskilled workers are now turned out by a work force divided into thirds made up of trained engineers and technicians, semiskilled workers, and unskilled workers. Engineering is the dominant occupation in robot manufacturing, about 23.7 percent, mainly mechanical, electrical, electronic, and computer engineers. In addition, large numbers of managers, officials, and entrepreneurs in robot manufacture are trained engineers. Engineering technicians account for an additional 15.7 percent of the robotics work force. In this industry, the unskilled and the semiskilled are being eliminated and the jobs created require substantial technical background.

In the new high-tech environment, brains not brawn will count the most. A recent study found that overall, during the 1950 to 1990 period, there has been an increase in work tasks requiring substantive complexity and social interaction, and a decrease in work tasks requiring both gross and fine motor skills. Work tasks defined by the term "substantive complexity" usually require numerical and verbal aptitude, abstract thinking, and lengthy training. Interpersonal relationships will be important in the workplace of the future as work teams become more prevalent. The old Taylorist approach discouraged thinking, but the complexity of the high-tech work environment will demand a mental contribution from everyone. With expensive equipment, mistakes will be costly and so job tension will be high. The sexes should be much more equal in skills and qualifications for high-tech work. However, those with inferior education and social maladjustment will be at a great disadvantage. Work groups will not be regular. Assignments will vary with task and technical requirements, making conventional organization impractical. Workers will have to get used to change and uncertainty, but the work ethic will be based on intrinsic as well as extrinsic rewards.

Workers will expect to be compensated for their performance and their contributions to the work rather than seniority. Workers in high-tech industries will be concerned with skill obsolescence and thus, their work ethic will include constant education and re-education. They will need to be retrained more often, and it will be beneficial for employers to recognize these needs and compensate employees for their retraining efforts. Management will need to consider workers who are flexible enough to be retrained as permanent employees, rather than seeking new employees every time technology changes. It is still not clear whether increasing technological complexity leads to deskilling, increasing skill requirements, or remains pretty much the same. However, the work ethic of the high-tech age will be one that will require workers to accept change and uncertainty along with new assignments and new challenges.

The essence of computer technology in manufacturing involves a twofold process identified by Shoshana Zuboff as "automate and informate" (1988:62–63). On the one hand, as manufacturing is automated, it removes the workers from physical contact with materials and tools. In the traditional work process, through their physical contact with products, workers developed senses of touch, sight, smell, and hearing. This experience with the material world became part of their skill and knowledge. A steel worker may not know the exact temperature of a heat of steel, but he knows from its color and even its smell if it is ready for a pour or ready to receive certain additives. He is tuned into cause-and-effect relationships based on physical contact with materials. With computerized production workers are removed from contact with materials while manipulating them from a remote control console.

The second element of computer technology is that information about the work process itself is now automated and recorded. Information technology (IT) automates an activity at the same time that it produces information about the activity. It both accomplishes tasks (automates) and translates the performance of tasks into information (informates). Information technology contributes to product manufacture while reflecting back on its activities. It not only produces action but also produces a method to symbolically represent events, objects, and processes to make them visible, knowable, and shareable in a new way. In its automating function, information technology perpetuates the logic of the industrial machine that rationalizes work and reduces dependence on human skills. In its informating function it can release dynamics that may reconfigure the nature of work and the social relations associated with work.

When hammers and wrenches are displaced by numbers and buttons, a whole new kind of learning must begin. We are at the edge of progress where action-centered skills are being replaced by intellective skills. As the concept of integrated production grows in importance, the web of communication for effective performance expands and both workers and managers must see the productive system as a whole. Unlike the previous industrial revolution that removed the craft worker from the total product and allowed him and her to only view and deal with a very small part of manufacturing, information technology permits and even requires that the worker must contribute his or her intellect by grasping the entire work process. This will be truly revolutionary if indeed it becomes part of the factory of the future. Then the worker, the work process, and the work ethic will be transformed and liberated. We are still a long way from arriving at this new stage of work, and history has a way of washing away our hopes and predictions. However, without visions and perspectives about the future of work we will be unable to devise methods and paths to arrive at our goals.

To date, only a few corporations have achieved major transformations of the workplace with accompanying performance improvements. As companies have downsized, the emphasis among workers and unions has shifted from job improvement to job saving. Furthermore, the institutional and political environment in the United States at the end of the 1990s provides virtually no support for transforming work systems. If anything, Congress is hostile to anything that encroaches upon private enterprise prerogatives. Today, the efforts of most corporations are piecemeal and marginal as profit continues to be the "bottom line." No workplace improvement will be tried if it does not enhance the company's quarterly report and the price of its stock. Workplace transformations continue to be at the discretion of management and can be cut back at any time to reduce costs. Corporations are attempting the impossible—downsizing the work force and creating insecurity in the workplace while trying to motivate workers to increase their productivity and their loyalty to their employers. Still, we need to explore some of the benefits that can accrue to workers with changes in the organization of factories of the future.

BIBLIOGRAPHICAL ESSAY

For a discussion of factory work, including its theoretical underpinning as well as specific case studies of work in factories, see Herbert Applebaum, ed., *Work in Market and Industrial Societies* (Albany: State University of New York Press, 1984), 33–69.

For evidence of resistance to factory discipline and work organization, see the Health, Education and Welfare Department (HEW) report *Work in America* (Cambridge, MA: MIT Press, 1975), 29–33, 81–91.

For the quote on the factory system, Taylorism, and human automatons, see Siegfried Giedion, *Mechanization Takes Command* (New York: W. W. Norton, 1948), 99. Giedion's book also has an excellent discussion of Taylorism and its methods, 96–106. On the assembly line methods of production in the twentieth century, as applied in the auto and meat packing industries, see Giedion, 115–127. Oliver E. Allen states that Taylor, as the originator of the scientific management approach to factory organization, has remained relevant and valuable down to the present time. For a review of Taylorism and his contributions, see Oliver E. Allen, "This Great Mental Revolution," *Audacity* 4, no. 4 (Summer 1996), 52–61. The aim of Taylorism was to transfer the knowledge of the work process from the worker to the supervisor. This is discussed in detail in Harry Braverman, *Labor and Monopoly Capital: The Degradation of Work in the Twentieth Century* (New York: Monthly Review Press, 1974), 85–152. Also see David Montgomery, *Workers' Control in America: Studies in the History of Work, Technology, and Labor Struggles* (New York: Cambridge University Press, 1979), 113–114, 116–117. There has been a criticism of Braverman's thesis about deskilling, specifically the fact that in his book, Braverman did not deal with worker resistance to deskilling and how that sometimes affected and even reversed attempts to deskill certain jobs in certain industries. Also there has been a critique of Braverman for not dealing with the gender aspect of deskilling. Another criticism of Braverman is that there is no single trend that encompasses all kinds of work, but that deskilling or upgrading of skills varies with industrial, occupational, and organizational setting. Others have argued that skill itself is a difficult concept that has a number of nuanced definitions which need to be accounted for in any discussion of the issue. For a discussion of Braverman's thesis and his critics, see Vicki Smith, "Braverman's Legacy: The Labor Process Tradition at 20," *Work and Occupa-*

tions 21, no. 4 (November 1994), 403–421. For an analysis of the concept of skill, see the entire issue of *Work and Occupations* 17, no. 4 (November 1990). That issue contains four articles: "The Concept of Skill," by Steven P. Vallas; "Skill: Meanings, Methods and Measures," by Kenneth I. Spenner; "What is Skill?" by Paul Attewell; and "Social Construction of Skill: Gender, Power and Comparable Worth," by Ronnie J. Steinberg.

For a discussion of the clash between the craftsman work ethic and the new factory ethic, see Daniel T. Rodgers, *The Work Ethic in Industrial America* (Chicago: University of Chicago Press, 1974), 1–29.

On the problems that Ford encountered when he introduced his assembly line and workers deserted him in droves, see Keith Sward, *The Legend of Henry Ford* (New York: Rinehart, 1948), 32; and Shoshana Zuboff, "The Work Ethic and Work Organization," in *The Work Ethic—A Critical Analysis* (Madison, WI: Industrial Relations Research Association, 1983), 162.

The introduction of the factory system was met with much resistance by workers on the shop floor where the struggle revolved around who was to control the manner and pace of the work. The craft worker in the early industrial workshop maintained a large degree of control over how their work was organized, and they fought management every step of the way as the latter slowly but surely, through technology and organization, wrested that control from the worker. On this important struggle, see David Montgomery, *Workers' Control in America*. Workers had their greatest successes in preserving their craft privileges in the railroad, printing, and construction industries which had a greater degree of trade union organization than in the mass-production industries such as steel, auto, rubber, and electrical before the 1930s. On this see Alan Dawley, *Struggles for Justice: Social Responsibility and the Liberal State* (Cambridge, MA: Belknap Press, 1991), 78–84.

For a picture of the work process in the early years of the automobile industry, with a good description of the technical aspects of producing automobiles with the existing technology of the time, see Joyce Shaw Peterson, "Auto Workers and Their Work, 1900–1933," *Labor History* 22, no. 2 (Spring 1981), 213–236. Also see Joyce Shaw Peterson's book, *American Automobile Workers* (Albany: State University of New York Press, 1987). Steve Babson provides a valuable history of the automobile industry through his history of industrial Detroit, in his fine study *Working Detroit: The Making of a Union Town* (New York: Adama, 1984). Babson's book provides excellent photos and carries the story from the early years of the auto industry, through the depression and the sit-downs, into the war years when women and blacks entered the auto industry, into the postwar years of the high points of the 1950s and 1960s, and then into the stagnation that set in after the 1970s. Both the text and the photographs provide the reader with a vivid survey of what happened to industrial America during the course of the twentieth century. Another study that deals with the automobile factory is that of Lindy Biggs, "Building for Mass Production: Factory Design and Work Process at the Ford Motor Company," in *Autowork*, edited by Robert Asher and Ronald Edsforth (Albany: State University of New York Press, 1995).

Ben Hamper provides a very funny but very realistic and detailed picture of life on the assembly line, based on his own experiences as an auto worker. It is a valuable picture of work in an automobile plant because Hamper has no theoretical preconceptions to present or defend. What he does have is an instinct for what the men on the line are thinking and why and how they go about their work. For a most enjoyable time, read his account, one that includes many insights, *Rivethead: Tales from the Assembly Line* (New York: Warner Books, 1991).

A strike at the Lordstown, Ohio assembly plant of General Motors received wide attention in the press. An analysis of that strike can be found in three studies: Stanley Aronowitz, *False*

Promises: The Shaping of American Working Class Consciousness (New York: McGraw-Hill, 1973); Barbara Garson, "Lordstown: Work in an American Auto Factory," in *Work in Market and Industrial Societies*, edited by Herbert Applebaum (Albany: State University of New York Press, 1984), 38–44; and in Shoshana Zuboff, "The Work Ethic and Work Organization," 167 ff.

For a study of the changes introduced in the automobile industry as a result of the challenge and competition of foreign auto manufacturers, see Ruth Milkman and Cydney Pullman, "Technological Change in an Auto Assembly Plant," *Work and Occupations* 18, no. 2 (May 1991), 123–147. Bringing the picture up to date in the automobile industry, is an article in the *New York Times* by Robyn Meredith, April 21, 1996, titled, "New Look for the Big Three's Plants," section 3, Money and Business. The article deals with the new kind of worker that management is seeking, along with the skills and education background that are now being sought for work in the automobile industry. The wages being offered are good by comparison with other blue-collar work, but the challenge for applicants is that they must have math and logical skills as well as social skills since they are now required to work in teams.

Another important industry, a crucial industry in the United States that went into decline in the 1960s and 1970s, was the steel industry. Once the foundation of America's industrial might, it went into decline because of foreign competition and because of the failure of steel executives to change their technology stemmed from their belief that their monopoly of the domestic United States market would last forever. For a picture of what happened in the steel industry there are several sources: see William Issel, Chapter 3 in *Social Change in the United States, 1945–1983* (New York: Schocken Books, 1987). Another is a book by Richard Preston, *American Steel* (New York: Prentice-Hall, 1991). There is also a book by David Bensman and Roberta Lynch, *Rusted Dreams: Hard Times in a Steel Community* (New York: McGraw-Hill, 1987). Thomas Geoghegan was an attorney for the steel union and wrote *Which Side Are You On? Trying to Be for Labor When It's Flat on Its Back* (New York: Farrar, Straus & Giroux, 1991). Finally, there is the book by Paul A. Tiffany, *The Decline of American Steel: How Management, Labor and Government Went Wrong* (New York: Oxford University Press, 1988).

On the conceptualization of the high-tech factory of the future, see Ross Bishop, "Computer Integrated Manufacturing: The Human Factors," in *The World of Work*, edited by Howard F. Didsbury, Jr. (Bethesda, MD: World Future Society, 1983). Edmund F. Byrne, in his book, *Work, Inc.*, has an excellent chapter dealing with robots, "Automation: Labor-saving or Dehumanization," 181–205. On the future factory and the future of work there is the important book by Shoshana Zuboff, *In the Age of the Smart Machine: The Future of Work and Power* (New York: Basic Books, 1988). This book has become a classic in the sense of providing insights into the use of automation and information technology in the workplace and has provided this author with many of the ideas in this chapter and the previous one.

On the future prospects of work and its transformations, see Harley Shaiken, *Work Transformed: Automation and Labor in the Computer Age* (Lexington, MA: Heath Lexington Books, 1986). Shaken worked in an auto factory and therefore is familiar with work first hand. Milkman and Pullman, "Technological Change in an Auto Assembly Plant," are also a good source for understanding how experiments in the workplace can affect work. For a most comprehensive analysis of workplace experiments, Appelbaum and Batt, *The New American Workplace* (Ithaca, NY: ILR Press, 1994), is a good source. Finally, for a projection of the workplace and work into the future, see Arthur G. Wirth, *Education and Work for the Year 2000: Choices We Face* (San Francisco: Jossey-Bass Publishers, 1992).

Deskilling theory argues that managements use automated technologies to fragment work tasks and transfer control over pacing from workers to machines. This, in turn, atomizes workers' shop-floor experiences and relationships, thereby reducing their collective capacities for resistance. For a test of this theory, James R. Zetka examines the effects of automation on the most militant workers in the United States automobile industry—the stamping, body-building, and trim workers. Industrial analysts have linked these workers' militancy to a distinctive labor process that (1) grants them collective control over their work pace; (2) links their interests to task-specific goals; (3) forces them to coordinate their efforts closely with one another in accomplishing these goals; and (4) thereby raises their group consciousness and commitment. See article by James R. Zetka, "Mass-Production Automation and Work-Group Solidarity in the Post–World War II Automobile Industry," *Work and Occupations* 19, no. 3 (August 1992), 255–271.

For a contrasting study of traditional factory organization, see Lindy Biggs, *The Rational Factory: Architecture, Technology and Work in America's Age of Mass Production* (Baltimore: Johns Hopkins Press, 1996).

16

FARMERS IN THE
TWENTIETH CENTURY

FARMERS' WORK ETHIC

Industriousness, independence, fair play, and honesty, traits that gain meaning and substance through hard work, comprise the central features of the traditional farmer's work ethic. Hard work for the farmer is more than keeping occupied. It is the basis for his or her respect and self-esteem. A farmer's esteem attaches both to work itself and the goals that work fulfills. These goals, short and long term, are pursued with great personal sacrifice to comfort and leisure. Farmers and their families endure working in the heat of summer, the bitter frost of winter, laboring during harvest from five in the morning till after dark, loading hay by searchlight, milking at midnight and dawn, driving long miles to market, and caring for family, farm, and animals in every kind of adverse weather. Farm work is physically exhausting. Yet, farm families have the satisfaction of calling the land their own and of watching nature procreate under their loving care. If not all farmers achieve this ideal level of respectability through dedicated work, it is the standard by which their peers judge them.

The traditional farmer faced many changes in the twentieth century. Yet, farmers are still around in the United States, though their numbers have declined drastically, both relatively and absolutely. They still represent a particular ethic that resonates in the American mystique, a way of life practiced with cultural and ritual complexity. Capital investments and modernization are important, but for traditional farmers, machines are often old and limited in quantity—a tractor with some accessories, spreaders and mowers that need replacing but are kept going by repairing, some hand tools, a second-hand pick-up truck, and hand-operated farm implements. Stock and storage buildings require constant maintenance. Farmers must be mechanics and carpenters who are constantly fixing if they are not to go broke. The traditional farmer survives by using all of his family's labor. The family, the church, and the community comprise the social world of the traditional farmer. Education is important but must give way in favor of the need for the labor of children, who will inherit the farm. When there are many children, some will migrate to the city or town to seek employment. Consumption within the family is limited to necessities during hard times and expands only with better times. Their way of life can be idealized as old-fashioned independence.

The modern farmer views farming work as a business. Market calculation rather than sentiment or tradition govern the work and mentality of the modern farmer who must calculate all the variables that enter into production efficiency. The significant variables of modern farm management are prices of farm product, amount of labor available, costs of running machinery, acquiring additional machinery, feed costs for livestock, costs of maintaining or constructing farm buildings, and capital to expand landholdings. Credit is important since few independent farmers have the capital for land expansion. This is different for the large agribusinesses who do have the capital and the credit line, as well as the financial sources for acquisition and expansion. Like the traditional farmer, the modern farmer seeks to make use of his own and his family's labor, but is also inclined to buy labor-saving machinery. The emphasis is on work and efficiency, using time as a standard that leaves little for the ritual so important to the traditional farmer. The modern farmer gears his life-style to economic expansiveness through hard work rather than simply wishing to maintain what he has, which is the position of the traditional farmer.

AGRICULTURE

American agriculture has been so productive that we take for granted or do not appreciate at all, the crucial importance of agriculture and farmers for our society. Since the dawn of time, three imperatives for human survival have remained the same. Humans must have pure air to breathe, clean water to drink, and nutritious food to eat in order to survive. In the United States, for all but a relatively small segment of the population, the task of securing food means no more than a trip to the nearby supermarket where we choose from more than 8,000 items to meet our food needs. One of our major food-related concerns today is how to eat less. For this reason most Americans have given little thought or concern about how to preserve the welfare of our farmers nor do they understand the essence of farm work with respect to either its difficulties or its rewards.

Agriculture involves a method for working and transforming plants through sowing, feeding, picking, and processing. It is also based on the care of domestic animals kept for meat and milk, and in earlier times, for use as work animals. Farms need large areas for plant and animal populations. Unlike factories that standardize work and product and insulate against weather, agriculture is diversified and must adjust to various conditions of climate, soil, weather, and temperature. No other type of work is faced with as much uncertainty as farming. With millions of producers, farmers face chronic problems of oversupply and falling prices. With increasing mechanization, farmers face increasing debt to finance equipment.

Finally, with so many government programs, farmers face the uncertainty of changing political fortunes as local and federal governments change administrations.

Farm work statistically is in decline. There were 10 million workers in agriculture in 1945. By 1992 the number had fallen to 4 million. In 1950 there were 5.4 million farms in the United States. By 1980 there were 2.4 million farms and by 1994, 2.04 million farms. The acreage in farms had reached its maximum of 1.161 billion acres in 1950, but has fallen since then to 975 million acres in 1994. Yet, the size of the average farm has grown from about 200 acres in 1945 to over 491 acres in 1992. Average acreage of corporate farms is 1,692 acres. In 1900, some 38 percent of the labor force was in farming. By 1990, the figure had fallen to just 3 percent. Today, there are two basic kinds of farms in the United States. There is the family farm, based on the labor of family and kin. And there is the agribusiness, or corporate farm or ranch, largely absentee-owned and based on the labor of wage earners.

WORK ETHIC: SMALL AND LARGE FARMS

The family farm is an icon of American life, a unique organization that combines workplace and dwelling. The family that lives and works together has a number of advantages, including a captive labor supply and an intergenerational access to credit and advice. The problems that plague family farmers have to do with the policies of banks that offer credit and corporations that sell them supplies and equipment. Farmers are also affected by economic trends and federal and local politics. Credit plays a crucial role in farming, along with farming methods, tenure, and inheritance. Small farms make up more than 80 percent of all farms, but account for only 20 percent of total farm output. Despite the lip service about maintaining small farming as a way of life, the crisis of farming in the 1980s and 1990s has reduced the numbers of small family farms. In many ways, the policies of Reagan and Bush aimed at eliminating the family farm. Small farmers were told that they were no longer efficient and that they should find other jobs, as if farming was a job rather than a way of life, as if farmers could be retrained to give up their value system and their life-acquired skills.

On the small farm, farming has remained a desirable way of life, a lifelong commitment to the soil. Small farmers are dedicated to farming values inherited from several generations before them. Small farmers virtually work on the shoulders of earlier generations who prepared the land and fenced it and divided the land between cropland and pasture, woods and meadows, cultivated and fallow. Small farmers love to watch things grow, they enjoy the peace and quiet of rural life, and the sense of independence that is part of farm culture. This is not to say that farm life is easy. Working ninety hours a week is not a life of leisure. Moreover, when economic conditions are bad farmers face low prices for their crops, pressure from creditors, threats of foreclosures, and a struggle to maintain their way of life. Still, building for the future with one's own land has had strong attraction for those who grew up on the land and have absorbed its ways. The difference between large and small farms is not only size but methods of operations. Small farm families work together, with husband and wife acting like partners, making joint decisions, and involving children in all phases of the work. Many small farmers deliberately resist expansion because they want to maintain the family cohesion and relationships and they do not want to hire farm laborers to perform work they can do for themselves.

In contrast to the operations of the small farm, superfarms are run by business managers who can predict their chance of making a profit before starting operations. The large-scale farm is more efficient than the small farm in production, marketing, finance, and business management. It is the place where experimentation takes place. Large-scale farm managers will try gene splicing and embryo transfer so they can produce more milk or they will conduct plant propagation research to grow disease-free plants. The superfarm managers have access to information and finances necessary to adopt the latest technology. In the farm belt in the 1970s and 1980s, large agribusinesses hired bulldozers to smooth the terrain and prepare it for thousands of center-pivot irrigation sprinkler systems. Level ground was required to permit long, sectional tubes radiating out from a central motor to ride on rubber wheels in a slow circular sweep. Irrigation systems like these were subsidized by the federal tax system and had the effect of consolidating many small farm enterprises into megafarms. The cost of one center-pivot system was $60,000, with up to half the investment recovered through investment tax credits. After four years, land improved by one center-pivot system can increase in value by $117,000 net profit. In central Nebraska, the Thunderbolt Ranch, owned by Herdco of Denver, had thirty center-pivot systems on five thousand acres. This kind of investment is beyond the means of the average farmer. Thunderbolt purchased land owned by three separate family-run cattle farms and got a loan from the Federal Land Bank guaranteed by the U.S. Treasury. The preference given megafarmers by the tax system implies that the government means to hurry family farmers off the land.

Family farms disappeared on a massive scale in the 1940s and 1950s, mostly through voluntary migration. A 1954 Iowa study showed that 28 percent of all farms in the state could not provide a family with a decent living. Corn-belt agriculture was on a course that stressed increasing farm size, use of big machinery, and a reorientation toward grain farming. Many families left dairying in Iowa agriculture in the 1960s and 1970s. The high labor and high capital requirements of dairying were considered disadvantageous by modern farmers who wanted a quick return. Cows must be milked every twelve hours and there is a need for storage space and expensive machinery. By the early 1980s, diversified farming, milk cows, and poultry nearly vanished. The emphasis was on grains. All these strategies adopted in the 1960s and 1970s led to a second revolution in agriculture and eventually it led to the disastrous downturn in agriculture during the Reagan administration of the 1980s.

Anne Williams (1981) studied small-scale farming. A large percentage of American farms, over one-half, are small-scale. Apparently, small-scale farming that is economically marginal and even part-time, continues to attract many Americans. Williams states that this suggests that there may be a culturally based value system that provides a foundation for agrarian life styles, despite their apparent economic irrationality. To test this hypothesis, Williams conducted research on small-scale farming in three western Montana counties, studying forty-three small-scale farmers. Williams points out that small-scale farmers come from all age categories and ethnic backgrounds, and are a mixed bag of conventional demographic characteristics.

All forty-three farm families studied by William adhered to a common set of values known collectively as the Protestant work ethic (307). Among the most important values emphasized were those of individualism, self-sufficiency, independence, thrift, hard work, planning ahead, and respect for property and the natural environment. These values, they believed, could be retained and strengthened by living an agrarian life style. The farms were all family enterprises and the family life cycle was the most important influence on giving cultural meaning to their lives. Williams concludes that small-scale agriculture is not populated by a single, homogeneous group of people. Small-scale farm families can be distinguished by their place in the family life cycle, their economic situation including their relative dependence on off-farm income, and their aspirations concerning the future economic role of the farm unit (310). Whether the farms were of the aspiring business enterprise type, or of the hobby and retirement type, all respondents emphasized the higher quality of life they believed an agrarian life style promised despite its economic uncertainties. The virtues of independence and self-sufficiency were continually extolled. They considered the agrarian life as the good life because it offered an opportunity to independently control and manage a farm operation in spite of the economic risks. Williams believes that the prognosis for the small-scale farm is not good, that is, that their numbers will continue to decline. The United States government has never formulated a policy to preserve the family farm and put into practice policies that encourage the small farmer. As long as the benign-neglect policy continues, that was the policy during the Reagan-Bush years, small-scale farming will cease to have an economically viable role in American agriculture.

A study by Ida Harper Simpson, John Wilson, and Robert A. Jackson, of Duke University (1992) provides an interesting analysis of factors other than farm technology on farm productivity. Unlike factory production, a specialized work force is not the most productive division of labor for farming. The scale of farming is relatively small, and even on large farms its varied work tasks are dispersed over a wide area. Production activities are far from uniform throughout the year and thus, specialization seems inappropriate as a strategy to organize farm activities. Further, with the dispersal of activities, farm workers have to work on their own. Most workers on a farm are family members whose family role expectations serve to control their work behavior. Thus, the close supervisory line organization found in manufacturing is inappropriate on farms (240).

The authors point to the importance of recognizing, at least for small farms, that farming is a family-based enterprise. Although wives do much farm work, including field work, father-son is the core familial relation of farming, in contrast to retailing, for example, in which the husband-wife relation is the core. The father-son relation constitutes a lineage partnership that gives the farm a collective identity, with both a past and an anticipated future. This generational linkage extends the longevity of the farm and institutionalizes it beyond the work life of the owner. To have a son in farming and to share farm work with him is to fuse family and farm and to make the family a producer organization (240–241).

The authors of the article point out that although farming is a traditional occupation linked to the family, it is also a scientifically based one, with universities, businesses, and state and federal governments involved in research to develop its knowledge and skills base. The occupation is highly rationalized with scientific advice available on every aspect of farming. Farm organizations, farm magazines, newspapers, bulletins, and national and local farm radio and television programs give information on technology, climate, markets, and other conditions that affect farming. These associations not only provide information for the planning of farm operations, but just as important, they are agencies of occupational community. They inculcate and sustain perspectives toward farming as an occupation. Through participating in these associations, farmers learn new ways to think about farm operations and to look to nontraditional sources of information for ideas. Their knowledge and perspectives are constantly broadened beyond their family and local communities (241).

Howard Kohn (1988), who wrote about his father's small farm, had seen bulldozers in Nebraska push over trees and move the earth into complete flatness for center-pivot sprinkler systems. On a contemporary megafarm there is no room for woods, no reminder of the past. On his father's forty acres of wooded land, Howard Kohn felt he was in the tick of history. In his father's woods, he saw the tree trunks, stout and gray, individually delineated, with round, healed bumps where branches had broken off. He also observed the bristling, pollarded bush, the green shoots of creek banks where muskrats dug spring dens. The woods had the illusion of a place awaiting discovery. A grub ax in these woods did not threaten the scene like a grunting bulldozer. One comes away from reading Kohn's book with the message that land is one of America's strengths that needs to be preserved. The settlement and peopling of America was in a significant way about land, and we threaten the future of American society if we do not care about the land and the farmers who cultivate it.

BIBLIOGRAPHICAL ESSAY

A good introduction into the nature of farm work can be found in the excellent book by Alan Pistorius, *Cutting Hill: A Chronicle of a Family Farm* (New York: Harper Perennial, 1991). Pistorius not only details the elements of work on a dairy farm in Vermont, but provides season-by-season, almost day-by-day accounts of the life of a farmer and his family. He also describes the workings of the various kinds of farm machinery, as well as the functions of the farm buildings on a dairy farm. All of the human interactions are intermingled with sensitive descriptions of the countryside, its fauna and flora, and the sense of what different seasons mean to the farmer.

Another detailed and insightful study of a small family farmer is that provided by Howard Kohn, *The Last Farmer: An American Memoir* (New York: Summit Books, 1988). Kohn describes the workings of his father's farm in upper Michigan. Like Pistorius's book, Kohn's volume describes all the struggles of a family farmer, from the finances needed to sustain the farm to the worries about who is going to run the farm after the farmer's retirement. Kohn also provides insights into large agribusinesses by contrasting the operation and thinking of corporate farming with family farming. A "family farm" can be briefly defined as a farm owned and operated by a family that provides most of the management and financial resources for the operation of the farm. The family on a family farm usually consists of the nuclear family, that is, husband, wife, and children.

For statistics on agriculture in the United States, there is the *Statistical Abstract of the United States* (Washington, DC: Government Printing Office, 1995), section 23, 669–692. There is also comprehensive information on farming and agriculture in the *Historical Statistics of the United States: Colonial Times to 1970* (Washington, DC: Bureau of the Census, 1975), 449–525.

For a history of American agriculture, see Willard W. Cochrane, *The Development of American Agriculture: A Historical Analysis* (Minneapolis: University of Minnesota Press, 1979). On the history of farming in the twentieth century, see Trudy Huskamp Peterson, ed., *Farmers, Bureaucrats, and Middlemen: Historical Perspectives on American Agriculture* (Washington, DC: Howard University Press, 1980). Also see Douglas Helms and Douglas E. Bowers, eds., *The History of Agriculture and the Environment* (Washington, DC: Agricultural History Society, 1993). For an excellent study of farming in Iowa and California and for an in-depth description of the farm crisis in the late 1980s, see Mark Friedberger, *Farm Families and Change in Twentieth-Century America* (Lexington: University Press of Kentucky, 1988). On the 1980s farm situation, also see Daniel Levitas, "Farm Crisis," *Rural America* 8, no. 4 (Winter 1983).

For a discussion of farming in the twentieth century, along with the historical, political, and social backgrounds of the various periods, see Harvey Wish, *Contemporary America: The National Scene Since 1900* (New York: Harper & Row, 1966), 267–273, 304–306, 419–421, 446–448, 492–494, 595, 663, 704–705, 751.

On the hardship of farmers during the Great Depression, see Milton Meltzer, Chapters 11 and 12, in *Brother, Can You Spare a Dime?* (New York: Facts on File, 1991), 82–102. Also, on farmers during the depression, see Joshua Freeman et al., eds., *Who Built America: Working People and the Nation's Economy, Politics, Culture, and Society.* Vol. 2 (New York: Pantheon Books, 1992), 322, 330–333, 342–343, 349–351.

On the farmer's work ethic and outlook on life, see Arthur J. Vidich and Joseph Bensman, *Small Town in Mass Society* (Princeton, NJ: Princeton University Press, 1968), 55–57, 67–69.

For a discussion on farming as a declining form of work in the United States, see William Issel, *Social Change in the United States, 1945–1983* (New York: Schocken Books, 1987), 63; and Richard H. Hall, *Sociology of Work* (Thousand Oaks, CA: Pine Forge Press, 1994), 76–77.

For a discussion of the small, family farmer and his way of life, see John A. Young, "Small-Scale Farmers," in *Work in Market and Industrial Societies*, edited by Herbert Applebaum (Albany: State University of New York Press, 1984); Friedberger, *Farm Families and Change*, 2, 16–17; and Kohn, *The Last Farmer*, 45–46. In addition see Dennis L. Poole, "Family Farms and the Effects of Farm Expansion on the Quality of Marital and Family Life," *Human Organization* 40, no. 4 (Winter 1981), 344–349. Poole found that increased mechanization and farm expansion among family farmers generated higher productivity and greater farm income, but at the expense of creating a faster, more hectic way of life that undermined the quality of marital and family life (348). Families on smaller farms often suffer from a lower economic standard of living. But, unlike their counterparts on larger farms, the smaller scale of their operation enhances the quality of life by promoting team involvement in the farm work, fewer management-related tensions and frustrations, and more time for family social activities and recreation.

For an anthropological study of small-scale and large-scale farming, see Walter Goldschmidt, *As You Sow: Three Studies in the Social Consequences of Agribusiness* (Montclair, NJ: Allanheld, Osmun, 1978); and by the same author, *As You Sow* (New York: Harcourt Brace, 1947). Goldschmidt supervised a comparative study of Arvin, a town dominated by large-scale absentee landlords and Dinuba, a town dominated by smaller-scale, farmer-owned farms. He found more retail trade, a better school system, and more religious organizations in Dinuba than in Arbin. Dinuba had paved streets, sidewalks, garbage collection, sewers, and public parks, all absent in Arvin.

New technology had a tremendous effect on the productivity of American farming as well as on their way of life. Evidence for the increase in output and the decrease in man-hours needed to produce food for American and overseas consumers can be found in the *Statistical Abstract* and the *Historical Statistics* cited above. For additional discussion of this subject, see Vernon Carstensen, "An Overview of American Agricultural History," in *Farmers, Bureaucrats and Middlemen*, edited by Trudy Huskamp Peterson, 19–20; Also see Deborah Fink, *Open Country Iowa: Rural Women, Tradition and Change* (Albany: State University of New York Press, 1986), 163–164. Also, see Orville, L. Freeman, "Perspective and Prospect," in *The History of Agriculture and the Environment*, edited by Douglas Helms and Douglas E. Bowers (Washington, DC: The Agricultural History Society, 1993), 3–11.

To gain an insight into the life of the rural South for blacks before World War II, see the book by Thordis Simonsen, ed., *You May Plow Here: The Narrative of Sara Brooks* (New York: W. W. Norton, 1986). Sara Brooks defined her life on the farm in southern Alabama, seeing the farm as a touchstone in her quest for meaning and fulfillment in her life.

An excellent novel that deals with country life and the struggles of women in a rural setting is that of Willa Cather, *My Antonia* (Boston: Houghton Mifflin, 1918).

For a discussion of the New Deal and its effects on farmers in the South along with the politics of the South, see Alan Dawley, *Struggles for Justice: Social Responsibility and the Liberal State* (Cambridge, MA: Belknap Press, 1991), 391–394. On the various programs during the New Deal that tried to help the farmer, see Freeman et al., *Who Built America*, 349–350; and Friedberger, *Farm Families and Change*, 4–5.

On farming as a desirable way of life, a lifelong commitment to the soil, see Angus Campbell, P. E. Converse, and W. L. Rodgers, *The Quality of American Life* (New York: Russell Sage, 1976). For a discussion of megafarms, see Kohn, *The Last Farmer*, 44–45; and Friedberger, *Farm Families and Change*, 246–247. On dairy farmers, see Pistorius, *Cutting Hill*; Friedberger, *Farm Families and Change*, 21–22, 26–28, 30–31; and Fink, *Open Country Iowa*, 163.

Farming in the Palouse areas of Northern Idaho and eastern Washington State is based on regional particularity, but in many ways it is representative of twentieth-century farming that changed as a result of new and advancing technology. For a picture of how agribusiness, farm technology, and railroads broke Palouse agriculture out of its subsistence phase and into its commercial, cash-crop phase in the twentieth century, see Corlann Gee Bush, 1987, " 'He Isn't Half So Cranky as He Used to Be': Agricultural Mechanization, Comparable Worth, and the Changing Farm Family," in *To Toil the Livelong Day: America's Women at Work, 1780–1980*, edited by Carol Groneman and Mary Beth Norton (Ithaca, NY: Cornell University Press, 1987).

An excellent study by a sociologist dealing with small-scale farmers in American agriculture can be found in an article by Anne S. Williams, "Industrialized Agriculture and the Small-Scale Farmer," *Human Organization* 40, no. 4 (Winter 1981), 306–312.

The article called "The Contrasting Effects of Social, Organizational and Economic Variables on Farm Production," by Ida Harper Simpson, John Wilson, and Robert A. Jackson, appeared in *Work and Occupations* 19, no. 3 (August 1992), 237–254. In their study, the authors identify important differences between farming and manufacturing.

During most of the twentieth century one of the most controversial issues of public policy has been the federal government's quest to eliminate America's farm problem. Efforts have been expended to raise farm income and sustain family farms through support of farm prices and assistance to disaster-stricken farmers. There have also been programs to conserve the soil, prevent erosion, promote farm exports, and develop rural life. Recently, farm programs have aroused opposition for their costs at a time when few Americans continue to farm and Washington struggles to cut spending. American agriculture in the 1990s, with its large and highly specialized farms dependent on machinery and chemicals, bears little resemblance to the farming system from 1900 to 1940. Farm families today are more heavily dependent on exports, face envrionmental and food safety challenges, and confront the system of agribusiness. The political position of farms has eroded as their numbers have declined and nonfarm lobbies are more powerful than the farm lobbies. For a review of agricultural policy in the postwar years and up to the present, see James T. Bonnen, William P. Browne, David B. Schweikhardt, "Further Observations on the Changing Nature of National Agricultural Policy Decision Processes, 1946–1995," *Agricultural History* 70, no. 2 (Spring 1996), 130–152.

17

WHITE-COLLAR AND PROFESSIONAL WORKERS IN THE TWENTIETH CENTURY

The clear trend in the United States during the twentieth century has been the relative expansion of nonproductive jobs and the contraction of goods-producing jobs. This expansion of nonproductive work is in part a consequence of America's increased capacity to produce, since it enables our society to support the growing managerial, professional, service, sales, administrative, financial, and white-collar sectors of our work force. It is also in part a result of the growing bureaucratization of work organizations that are monitored and controlled by an army of office workers, managers, and administrators. Huge bureaucracies have been created in private industry, government, education, health, service, and leisure industries. The Bureau of Labor Statistics groups nonproduction workers into three broad categories: managerial and professional; technical, sales, and administrative support; and service occupations. In 1992 these three categories comprised 78 percent of the work force. The other two broad categories that made up the productive sectors of the work force, precision, production, craft, and repair; and operators, fabricators and laborers, comprised 22 percent of the work force.

Although nonproductive workers do not produce goods, their work is indispensable to an industrial society. Without workers to produce and process paperwork, make up payrolls, type letters, answer phones, send out invoices, and file records, the productive work process could not function. Materials have to be ordered and shipped, parts have to be replaced, costs of labor and materials have to be monitored and recorded, finished products have to be shipped, sales of finished goods recorded, and financial accounts have to be tracked, recorded, monitored, and analyzed. All of this work and all of the paperwork produced (today mostly by computers) must be prepared in a form that enables managers and administrators to make decisions regarding products to be manufactured, numbers of people to be employed, and markets to be found for sales of company products.

The growing numerical strength and functional importance of administrative, sales, service, and clerical workers has been accompanied by the rationalization of their work. The standardization and mechanization of clerical and office work to increase speed, efficiency, and productivity have followed similar patterns found in the rationalization of blue-collar work. Just as factory work is streamlined through subdivision of tasks and use of machines, so clerical and office workers are subjected to this process. The rationalization process is a reflection of bureaucratization, which in turn is based on the accumulation of incredibly huge sums of capital within the control of financial and industrial corporations that require administration by an army of office workers, managers, and administrators who monitor paper, money, and each other.

WHITE-COLLAR WORKERS

The term "white collar" refers to office, technical, administrative, and professional workers. It is a carryover from the past when clerks and office workers were people in managerial positions in enterprises and firms. They were close to owners, were usually well paid, and many eventually went into their own businesses. They were middle class in income, outlook, attitude, and life style. This is no longer true. Most white-collar workers today are workers, not middle-class managers. In income and life style they are closer to blue-collar workers than to owners, and most of them earn less than unionized blue-collar factory workers and skilled craftsmen. Most office work is repetitive, manual, monotonous, and mechanical rather than intellectual and mentally creative.

Much that is characteristic of America in the 1990s is characteristic of the white-collar world. Its workers have risen to numerical importance and carry many of the themes of our time—they are split and largely unorganized; they largely accept their way of life and do not threaten anyone; they live in suburbs and are either homeowners or aspire to be so; they are burdened by taxes; they do not practice an independent way of life but are dependent upon employers and politicians for the decisions that affect their life style. By examining white-collar culture it is possible to learn something about typical American culture in the 1990s. American society may be seen as a giant salesroom, an octopus shopping center, an enormous fileroom, an incorporated computer brain, a new universe of management and manipulation. White-collar men and women have no culture to lean on except the contents of a mass society that has shaped both genders and seeks to manipulate them. White-collar people seek to attach themselves somewhere, but no organization or ideology seems to be thoroughly theirs. This isolated position makes them subjects for synthetic molding in the hands of the popular culture. White-collar workers do not make anything. They handle products made by others. Like others, white-collar workers are bored at work, restive at play, and forever worn out. They turn to leisure and ersatz diversion that partakes of synthetic excitement that neither eases nor releases. As an employee, he and she must smile and be personable while standing behind the counter or working in the office. White-collar employment traits such as courtesy, helpfulness, and kindness, perhaps once real and intimate, are now part of the impersonal rules required to keep one's job. When white-collar people get jobs they sell not only their time and energy but their personalities as well. They sell their smiles and kindly gestures while they must practice repression of resentment and aggression. In many cases they cannot repress their feelings and so they utilize indifference as their face to the consumer.

White-collar workers are employed in several kinds of occupations. There are the managers and administrators who are part of the control systems of major corporations. There are the established professions—doctor, lawyer, engineer, architect, pharmacist, dentist, nurse, teacher, social worker, clergy, computer analyst, biomedical researcher. There are scores of sales people from the auto salesman to department store clerk, from insurance salesman to real estate broker, from Wall Street broker to telephone hawkers. There are office workers—secretaries, typists, clerks, office machine operators, receptionists, telephone operators, mail room sorters and deliverers, bookkeepers, purchasing clerks, estimators, and so on. The service sector contains many white-collar workers, but also has many blue-collar workers. This sector includes food service and supermarket employees, warehouse workers, health service employees, domestic workers, janitors and cleaners, guards, barbers, police, firefighters, correction officers, dental and medical assistants, amusement attendants, and many others in the advertising industry, hotel and lodging places, repair shops, hospitals, and social services.

The Modern Office

Millions of people every day enter the skyscrapers of New York, Chicago, Boston, Houston, San Francisco, Philadelphia, Atlanta, and other cities. These tall buildings are monuments to our American office culture. Row upon row of office workers take their places in the system of paper production and money watching, working computers and machines that record the activities that make up the country's daily round of work and commercial exchange. They transmit the printed record to the next day's round of work and exchange. This paper-and money-culture is housed in giant headquarters of steel and glass that serve as centralized offices overseeing a nationwide network of offices, plants, mines, shopping centers, and even farming operations. Increasingly, these systems stretch overseas and touch every corner of the globe. One of the main functions of an office and its occupants is to direct and coordinate the activities of far-flung enterprises and governments. Every business enterprise and factory is tied to some office where money and decisions coalesce.

The modern office with its tens or hundreds of thousands of square feet and its factory-like flow of work, is not the informal, friendly place that it once was. The beat of the work, the production-like atmosphere, requires that time be accounted for and anything other than business be eliminated. The office manager began to appear in the larger offices by the late 1920s. He had to know the routing of all departments, be able to design and adapt new administrative schemes and to train new employees. As office machinery was introduced, the number of routine jobs increased and positions requiring initiative decreased. Mechanization resulted in a clear division between the managing staff and the operating staff, just like in the factory. The key advantage of mechanized offices is that they permit greater speed and accuracy and require cheaper labor, less training, and replaceable employees. The rationalization of the office has created a mass of clerical workers and machine operators and the specialized manager or administrator who operates the human machinery of the office.

SOCIAL SERVICES

Social services, both public and private, are a growing segment of American society and culture, and organizations devoted to providing social services are employing a larger proportion of the American work force. In the early part of the twentieth century, social services were provided by private and voluntary organizations. The decade of the New Deal accomplished a nonviolent revolution in the role of government in providing social services. The New Deal provided the conceptual foundation for the welfare state, a conception based on the principle that society as a whole, through its government and private agencies, accepts responsibility for its poor, its aged, its unemployed, and other disadvantaged groups. Full employment became a key element of this policy. Americans may argue against the so-called handouts of welfare programs, but everyone is in favor of the idea that all those who are willing to work should be able to find a job. Americans believe that while people are helping themselves, government should also help the unemployed to acquire the jobs through which they can then get ahead through hard work. Attempts have been made since the New Deal to use the federal government to coordinate such policies to guarantee full employment. Most of these attempts have failed, but today, the idea that work rather than welfare is the answer for the poor is prevalent once again.

The climax of the idea that government has responsibility for the poor and the disadvantaged came in the 1960s with the War on Poverty commenced by the Kennedy and Johnson presidencies. Since the 1970s, especially during the Reagan–Bush era of the 1980s, there has been a furious debate about the role of government in society. The welfare state is still intact because essentially that is what the American people desire. Conservative Republicans and others have not been able to dismantle it because it would be political suicide.

There are an enormous number of people engaged in social services, as many as 7.7 million employed by firms. Private expenditures for social welfare in 1992 amounted to nearly $825 billion, or 13.7 percent of our gross domestic product, up from 11.7 percent in 1987. There are today a half million religious, charitable, and social welfare organizations dispensing help to the disadvantaged. The Bureau of the Census records that 47.7 percent of the American population 18 years and over did volunteer work in 1993, averaging 4.2 hours a week. Females volunteer more than males, whites more than blacks, and those with a higher education and more income more than those with less education and less income (*Statistical Abstract of the United States*, Table 619, p. 392). The fact that such large numbers of Americans volunteer their time to help others, and the fact that the overwhelming majority of Americans want the social safety net to remain in place, shows that the United States is still a nation with a population that cares for others. One observer stated (Davidson and Davidson, 1988, quoted in Cherny, Gordon, and Herson, 1992:61) that

[a] civilized society shows compassion and caring for all members of the community, and provides opportunity for all to earn a livelihood. The art of civilized government is to combine self-interest with civic values (the two major types of human motivation) so that society reaps the benefits of each.

PROFESSIONALS

The Bureau of the Census breaks down professionals into the following groups: architects, engineers, scientists, physicians, dentists, nurses, pharmacists, therapists, teachers, social scientists, social workers, lawyers, writers, and artists.

Professionals claim to possess the following traits:

1. A systematic body of knowledge learned within the university and known only to members of the occupation
2. A norm of autonomy that requires that professionals be free of external control as outside interference reduces the quality of professional service offered to the community and to clients
3. A norm of altruism that includes an ethical code requiring members to place the interests of clients and community before self-interest
4. A distinctive occupational culture manifested in associations, training schools, and organizations that reinforce professional norms within the profession and enforce punishments against those who violate those norms

These attributes combine into an ideal model that represents a societal and political mandate granted to a group to provide essential and expert services and organized to protect a vulnerable and unknowledgeable public. However, the forces that coalesced during the first half of the twentieth century in favor of professions are now being countermanded by other forces that threaten the bases of professionalism. These include the increasing bureaucratization of professional employment that threatens the autonomy of professionals, consumerism that takes a hard look at the ethical behavior and selfish actions of professionals, and encroachments of other groups upon the practices of professionals.

Recently, client awareness of too much self-interest and abuse of privileges among professionals has led to closer scrutiny by individuals, consumer groups, and state legislatures over the practices and privileges of professionals. This has tended to reduce the autonomy and monopolistic positions that professionals formerly enjoyed. In addition, allied occupations have encroached upon the once exclusive jurisdictions of professional groups. Realtors and title insurers now perform work previously done by lawyers. Nurses perform functions such as giving shots and administering medicines once done by doctors. Drug companies now make over-the-counter medicines once dispensed by pharmacists. For half of the twentieth century professionals enjoyed an autonomy over their practices as most of them were in their own private practice. Doctors lived in neighborhoods and came to a client's home. Lawyers were individual practitioners, except for the corporate attorneys. The pharmacist practiced in the corner drugstore. The dentist was within walking distance. And there were few specialists, as most professionals were generalists. However, from 1950 to the present, there has been a shift from self-employment to salary status for many professionals that has partially under-mined this professional autonomy.

There has been a growing subordination of professional markets to state-con-trolled and corporate-dominated markets in which professional services are em-ployed. Professional groups such as engineers and school teachers have normally been salaried and subject to managerial control. In the medical field, where doctors once were free agents, power over medical work has shifted significantly from entrepreneur physicians to hospital administrators and health management organi-zations (HMOs). The same process of bureaucratization and control has occurred in other professional settings—law, research, physical sciences, social and human services, and so on. Bureaucratic control yokes professionals to organizational objectives and procedures shaped by administrators and managers making budget-ary and policy decisions. Managers seek to control professionals through perform-ance evaluations, job security reports, merit raises, and through control of technologies owned and administered by the organization, not the professional. Still, there are some professionals who prefer to work for organizations rather than themselves. They do not have to worry about paperwork and business decisions that are made by others. They know they will have a paycheck coming in every week or two weeks. They do not have to solicit clients. Thus, they can be free to devote themselves to their professions without bothering about all the business and management aspects of their practice. They exchange a certain amount of freedom and autonomy for freedom from matters extraneous to their practice.

As society is increasingly ordered by scientific and rational standards, people who create, disseminate, and supply new scientific knowledge have a strategic role to play in society's work ethic. Such people are professionals. As self-proclaimed arbiters of what is scientifically, rationally, and legally appropriate, the professions have increased their power. If the trend continues in which knowledge is the essential ingredient in productive capacity, then the relative power of professionals will be enhanced. On the other hand, there has been an erosion of professional autonomy as many professionals now work in organizations and firms where policy-making is in the hands of administrators, not professionals. Furthermore, many professions are viewed by the public as having more interest in their own well-being, status, power, and income than in the well-being of their clients or the community at large. Thus, while professionals have certainly gained in status, income, and power, their role in today's society is viewed as having a mixture of positive and negative attributes. The American consumer no longer accepts entirely the self-proclaimed professionalism of professionals, while relying upon their services to a greater extent than at any time in America's history.

SALES

Another large category of white-collar work is sales work. Sales link business with the cash nexus of society. It is a marketing technique that has increasingly become our way of life. Most of us must constantly "sell ourselves" if we want to keep our jobs or find new ones. So deeply has the sales ethic infiltrated American life, so potent is selling and advertising, that it may be viewed as a metaphor for American culture. As we enter the twenty-first century the consumer is king in the United States. The presence of the advertising industry is everywhere, and the media is dominated by corporations bent on selling products. Indeed, selling and consumption have become the very foundation of our economic health. Every year, economic analysts and forecasters watch the annual Christmas sales figures for indications of consumer confidence, which has become one of the key factors in marketplace health. Recent polls show that shopping has become the number one leisure activity. Buying and selling is a major part of American culture and every other institution is governed by it, including our politics and including areas once considered beyond such commercialism, like religion, the family, and the creative arts. Salesmanship has become an abstracted value, a science, and an ideology competing with the work ethic.

THE FUTURE OFFICE AND THE WORK ETHIC

One of the questions regarding the office of the future is how the new technology will affect it. It is possible that computer technology will be used to monitor job performance, increase managerial control over workers, subdivide and standardize jobs, regulate work schedules and pace, and substitute computer routines for employee decisions and judgments. Such application of computer technology has already been used with regard to secretarial work and among clerks in large, commercial enterprises. In short, these applications of computer technology is the equivalent of scientific management principles from the industrial age applied to the information age. It exhibits the same concepts of work values with the same dehumanizing effects as occurred on Henry Ford's assembly line.

Another scenario rejects the rigidly structured, machine-like control as applied to office work and moves toward more flexibility in office work tasks. Work hours and work location would be organized in a less rigid fashion and office workers themselves would be involved in decisions about all aspect of their work. To the degree that employees have control over the scheduling, location, pacing, and nature of their work there is less stress and more satisfaction. Where workers are given more discretion and more participation in planning and organizing their own work they are more active and participatory in their nonwork lives, engaging in political, voluntary, and community affairs.

Given the direction of society as we move toward the twenty-first century it will be difficult for future enterprises to function with the old bureaucratic, pyramid-style organization where various layers of managers regulate obedient hourly workers based on standard operating procedures. Work in future enterprises will require problem solvers and problem identifiers who will need to be in constant communication with each other. Routine service skills will be replaced by skills to enable white-collar workers to see the entire system in order to identify and solve problems. They may work alone or with small teams. They will need to communicate constantly, often informally, to see that ideas are evaluated quickly and critically. White-collar workers will need to develop skills in conceptualizing problems and solutions.

It appears certain that in the future the transmission and exchange of information will be crucial in all aspects of economic life and in all kinds of enterprises. The dispensing of information and knowledge is now an industry, with its own technology, its own methods of work, and its own work ethic. The white-collar sector of the economy, the one that includes the gathering, storing, and diffusion of information, has now become and will be an increasingly dominant aspect of the work life of American citizens. As it grows, the number of specialties will grow that are based on the mastery of a body of knowledge. The new work styles and the new work ethic will require more dedication to mastery of the whole system, to working in teams, to knowing how to communicate and exchange information and knowledge, and to developing a work ethic that reaches beyond the workplace, one that integrates work with all of life, with all of society. In short, it will be a work ethic that can be truly self-fulfilling for each individual as well as benefiting the society at large.

BIBLIOGRAPHICAL ESSAY

For a listing of the white-collar occupations that includes managers and administrators, the professions, technical and sales workers, and service occupations, see Table 649, "Employed Civilians, by Occupations, 1983 and 1994," in the 115th edition of the *Statistical Abstract of the United States* (Washington, DC: Bureau of the Census, 1995), 411–413.

The quote on a civilized society is from Greg and Paul Davidson, *Economics for a Civilized Society* (New York: W. W. Norton, 1988) as quoted in Julius Cherny, Arlene R. Gordon, and Richard J. L. Herson, *Accounting—A Social Institution: A Unified Theory for the Measurement of the Profit and Nonprofit Sectors* (New York: Quorum Books, 1992), 61.

One of the best theoretical and cultural analyses of white-collar workers was done by C. Wright Mills, *White Collar* (New York: Oxford University Press, 1953). The book is more than forty years old, but it contains many brilliant insights into the nature of white-collar work as well as the perspectives and cultural aspects of white-collar workers. C. Wright Mills also foretells of the growing importance of white-collar work along with the occupational dilemmas faced by these workers.

For a breakdown of the category "clerical" as used by the Bureau of Labor Statistics, see *Fortune*, July 12, 1993, 55.

On the unionization of white-collar workers, along with an analysis of the prospects for unionization among these workers, see Daniel B. Cornfield, "Union Decline and the Political Demands of Organized Labor," *Work and Occupations* 16, no. 3 (August 1989), 294–295.

For a discussion of social services as a growing occupational category, along with a discussion of the welfare state and the increased importance of social services in modern American society, see the following: Cherny, Gordon, and Herson, *Accounting—A Social Institution*, 52–53, 60–61; Arthur M. Schlesinger, Jr., *The Cycles of American History* (Boston: Houghton Mifflin, 1986), 23–48; John Rawls, *A Theory of Justice* (Cambridge, MA: Belknap Press, 1971), 523–529; Edmund F. Byrne, *Work, Inc.: A Philosophical Inquiry* (Philadelphia: Temple University Press, 1990), 85–110.

On social work as a white-collar occupation and the changes that have occurred with regard to that occupation and the welfare system, see Barbara Garson, *The Electronic Sweatshop: How Computers are Transforming the Office of the Future Into the Factory of the Past* (New York: Simon and Schuster, 1988), 74–75, 102–103, 114–116.

There are many fine descriptions and analyses of the professions and the work ethic associated with the professions. Of course, each profession has its own body of knowledge and skill, but all have a similar or general set of ethics that can be said to apply to professional work. For a fine overview of the professions and their work ethics, see Andrew Abbott, *The System of Professions* (Chicago: University of Chicago Press, 1988). For an excellent summary of the professions and their characteristics, see Harrison M. Trice, *Occupational Subcultures in the Workplace* (Ithaca, NY: ILR Press, 1993), 54–58. For another overview of professionals, see Charles Derber, "Professionals as New Workers," in *Professionals as Workers: Mental Labor in Advanced Capitalism*, edited by Charles Derber (Boston: G. K. Hall, 1982), 3–19.

There is an extensive literature on lawyers as professionals, since the legal profession along with the medical profession, are the prototypes of professional occupations. For a fine overall analysis of lawyers-at-work, see Eve Spangler and Peter M. Lehman, "Lawyering as Work," in *Professionals as Workers: Mental Labor in Advanced Capitalism*, edited by Charles Derber. Robert A. Rothman provides an analysis of some of the latest trends in the legal profession, particularly with regard to challenges to the traditional aspects of the lawyering profession as far as its body of expert knowledge, autonomy, group solidarity, self-regulation, authority over clients, and its work ethic. See Robert A. Rothman, "Deprofessionalization: The Case of Law in America," *Work and Occupations* 11, no. 2 (May 1984), 183–206. Rothman concludes that the process of "deprofessionalization" challenges traditional values in the legal profession. It will continue to result in a decline in their power in the state legislatures, where the major struggles for monopoly and autonomy for professions take place. At the same time, the legal profession is working hard to neutralize external threats to its expertise and its earning power. As the rate of litigation continues to rise, the role and importance of lawyers is predicted to continue to be strong into the future.

Another good summary of the legal profession can be found in an article by Sharyn L. Roach Anleu, "The Legal Profession in the United States and Australia," *Work and Occupations* 19, no. 2 (May 1992), 184–204. The author deals with four significant changes in the legal profession: (1) increases in the number of lawyers, giving rise to increased bureaucratization of work settings and continued specialization; (2) the emergence of managing attorneys in large law firms that separates the administrative aspects from professional practice, thereby reducing the scope of collegial management and review; (3) the increased hiring of lawyers by government and business corporations; and (4) relaxation of prohibitions on advertising and determination of fees. All of the above trends are leading to a more complex and stratified legal profession that is hard to characterize by a single work ethic.

The American Bar Association appointed a Commission of Professionalism to study and make recommendations regarding the commitment of practicing attorneys to the norms and values of professional legal practice. Amid allegations of too much litigation, rapidly increasing attorneys' fees, advertising by attorneys, and increasing competition by attorneys for jobs and clients, it was feared that the profession was in a state of crisis and that commitment to service was giving way to commercialism. For an analysis of the finds of the commission and the state of the legal profession, see Jerry Van Hoy, "Intraprofessional Politics and Professional Regulation: A Case Study of the ABA Commission on Professionalism," *Work and Occupations* 20, no. 1 (February 1993), 90–109.

The highly segregated character of the early American legal system and the absence of a black bar contributed to the denial of justice for black citizens. Although 1954 marks the year when the legal system shifted from an oppressive mechanism to an instrument of progressive change, black citizens still use lawyers and courts less frequently than whites to solve disputes. Thus, the number of black lawyers is a demographic fact of great social significance. In 1972, nonwhite lawyers accounted for nearly 2 percent of lawyers in the United States. By 1981, nonwhite lawyers comprised almost 5 percent of the 558,000 lawyers. For a study of black lawyers and how and where they practice, see the article by Charles L. Cappell, "The Status of Black Lawyers," *Work and Occupations* 17, no. 1 (February 1990), 100–121.

For a picture of lawyers in large law firms, see Spangler and Lehman, "Lawyering as Work," 79–83; and Trice, *Occupational Subcultures*, 172. For lawyers in corporations, see Spangler and Lehman, "Lawyering as Work," 84–87; and Trice, *Occupational Subcultures*, 165–166. For lawyers who work for the government, see Spangler and Lehman, "Lawyering as Work," 87–89. For lawyers who work as public defenders and in neighborhood legal assistance, see Spangler and Lehman "Lawyering as Work," 90–93.

For figures on the number of doctors of all types in the United States, from 1900 to 1970, see *Historical Statistics of the United States: Colonial Times to 1970* (Washington, DC: U.S. Government Printing Office, 1975), vol. 1, Table Series D, 233–682, 141. For figures on doctors for years 1983 and 1994, see *Statistical Abstract of the United States* (Washington, DC: Bureau of the Census, 1995), Table 649, "Employed Civilians," p. 411.

For an overview of physicians as an occupation and its work ethic, see John B. McKinlay, "Toward the Proletarianization of Physicians," in *Professionals as Workers: Mental Labor in Advanced Capitalism*, edited by Charles Derber. McKinlay deals with the growth of specialization in the profession, along with the bureaucratization of the profession as more and more doctors find themselves working in organizations.

For an excellent study of the changes in the health care industry in the last three decades, with particular emphasis on physicians, see the article by Timothy J. Hoff and David P. McCaffrey, "Adapting, Resisting and Negotiating: How Physicians Cope with Organizational and Economic Change," *Work and Occupations* 23, no. 2 (May 1996), 165–189.

A more extensive and exhaustive analysis of the medical profession that is somewhat outdated because it was published more than twenty-five years ago is the work by Eliot Friedson, *The Profession of Medicine* (New York: Dodd, Mead, 1970). A more up-to-date work is that of P. Starr, *The Social Transformation of American Medicine* (New York: Basic Books, 1982).

An impressive set of satellite occupations has arisen around physicians and make up the allied health delivery system. It has been estimated that by the 1970s, there were over 500 allied health care occupations, with many of these specialties creating subspecialties. For a review of these satellite occupations in the health care industry, see Harrison M. Trice, *Occupational Subcultures*, 205–210.

HMOs and administered medicine are becoming increasingly significant in the health delivery field. For an analysis of how doctors practice their profession in these organizations and what their attitudes are toward such organizations, see Kathleen Montgomery, "A Prospective Look at the Specialty of Medical Management," *Work and Occupations* 17, no. 2 (May 1990), 178–198.

The increase in malpractice suits has caused profound changes in the way doctors practice their work and in their attitudes toward their profession, toward the government and toward their clients. For a study of physician reaction to malpractice suits, consult the article by Stephen L. Fielding, "Physician Reactions to Malpractice Suits and Cost Containment in Massachusetts," *Work and Occupations* 17, no. 3 (August 1990), 302–319. Also see P. M. Danzon, *Medical Malpractice* (Cambridge, MA: Harvard University Press, 1985).

On the profession of engineering and how it is viewed as an occupation and a profession, see the article by Peter Meiksins and Chris Smith, "Organizing Engineering Work: A Comparative Analysis," *Work and Occupations* 20, no. 2 (May 1993), 123–146. The authors examine the various ways in which the engineering occupation has been organized, based on whether it identifies with the technical occupations, whether engineers identify with the organizations that employ them, or whether they seek solidarity with other engineers as part of a professional community.

With regard to the office of the future and how it will affect white-collar work, see Don Mankin, "Autonomy, Control and the Office of the Future: Personal and Social Implications," in *The World of Work*, edited by Howard F. Didsbury, Jr. (Bethesda, MD: World Future Society, 1983).

18

SKILLED AND CRAFT WORKERS IN THE TWENTIETH CENTURY

The 1995 *Statistical Abstract of the United States* shows that the total number of skilled workers rose from 12,328,000 to 13,489,000 between 1983 and 1994. Skilled workers numbered three million in 1900, six million in 1940, nine million in 1960 and eleven million in 1970.

Skilled workers, craft workers, and foremen have composed a remarkably stable component of the labor force—10 percent in 1900, 14 percent in 1950, 12 percent in 1990, and 10 percent in 1994. The building trades constitute the largest single portion of skilled labor in the United States. Skilled workers in industrial settings include tool-and-die makers, machinists, pattern makers, printers, upholsterers, cabinet makers, clothing cutters, furriers, jewelers, clock makers, glass blowers, engravers, and others. In transportation, railroad engineers may be considered skilled workers. Other skilled workers include mechanics, repairmen, technicians, weavers, chefs, wood carvers, coppersmiths, and artists.

CRAFT WORK ETHIC

The work ethic of craftspersons and skilled workers includes the following elements:

1. A sense of accomplishment and craft pride in the work performed
2. Exercising control over entry into the skill or craft through unions and organizations, based on the premise that it is a privilege to practice a craft, a privilege that must be earned through apprenticeship, training, and education
3. Quality of workmanship
4. Honesty in dealing with customers, suppliers, employers, and employees

5. Resistance to change that undermines skill, particularly technological and organizational change

The culture of craftspersons tends to merge their work life with their nonwork life. Practicing a craft is more than a job or occupation, it is a way of life. Their craft or trade defines the way craftspersons think, what they think about, who their friends are, what they do in their off hours. Many workers with a skill or craft built their lives around their work, extending their work relationships into their nonwork lives, preferring to be friends with colleagues and encouraging and helping family members join their craft. Craftspersons share work-based beliefs about the world, trust most those who share their craft and their work. Craftspersons tend to spend leisure hours with members of their occupation. Often they live near one another and link their families through marriage, while encouraging children to follow parents into the trade. This has been true among craftspersons and mechanics from earliest colonial days right up to the present, and there are still many examples of crafts, trades, and skilled workers who follow this pattern of merging their work and nonwork lives.

Technology and Skilled Workers

There is much debate about whether and how technological change alters the skill requirements of work. Technology has substantial effects on the composition and content of work, but these effects vary for different dimensions of skill, for different occupations, industries, and firms, and for different technologies. There are three views on how technological change alters the numbers and quality of jobs: the upgrading thesis, the downgrading thesis, and the mixed-change and conditional thesis.

The upgrading thesis argues that the division of labor in the twentieth century evolved along lines of greater differentiation and efficiency. As technology increases productivity and expands markets, it requires a broader variety of skills and a higher average of skill from the labor force. One version of this thesis is that the postindustrial economy increasingly relies on highly automated environments that require new skills such as monitoring, adjusting, and visualizing the whole production process and responding to emergency situations.

The downgrading thesis focuses on the deterioration in the quality of work because of changes in the labor process in which technology is a key instrument in fractionating and deskilling jobs. Management uses scientific management, numerical control, automation, and the redesign of jobs to separate the conceptualization of work from the carrying out of work. The result is a polarized work force, with unskilled and semiskilled workers at the bottom and an elite of managers and professionals at the top. Both manual and white-collar workers are seen as being subjected to this deskilling process. There is a version of this thesis that sees a growth of low-skill occupations and industries and a relative decline of the demand for workers with skills and education. In recent years, there has been a focus on deskilling and downgrading as a result of companies downsizing their operations and their work force. Workers who are displaced and who are the subjects of structural unemployment, find that when they return to work they cannot find jobs that match the skill or the wage or salary level they formerly enjoyed. Deskilling is viewed as a consequence of downsizing and deindustrialization in the United States economy.

The third thesis in the debate about skill levels is that the effects of technological change or changes in the labor process are mixed and offsetting. The effects depend on the level of automation, the organizational environment, the way management chooses to implement and utilize technological changes, and the larger demographic and economic forces. Those adhering to this view believe that the outcome is little net change in skill requirements of work or offsetting trends on the composition of the occupational structure, so that some sectors and jobs experience upgrading while others are faced with downgrading. For example, in the telecommunications industry, one that is especially a focus for the introduction of the latest automation and microprocessor technology, survey data on job content suggest the existence of an upgrading tendency during the 1950–1980 period. However, during more recent years survey data indicate that a degradation of work has emerged. If a degradation effect has taken hold, it has not uniformly affected the workers in this industry. Two worlds of work seem to persist within the communications industry. In one, a growing proportion of craft occupations have been relatively insulated against the degradation process. In the other, the clerical labor seems to bear the brunt of the degradation effect. Thus, the industry is characterized by a polarization of skill levels rather than the emergence of simple, undifferentiated labor. It appears that the solidarity of the craft workers and their union representation has modified the effect of new technology and prevented it from leading to a degradation of skills among craft and skilled employees (Vallas, 1988).

In general, those studies that have focused on the overall occupational structure for the U.S. economy as a whole, have found little or no change, or even a slight upgrading of skill. Those researchers who have focused on particular industries or occupations have generally found a downgrading of skills. Finally, there are commentators who believe that the methodologies and the empirical evidence are so mixed that no definite conclusion can be made regarding changing skills levels in response to changing technologies.

SKILLED WORKERS AND THEIR CHARACTERISTICS

The practice of a skill ordinarily takes place within the context of a social structure, an organization, and a culture that determines in large part what kind of work will be valued. This influences both the wages for skilled work as well as the way that crafts and skilled workers are organized. During the twentieth century, the introduction of automated machines reduced the use of craft and skilled labor in a number of industries. On the other hand certain industries, like construction, have been able to maintain its traditional crafts and its hand-tool methods of production. In addition, the introduction of new industries producing electronics, microprocessors, communications, and computers have led to upgrading of skills and the use of new skills such as programming and computer analyzing. These new industries have grown spectacularly percentage-wise, but starting from a small base their growth in numbers has not offset the fall in skills in other industries such as printing, longshore, chemical, machine tools, office machines, and others.

Skilled workers and craftspersons share certain characteristics with professionals, such as a body of knowledge, a system of training, and organizations that seek to confine the practice of the craft to members only. Some crafts also enjoy licensure, as in the case of electricians and plumbers, but this is the exception rather than the rule. Craft unions provide skilled workers with more control over their work than industrial unions. Craft unions set standards for recruiting individuals into their apprenticeship programs, thus monitoring entry into the craft through entry into the apprenticeship programs. Still, craft unions have no control over whom employers may hire or to whom they give work assignments.

SKILLS FOR THE FUTURE

Craft knowledge and expertise fosters a feeling of occupational solidarity among skilled workers. Socialization in a craft or skilled trade creates the feeling that such knowledge, skills, and abilities require a lifelong commitment to a set of principles and values that identify one with an occupation regardless of what kind of firm or organization in which one is employed. Occupations that are rich in craft traditions have a socialization process that fosters a work ethic that stresses honesty, dedication to craft, and quality of workmanship. Skilled trades require a long and arduous training period before the new recruit is accepted into the craft. It is an acceptance that apprentices must earn so the new recruit will treasure what he or she has attained. However, as technological innovations and the bureaucratization of work advance as the twenty-first century approaches, it will be increasingly difficult for the crafts and skilled trades to maintain their position in the world of work.

While there is much talk about the future of work in the United States requiring higher levels of skill and education, trends in contemporary America seem to run counter to these projections. Most of the jobs being created are in the service rather than in the manufacturing sectors of the economy and these are jobs that require lower levels of skill. We are creating more jobs for janitors and guards than for computer analysts, more jobs for fast-food workers and kitchen help than for machinists. While the new technology will not eliminate the most skilled, creative, and demanding forms of work in future society, corporations find it more profitable to employ technologies to eliminate high-paying, high-skill jobs and replace them with jobs that they can fill with lower-skilled workers. As long as the so-called bottom line is profit, high-priced labor, whether blue-collar or white-collar, is vulnerable to restructuring and downsizing that will eliminate such jobs. What seems to exist in all industrial countries, including the United States, is that there is a core of skilled workers who have well-paying jobs that require a high level of training and education. This skilled elite, which includes professionals, managers, and skilled workers, comprise not more than 20 or 25 percent of the work force. The balance of the working population have low-skilled jobs that require little education and little mental or physical dexterity. Individual case studies of firms or sectors of industries may show some upgrading of skills, but the overall picture of the U.S. work force indicates a continually declining proportion of manufacturing and skilled jobs as compared with service, sales, retail, and unskilled jobs requiring minimum education or minimal training.

TWO ROADS TO THE FUTURE

As we approach the twenty-first century, we see America at a critical juncture. How will it organize itself for engagement in the global market? How will it cope with a high-tech society? At the present time, there is a clear gap between the elite 25 percent whose children get the education required for the future and the rest of the work force who struggle to make ends meet and provide a proper education for their children. In response to this dualism we face a choice between two courses of action. One is that with the present level of skills we can design, administer, and operate the high technology of the future and nicely hold our own. Those at the higher levels will probably turn their eyes away from the growing segregation of Americans by income and ignore the embarrassing social disarray of those at the bottom. This option, and one we seem presently to have chosen, would permit most workers to get by with only mediocre training, skills, and education. The main body of workers would be partially educated by standardized schooling, while the skilled elite would continue to occupy the best jobs based on higher skills and education. This option is based on the bet that the middle classes can be kept in line with an insecure standard of living, by the diversions of consumerism and entertainment, and by playing on their fears regarding the lower classes, minorities, immigrants, criminals, and the underclass. If current trends continue, in twenty years the top 25 percent will earn more than 60 percent of American income and the bottom will earn 2 percent of national income. The elite will withdraw further into their secure enclaves, with good jobs, excellent health care, challenging work, and effective schools (mostly private). They will tolerate the disorder beyond the pale by walling themselves off from those left out, investing in electronically equipped security forces, more high-security prisons, stepped up executions of criminals, and having less and less contact with the majority of society. The urban and rural poor will live largely out of sight in their own decaying sectors, with the despair and hopelessness of their children accepted as a way of life.

The second option would require a major shift in the nation's priorities. A decision would have to be made to counter the growing gap in education, skills, and income by adopting policies to insure that all American children would be given opportunities to learn and acquire the skills necessary for the future high-tech society. This would give them a chance to become responsible participants in the institutions of the future. It would require a commitment by the presently favored 25 percent of American society to make resources, education, and skills available to all. Such a choice would recognize that in the long run a dangerously divided society is an intolerable threat to the country's moral and material well-being. It would require a decision to combine the new technology with the democratic values of American society. Regarding work, it would require a commitment to spend the money to develop an educated and skilled work force and offer jobs that are challenging and satisfying. If this image of a trained work force seems unrealistic it shows how far we are from becoming serious about the human resources we need for the future. We will not achieve our goals without a major commitment from all levels of society, including a leading role from the federal government, to provide the resources to create a skilled, knowledgeable, and well-paid work force.

Providing Skills for Future Workers

Since we will be living in a world where the flow of data and information will be crucial in the workplace, workers will have to be trained to grasp entire systems and to make choices and decisions based on a holistic view of the production process. This is counter to what has happened during the industrial age when work and thinking have been broken into small parts to be learned and mastered in isolation of the entire production system. Only the managers, according to Taylor and those who followed his philosophy, were to have the overall view, the better to control workers and the production process. In the information workplaces of the future, workers and managers are going to have to learn to collaborate as problems will be confronted by teams seeking new solutions, new strategies, and new designs for new products. Mutual learning of skills occurs when workers share insights, experiences, puzzles, and solutions. The skills of communicating ideas will have to be developed so that other teams and individuals in the productive system can benefit. In addition to these new skills, workers young and old, will have to develop a renewed commitment to discipline. In work, as well as in school, we will need to take responsibility for defining desired goals and delaying immediate gratification so as to make sustained efforts and sacrifices for the future. In the future world of work, the work ethic should include quality along with quantity and should be made a concern of firms, institutions, individuals, and society at large. There are no blueprints to bring about the workplace of the future to meet the challenges of the future. One thing is certain: A skilled work force is necessary, one skilled in mental and manual dexterity, skilled in thinking in holistic terms. It will be a work force with an ethic designed to meet the needs of a society that provides opportunity for all sectors of the population.

BIBLIOGRAPHICAL ESSAY

For a listing of skilled workers categories under Precision Production, Craft, and Repair, see the *Statistical Abstract of the United States* (Washington, DC: Bureau of the Census, 1995), Table 649, p. 413. The *Historical Statistics of the United States: Colonial Times to 1970* (Washington, DC: U.S. Government Printing Office, 1975) contains a much more detailed breakdown of skilled workers and uses the heading, "Craftsmen, Foremen and Kindred Workers, Table Series D 233–682, pp. 142–143. Seventy-five categories of skilled workers are listed.

For a brief description and statistics on skilled workers, see Richard H. Hall, *Sociology of Work* (Thousand Oaks, CA: Pine Forge Press, 1994), 68–69. For an introduction to the nature of skilled workers, see Harrison M. Trice, *Occupational Subcultures in the Workplace* (Ithaca, NY: ILR Press, 1993), 42–43, 53, 127–128, 152.

Work and Occupations 17, no. 4 (November 1990), devotes an entire issue to a discussion of the theoretical concept of skill and how it is to be identified and measured. The issue is edited by Steven P. Vallas and provides the reader with a good idea of how difficult and complex the notion of skill is with regard to the study of work. See also Stephen P. Vallas, "New Technology, Job Content, and Worker Alienation" in *Work and Occupations* 15, no. 2 (May 1988), 148–178.

On the merging of their work and nonwork lives among skilled and craft workers see, Harrison M. Trice, *Occupational Subcultures in the Workplace*, 33–36; Herbert Applebaum, *Royal Blue: The Culture of Construction Workers* (New York: Holt, Rinehart and Winston, 1981); Frederick C. Gamst, *The Hoghead: The Industrial Ethnography of a Railroad Engineer* (New York: Holt, Rinehart and Winston, 1980); and Seymour M. Lipset, Martin A. Trow, and James S. Coleman, *Union Democracy* (New York: Free Press, 1956). On the declining role and need for skilled labor in the current labor market, see Edmund F. Byrne, *Work Inc: A Philosophical Inquiry* (Philadelphia: Temple University Press, 1990), 70–71.

Construction work has been a subject for many researchers and there is a rich literature dealing with skilled trades and the organization of work in the construction industry. The following is a list that is by no means exhaustive: Herbert Applebaum, *Royal Blue*; Herbert Applebaum, "Construction Management: Traditional Versus Bureaucratic Methods," *Anthropological Quarterly* 55, no. 4 (Winter 1982), 224–234; Thomas L. Steiger and William Form, "The Labor Process in Construction: Control Without Bureaucratic and Technological Means?" in *Work and Occupations* 18, no. 3 (August 1991), 251–270; Bob Rechman, "Carpentry: The Craft and Trade," in *Case Studies on the Labor Process,* edited by A. Zimbalist (New York: Monthly Review Press, 1979), 73–103; Jeffrey W. Riemer, *Hard Hats: The Work World of Construction Workers* (Beverly Hills, CA: Sage Publications, 1977); Jeffrey W. Riemer, "Worker Autonomy in the Skilled Building Trades," in *Varieties of Work*, edited by P. L. Steward and M. G. Cantor, 225–234; Marc L. Silver, *Under Construction: Work and Alienation in the Building Trades* (Albany: State University of New York Press, 1986); Marc L. Silver, "The Construction Industry," in *Varieties of Work*, edited by P. L. Steward and M. G. Cantor (Beverly Hills, CA: Sage Publications, 1982), 235–252; A. L. Stinchcombe, "Bureaucratic and Craft Administration of Production: A Comparative Study," *Administrative Science Quarterly* 4 (Winter 1959), 168–187. For detailed statistics on the construction industry, see United States Department of Commerce, *1987 Census of Construction Industries*, Bulletin CC87–I–28(P) (Washington, DC: U.S. Government Printing Office, 1989).

For a description of the changing nature of construction projects, see Marc Silver, *Under Construction,* 40–41. On the need for quick decisions and decentralized problem-solving on a construction project, see Marc Silver, *Under Construction,* 57–58, 64–65.

Regarding a listing of the work ethic among craft workers that was used in this chapter and the sanctions against those who do not conform to them, see Harrison M. Trice, *Occupational Subcultures in the Workplace*, 198–199.

Printing is another industry that has been studied in order to analyze the nature of craft work and the effects of technology on craft workers. For statistics on the printing industry and the number of production workers versus the total employment in the industry, see the 1995 *Statistical Abstract of the United States*, Table 668, p. 477, "Nonfarm Industries,

Employees and Earning: 1980 to 1994." For additional statistics on printing trades, see *Fortune*, July 12, 1993, p. 55.

Two works that deal with craft workers in the printing industry are as follows: Robert Blauner, *Alienation and Freedom* (Chicago: University of Chicago Press, 1964); and Andrew Zimbalist, "Technology and the Labor Process in the Printing Industry," in *Case Studies on the Labor Process*, edited by Andrew Zimbalist (New York: Monthly Review Press, 1979).

For a discussion of the deskilling of trades in the printing industry, see M. Wallace and A. L. Kalleberg, "Industrial Transformation and the Decline of Craft: The Decomposition of Skill in the Printing Industry, 1931–1978," *American Sociological Review* 47 (Spring 1982), 307–324; and Arne L. Kalleberg, Michael Wallace, Karyn A. Loscoco, Kevin T. Leicht, and Hans-Helmut Ehm, "The Eclipse of Craft: The Changing Face of Labor in the Newspaper Industry," in *Workers, Managers and Technological Change*, edited by Daniel Cornfield (New York: Plenum Press, 1987), 47–71.

Steve Babson, *Working Detroit: The Making of a Union Town* (New York: Adama, 1984), has provided a fine study of working people in the city of Detroit. Besides the excellent picture of the automobile workers, Babson deals with a number of other occupations, in particular, the printing trades. For his remarks on the printing trades, see pages 190–191.

On printers as an occupational community with a proud craft tradition before the deskilling process see Seymour M. Lipset, Martin A. Trow, and James S. Coleman, *Union Democracy.*

Longshore work was considered a skilled trade, using hand methods and slings to stow cargoes in ships. Then, the container was introduced into the industry, using standardized containers already loaded with goods for shipment overseas. The job of stowing ships then became a matter of using cranes and signalmen and the older craft skills became obsolete. An excellent case study of longshoremen that provides a picture of the industry before its massive mechanization and containerization is provided by William Pilcher, *The Portland Longshoremen* (New York: Holt, Rinehart and Winston, 1972). Pilcher himself was a longshoreman and provides a picture of longshoremen from the viewpoint of an insider. For a more up-to-date study of longshoremen, see William DiFazio, *Longshoreman: Community and Resistance on the Brooklyn Waterfront* (South Hadley, MA: Bergin and Garvey, 1985). For an excerpt from Pilcher's book that deals with their skills, work socialization, cultural norms, pilfering, and other characteristics of the trade, see William Pilcher, Chapter 8, in *Work in Market and Industrial Societies*, edited by Herbert Applebaum (Albany: State University of New York Press, 1984), 120–129. For a study of the technological changes in the longshore industry, see Gordon Betcherman and Douglas Rebne, "Technology and Control of the Labor Process: Fifty Years of Longshoring on the U.S. West Coast," in *Workers, Managers and Technological Change*, edited by Daniel B. Cornfield, 73–89.

Miners may be classified among skilled workers because of their work habits and the independence they have traditionally displayed in the workplace. One of the finest studies of the mining industry and its history, including the effects on miners through the introduction of new technology is provided by Keith Dix, *What's a Coal Miner to Do? The Mechanization of Coal Mining* (Pittsburgh, PA: University of Pittsburgh Press, 1988). For a close-up view of miners and their work, their solidarity, and their occupation as a culture of danger, see John S. Fitzpatrick, "Adapting to Danger: A Participant Observation Study of an Underground Mine," *Sociology of Work and Occupations* 7, no. 2 (May 1980), 131–158. In the same volume of *Sociology of Work and Occupations*, see the article by Charles Vaught and David L. Smith, "Incorporation and Mechanical Solidarity in an Underground Coal Mine," 159–167.

There have been many studies on John L. Lewis, the coal miners' union leader from the 1920s to the 1960s. For an excellent review of the history of the miner's union under his leadership, see David Brody, Chapter 4, *In Labor's Cause: Main Themes on the History of the American Worker* (New York: Oxford University Press, 1993), 131–174. On the reduction in the number of miners in the United States, see Richard A. Souto, "Changing Technologies and Consequences for Labor in Coal Mining," in *Workers, Managers and Technological Change*, edited by Daniel B. Cornfield, 180. On John L. Lewis's use of the legislation of the New Deal to build his mine workers' union as well as the CIO, see Robert H. Zieger, Chapter 2, in *American Workers, American Unions, 1920–1985* (Baltimore: Johns Hopkins Press, 1986).

Men's clothing is another industry where skilled trades are important. On the men's clothing industry, see Steve Fraser, "Dress Rehearsal for the New Deal: Shop-Floor Insurgents, Political Elites, and Industrial Democracy in the Amalgamated Clothing Workers," in *Working-Class America: Essays on Labor, Community and American Society*, edited by Michael H. Frisch and Daniel J. Walkowitz (Urbana: University of Illinois Press, 1983), 212–255. Also see Steve Fraser's article, "Combined and Uneven Development in the Men's Clothing Industry," *Business History Review* 57, no. 4 (1983), 522–547. Sidney Hillman was a key figure in building the Amalgamated Clothing Workers union, as well as being influential in providing labor support and ideology for the New Deal. For a biography of Sidney Hillman, see Matthew Josephson, *Sidney Hillman: Statesman of American Labor* (Garden City, NJ: Doubleday, 1952). On the practices and methods of the petty garment manufacturer, see Irving Howe, *World of Our Fathers* (New York: Simon and Schuster, 1976), 155–159. In spite of their strong craft traditions and their pride in their autonomy and independence, the cutters local in the Amalgamated Workers Union came under the control of racketeers and gangsters in the early 1920s and not until ten years later did the national union leadership mobilize enough power to end it in cooperation with fair-minded employers and Mayor Jimmy Walker. For a description see Howe, 337.

On the future of work and the skills that will be required in the high-tech economy of the future, see Henry M. Levin and Russell W. Rumberger, "The Future Impact of Technology on Work Skills," in *The World of Work*, edited by Howard F. Didsbury, Jr. (Bethesda, MD: World Future Society, 1983). Also see Russell W. Rumberger, "The Changing Skill Requirements of Jobs in the U.S. Economy," *Industrial and Labor Relations Review* 34 (July 1981), 578–590.

For an analysis of the impact of computer technology on work and work skills, see Shoshana Zuboff, *In the Age of the Smart Machine: The Future of Work and Power* (New York: Basic Books, 1988).

On the two options facing American society with regard to work, education, and training, see Arthur G. Wirth, *Education and Work for the Year 2000: Choices We Face* (San Francisco: Jossey-Bass, 1992), 197–203. On the same subject, see Rushworth M. Kidder, "Ethics: A Matter of Survival," *The Futurist* 26, no. 2 (March–April 1992).

19

WOMEN IN THE
TWENTIETH CENTURY

To introduce this chapter on women's work in the twentieth century it may be useful to summarize a news report called "Working Women Count" (*New Jersey Star Ledger*) on a survey of 250,000 women expressing opinions about juggling jobs and family responsibilities. It sought female opinions on job satisfaction, wages and salaries, benefits, and opportunities for advancement. The report concluded that "America's working women are exhausted." The study showed that women are angry at not getting a fair deal, revealing that most women are still segregated in low-paying, traditionally female jobs in clerical, sales, and service occupations. Women who hold professional positions are still clustered in fields like education, social work, and nursing, where wages are much lower than in business, law, engineering, medicine, and other professions where men dominate. Nearly three-quarters of women in their forties holding professional and management jobs listed stress as the most-mentioned problem, as did more than two-thirds of single working mothers. Not surprisingly, women also complained of being paid less than men and of having fewer opportunities for advancement.

WOMEN IN THE WORK FORCE

The rapid growth of the service sector in the twentieth century—particularly clerical and sales positions—was a crucial factor for the growth of females in the labor force. Between 1900 and 1960, the number of secretaries, stenographers, and typists grew twenty times, absorbing over 2.1 million workers, 96.5 percent of whom are female. By 1960, almost one of every three employed women worked in a clerical job. Women are still entering jobs construed as feminine gendered—elementary and high school teachers, nurses, social workers, librarians, and office workers.

Some women attempted to gain entrance into the crafts, but their progress has been very slow given the resistance of craft unions to accept women. The Parnest study of occupational choices found that non–college-educated women who chose masculine jobs was only 19 percent in 1973 for whites and 13 percent for blacks. Young college women were more likely than older women to choose jobs that were dominated by males.

In 1994, women were 38.1 percent of machine operators, assemblers, and inspectors. However, they were 86 percent of textile sewing-machine operators, 62.8 percent of pressing-machine operators, and 52.9 percent of production inspectors, testers, samplers, and weighers. Of fabricators, assemblers, and hand-working occupations, women were 31.5 percent. In transportation as a whole women were only 9.4 percent and as laborers, except construction, they were 18.2 percent.

As the twentieth century advanced women were able to gain greater access to an education that would prepare them for the professions. From 1890 to 1920, women's participation in the paid professions increased by 226 percent. Women college graduates combined career and family, not simultaneously, but as part of their life cycle—from college to work to marriage to homemaking, and later back to the work force when their children were grown. The labor-force participation rate of married college-educated women rose from 9.8 percent in 1900 to almost 59 percent in 1974. The entrance of women into colleges and their education alongside men proved they were equally capable of intellectual achievement and thus eligible for entrance into the professions. By 1950, educated women had broken down many of the formal rules barring their employment into men's professions. Professional women wanted more from their jobs than simply money for their families. They wanted self-expression and this led them to shun "female" jobs and seek entrance into what were considered male professions. They became lawyers, doctors, scientists, and researchers. Many chose to become owners of business and managers. Today, female stock and bond salespersons are about 15 percent of those professions, women doctors about 19 percent, and female lawyers about 23 percent. Women are advancing in both position and income. The number of working wives outearning their husbands increased from 16 percent to 21 percent between 1981 and 1991.

Women who sought entrance into male-dominated occupations had to face hostility from employers and fellow employees, disbelief from customers, difficulty on the job, and conflicts at home. To succeed in these male-dominated jobs women must work hard, demonstrate determination, maintain a cooperative attitude despite taunts and harassments, and not be dissuaded from their purpose. Males find it hard to interact with women, to ignore their gender and their femininity. Many men can only interact with women by flirting, fathering, or seeking mothering. Many women in the workplace find that whatever role they take they are prevented from participating equally on the job with men. Women in male-dominated jobs have to walk a thin line, striking a balance between being assertive to command respect, and not being too aggressive in order to be accepted.

In a study of reactions to blue-collar work by women, Karyn A. Loscocco (1990) points to the differing points of view regarding women in the workplace: (1) women have different attitudes toward work than men because of gender role differences that they bring to the workplace; or (2) there are few gender differences in work attitudes and that such variation as exists is due primarily to differences in work characteristics. Loscocco finds that both the gender and the job models are involved in female attitudes toward work. Like men, blue-collar women react more positively to jobs and companies that provide challenge, variety, and autonomy. Women are motivated by financial rewards as well. The traditional view that women are more devoted to family than to work has been used by management as an excuse not to promote women. Loscocco's conclusion is that women take paid work very seriously. They form their attitudes about their jobs and companies primarily on the basis of their judgment of how well they are rewarded. Despite different positions in the gender stratification system, women and men react to their jobs and companies in a remarkably similar fashion in the blue-collar world (1990:173).

Most women seek self-expression and recognition from others in their jobs. To compete, women must place their jobs and its demands first and structure their family life around the time constraints of their jobs. This conflicts with their role as homemakers. They can resolve the conflict by either giving up one of their careers, or they can settle for less advancement in their work to get more flexibility in hours or work location; they can try to change the division of labor in their families by getting their husbands and children to share the homemaking. But the ambivalence remains, and the resolution of the conflict often falls mainly on the shoulders of women.

The entrance of married women into the labor force has transformed the average American family from a one-earner to a two-earner family. By 1979, both husband and wife were in the labor force in over half of the husband-wife families. Only 33 percent followed the traditional pattern of husband in the labor force and wife in the home. Today, the two-earner marriage is the predominant form. The entrance of women into the labor force involves husbands more actively in the family and provides an opportunity for men to share in the housework as well as participating in the care of the children. However, the evidence on the amount of time men spend on housework or on feeding, clothing, bathing, or transporting children is quite minimal. A more symmetrical marriage could offer a man more companionship and understanding from his wife on the basis of shared experiences—mutual acceptance, respect, advice, and love of two people who are both participants in the world of work. However, it appears that in most cases women who work must take on the burden of most of the work at home in addition to having a career.

From 1969 to 1987, yearly household working hours for working women fell by 145 hours, while yearly household hours for working men rose by 68 hours. To some extent women have been able to substitute commercial services for their own labor by using part of their paychecks for this purpose. Expenditures on precooked food, professional child care, and dry cleaning have risen rapidly in recent years. Both for two-earner families and single mothers, the reduction in women's time at home has led to children left in the care of others or even by themselves. Unless husbands pick up the slack, these changes in child care will continue as women just do not have the time. Families are having fewer children, which reduces domestic hours as children require tremendous amounts of time, particularly when they are young. From 1970 to 1990, the married proportion of the population fell from 70 to 60 percent and the average number of children declined from one child per person in 1969 to slightly over one-half child in 1990. By 1987, only one-third of the population had children under eighteen years of age, and in 1995, only 25 percent of American households were composed of husband and wife with children living at home. Increased female employment has been accompanied by fewer births and later and shorter marriages. The white female labor-participation rate in 1994 was 58.9 percent compared to 75.9 percent for white males. The black female participation rate was 58.7 percent compared to 69.1 percent for black males.

One-fourth of all working women are found in only five occupations: secretary, bookkeeper, elementary school teacher, waitress, and retail sales clerk. Half of all employed women are in just seventeen occupations. The contribution of women to family incomes by wives who work full time is 40 percent of total family income. For single, divorced, or separated women, working is usually their sole means of support. Despite the importance of a wife's work to family finances, the husband's work often takes priority when conflicts arise. A husband's job may require absence from home for long periods of time, such as long-distance truck driving or being a traveling salesman, which makes it difficult for these wives to work, especially if there are small children and inadequate child-care arrangements.

Occupational segregation, coupled with discontinuous career patterns and part-time work, depress the earnings of females. Although segregation of women has declined in the public sector to some extent, significant wage differentials still exist in both the private and public sectors of the economy. Work done primarily by women is systematically undervalued. For example, male managers are perceived as running offices and departments. Yet, the daily indispensable work of secretaries in passing on messages, responding to emergencies, training new employees, and coordinating schedules for meetings remains invisible. Female ward clerks are thought to perform routine clerical functions. Yet, one of the things they do routinely is handle the family of a patient in a crisis situation, allowing the medical staff to treat the patient. The skills of firefighters in handling emergencies are central to an understanding about their job and they are fully compensated for this type of work. Female flight attendants are trained to work with passengers in case of an emergency, in addition to having communication and food distribution skills. Yet the emergency skills of the flight attendant remain invisible and uncompensated.

In the years preceding Pearl Harbor comparatively few women were hired by industry, but with America's entry into World War II massive campaigns were launched to convince women to take defense jobs. Women poured into the factories. Between 1940 and 1945, the number of women in the labor force expanded from less than 14 million to more than 20 million, from 25 percent of the work force to 38 percent. Before the war, 85 percent of female factory labor was employed in nondurable goods industries—textiles, apparel, leather, food, and paper. With the war, increasing numbers of women worked in durable goods and basic industries—communications and electrical equipment, small-arms ammunition, iron and steel, automobiles, rubber, scientific equipment, and weapons. Women became welders and shipbuilders; they built airplanes and produced ammunition; they made complicated electrical equipment; and they riveted the sides of tanks. By the end of the war, women had entered every phase of industry and almost all areas of manufacturing.

In the postwar period there was a rapid rise in government, services, and retail jobs. Between 1950 and 1970, 9 million jobs opened up for secondary school teachers, hospital support staffs, and local government office workers, all jobs in which women were prominent. The growing demand for consumer goods spurred the creation of new department stores and supermarkets, staffed by 3 million additional employees, many of whom were female. Finance, real estate, and insurance companies added 4 million new workers between 1950 and 1970, again areas in which female employment was significant. The American economy's shift into service and office work would not have been possible without the influx of 20 million women into the postwar work force.

WOMEN AND THE WORK ETHIC

Women have sought entry into men's jobs on the basis of their qualifications, directly challenging the gender division of labor based on the spurious arguments that women are not qualified for men's jobs. The rationale for the gender division of labor has been undermined. Women have demonstrated to policy makers that opposition to the employment of an individual solely on the basis of gender is unfair, contrary to the principles of free choice, and violates laws providing for equal opportunity for all regardless of gender. In the last decade or two, the contention that males and females are naturally different in abilities, once an unquestioned part of the general work ethic, has been rejected by the American legal and social structure. Women themselves, in the past, accepted male concepts of work and excluded themselves from men's jobs and sought out women's jobs. But this is changing as males and females move into all sectors of the work force.

More than 50 percent of married women are now in the work force. They are faced with the need to straddle the work ethic of the public world with the family ethic of the private world. In the past, the two spheres of social life have been viewed as the exclusive vocations of men and women, respectively. The traditional work ethic regarding women was that they could only succeed in the masculine job world by giving up their commitment to their families and dedicating their lives to job advancement, on the premise that it was impossible to be successful in both the economic and family spheres. Recently, in a number of custody cases, children were awarded to the father who was less successful and earned half the salary of the mother. The reasoning in these cases was that the best parenting may come from the parent who is less successful and does not have the burden of long hours of work. This too is changing, except that the burden of straddling the two spheres has fallen upon women, along with the burden of breaking through male-dominated occupations despite the opposition of males.

When we speak about males and their work ethic, we assume that we are dealing with men and their jobs, based on commitment to one's occupation, along with the self-esteem and satisfaction that comes from one's occupation, skill, or craft. When we speak about women and the work ethic, we do not separate the spheres of work and home as we do for males. Women's work for those who are in the job market includes jobs for which they are paid and household work for which they are not paid. We denigrate household work because it does not command a wage, except when done by commercial companies. The female work ethic, like the male work ethic, includes commitment to one's work and seeking self-esteem and satisfaction from one's occupation, skill, or craft. A woman's self-esteem is judged both by her occupation as well as her role in her family and household. Whether she will gain satisfaction from both workplace and household depends on the nature of her occupation and the quality of her marriage and family. Both are equally important to her. However, the basis for judging her work in the workplace and in the family must be different as the work environments are different, along with the discipline in each sphere and the nature of the tasks in each sphere.

For most of the nineteenth century and for almost half of the twentieth, among nonfarm households there was a separation between home and work. Nonfarm men left their homes in the morning for the factory, mill, or office to perform "work," defined as those physical and mental tasks for which one was paid. Women were expected to remain at home. The nineteenth-century fight for a family wage was simultaneously a fight for a social order in which men could support families and receive the services of women, and women, dependent on men, could stay out of the labor force. Both labor unions and management continued to agree with these assumptions in the twentieth century. The persistence of the wage gap over the twentieth century attests to the strength of these views of sex roles and to their institutionalization in a two-tiered wage structure.

While husbands were at work outside the home, women were at work inside the home, cleaning, caring for children, doing laundry, preparing meals, shopping for household supplies, mending or making clothing, and if they had time, socializing with family, friends, and neighbors. The crucial difference between men's and women's work was that men were paid, had no choice over their assigned tasks, and were constrained by supervisors and discipline. Women, on the other hand, were not paid, had free choice as to how to do their work, what work to do, and when to do it. Women were constrained by their children's routines in school, by when they had to feed and transport their children, and by when they had to have family meals ready.

As married women entered the workplace in larger and larger numbers, the separation of spheres began to break down. The two-wage-earner family is now the norm. Women must bridge the two spheres, while men, at least in the majority, still separate themselves from household work and concentrate their energies and interests on their work, and look to their households as places to relax and interact with their families. It is the woman who must arrange and organize her time to bridge both worlds rather than the man. It has been the female work ethic that has been largely affected by the female entry into the work force on a mass scale, while the male work ethic has remained largely unaffected. Only when men begin to assume more housework responsibilities will the entry of females into the work force affect the male work ethic. In short, there is a female work ethic that seeks to bridge the two spheres of household and work, while the male work ethic remains what it has been traditionally, that is, concentrating on work.

The second aspect of the female work ethic relates to how females in the work force may change the habits and mind-sets that presently exist in the workplace. Traditionally, the male-dominated workplace has been characterized by competition, aggression, ambition, and power seeking. The male work ethic, along with its forms of management, stresses authoritarian decision making, hierarchy, dominant and subordinate relationships, and formalized systems of communication. Female behavior, on the other hand, enmeshed with caring for family members, has been characterized by cooperative decision making, nurturing relationships, and communication based on a caring ethic. Women are more likely than men to listen to others, to seek advice, to be less opinionated, and to be less authoritarian in relation to other adults. It could be that female entry into the workplace will change it in the direction of a caring ethic to be combined with a work ethic. This could be beneficial for the workplace of the future that will require cooperation and exchange of information. If males begin to participate more fully in the household it could affect their behavior at work, making them more sensitive to others and more caring. It could be beneficial to society at large if total commitment to work is modified so that all workers, male and female, take a larger interest in community and family. It could make Americans better citizens and the country a more participatory society.

It is important to note that work life norms in industry were created by men. These norms demanded a continuous work life, the eight-hour day plus overtime and shift work, interrupted only by weekends, holidays, annual vacations, or brief sick leaves. When women entered industry, they were expected to satisfy these norms. Any deviation was considered a weakness that made corporations think twice about hiring women. Since working mothers can hardly conform to these norms and since many women workers are mothers, employers who are usually males, still regard female labor with strong reservations. Changing the norms of work life for working mothers may benefit them and our entire society. Working mothers seldom conform completely to male norms—they have to leave work in emergencies, many work part time, and many interrupt their work life for some years. For all this they are penalized. They receive lower pay, they lose seniority rights through interruptions, and they lose pension rights. Many women have no job security and are the first to go in a general layoff. And frequently women are excluded from either training or promotion based on management's excuse that they may have to quit because of their family obligations.

Women are still grossly underrepresented in management positions, especially in upper management. As they begin to fill these positions it will be important to see if they can bring a new, more caring style of management to corporate America. Only time and future trends will provide the answer. In the meantime, we can only hope that women will have a positive and beneficial effect on the American work ethic as a whole.

In the study of women's work, it is crucial that both the unpaid labor as well as the wage labor of women's work be seen as a continuum rather than a dichotomy, with many intermediate stages linking the two poles. The studies of women's work are not simply an extension of the study of men's work, but must be reconceptualized so that they apply to women and their circumstances. Women's work has always been linked in some way to their families and often to their communities. The nature of women's domestic responsibilities, coupled with their race, ethnicity, marital status, and ties to kin and community has largely determined the kind of work they do, whether paid or unpaid, whether performed inside or outside the household. The conceptualization of women's work is part of the history of women in the United States. Such conceptualization will lead to an increased understanding of not only women's work, but of men's work as well.

Through language and other means, Deborah Tannen (1994) has identified certain patterns of behavior between men and women that define different patterns of workplace relationships. Tannen shows unmistakably that female postures and behavior in the workplace is softer, more caring, less aggressive, more listening, more respectful of others, more group-minded than males, who are harder, more competitive, more selfish and self-centered, and more individualistic in their workplace orientations. The male metaphors revolve around the military and sports, the female metaphors revolve around family and the group. In the text, it was mentioned that few women are found in management positions in American corporations. In the top 1,000 companies in 1989, only 5 percent of those in executive management positions were female. Evaluations of women by men consistently state that men believe women lack confidence, in spite of their credentials or good performance. In a sampling of 94 companies of the top 1,000 companies, although women were 37 percent of the employees, only 6 percent were in management positions. Women always tended to say "we" with regard to their accomplishments, whereas men tended to say "I." Thus, many women found that their good work and their efforts went unrecognized, thus reducing their chances for promotion. If women are aggressive and assertive in the workplace then men tend to resent them and say they would not want to work for women. Tannen goes into greater detail citing specific instances to illustrate the fact that while men and women want the same thing as far as good wages, recognition, and career goals, females have their own ethic as far as how to interact with others in the workplace that is distinctly different from that of males.

BIBLIOGRAPHICAL ESSAY

For women in the labor force in the period 1960 to 1994, see the *Statistical Abstract of the United States* (Washington, DC: Bureau of the Census, 1995) as follows: For "Labor Force Participation Rates by Marital Status and Sex," see Table 636, p. 405. For marital status of women in the labor force, see Table 637, p. 405. For the employment status of women by marital status and presence and age of children, Table 638, p. 406. For the overall civilian labor force and breakdown of employment by sex, race, and age, see Table 640, p. 407. On the employment of civilians by occupation, broken down by sex, race, and Hispanic origin, see Table 649, pp. 411–413. On female unemployment, see Table 659, p. 421. On the educational attainment of males and females from 1970 to 1991, see Table 662, p. 422. On median weekly earnings for male and female for years 1983 to 1994, see Table 677, p. 433.

On the report of the study "Working Women Count," see the *New Jersey Star Ledger*, October 15, 1994, 3. On women and the rise of consumerism, see "Decline of Thrift," *The Futurist* 26, no. 2 (March–April 1992). Also see Kathleen Burke, "Winning the Hearts and Minds of an America Facing War," *Smithsonian* 24, no. 12 (March 1994).

For a history of women in the work force during the twentieth century, see Julie A. Matthaei, *An Economic History of Women in America: Women's Work, the Sexual Division of Labor, and the Development of Capitalism* (New York: Schocken Books, 1982), 235–236, 242–248, 254–272, 281–299, 301–309. Also see *The Futurist* 28, no. 1 (January–February 1994).

On women at work in the household, see Ruth Schwartz Cowan, *More Work for Mother* (London: Free Association Books, 1989).

On married women in the work force and the burden of work at home and the caring of children, see Mirra Komarovsky, *Dilemmas of Masculinity* (New York: W. W. Norton, 1976), 35–36; also Ruth Cowan, *More Work for Mother*, 200–216.

For statistics on United States households and the number of married couples with children at home, see the *U.S. Bureau of Census Bulletin* 31, no. 6 (June 1996), 1. That report showed that only 25.2 percent of all U.S. households are married couples with children at home.

Juliet Schor provides data on working women with respect to the number of hours devoted to housework and the solutions that women must seek in order to meet their household obligations and still remain in the workplace. See Juliet B. Schor, *The Overworked American: The Unexpected Decline of Leisure* (New York: Basic Books, 1991), 35–38. Schor points out that for women, the acquisition of a husband leads to more work at home such as home-cooked meals and bigger houses and apartments to care for. Married people try to save more, and that cuts down on the purchasing of services. For women, gaining a husband adds about five hours of domestic work per week. Men, at least into the 1980s, did not do any more housework when they got married.

Data on the various occupations in which women's work can be found in Richard H. Hall, *Sociology of Work* (Thousand Oaks, CA: Pine Forge Press, 1994), 195–203. Also see Barbara F. Reskin and Patricia A. Roos, eds., *Job Queues, Gender Queues* (Philadelphia: Temple University Press, 1990), 17–19.

On the evaluation of women's work in the job market, see Ronnie J. Steinberg, "Gendered Instructions: Cultural Lag and Gender Bias in the Hay System of Job Evaluation," *Work and Occupations* 19, no. 4 (November 1992), 387–423. In her article, Steinberg cites S. Taylor, "The Case for Comparable Worth," *Journal of Social Issues* 45, no. 4, (1989), 23–37, who stated that "[e]mployers routinely placed men and women in sex-typed job classes and assigned lower pay rates to women than men, regardless of the similarities of their work" (25–26). Regarding women who enter managerial jobs, Steinberg points out that these jobs are designed for privileged white men whose wives perform unpaid work in the home. And, despite all the attention paid to women in management, the overwhelming majority of women engaged in paid employment continue to work in nonmanagerial jobs. In another article on the evaluation of women's work, Steinberg points out that there has been a pervasive invisibility of skills historically associated with women's work. See her article, "Social Construction of Skill, Gender Power, and Comparable Worth," *Work and Occupations* 17, no. 4 (November 1990), 449–482. Steinberg points out that taken-for-granted formulations have advantaged men in the labor market, legitimizing and rationalizing the wage gap. Human relations and caretaking skills of women are undervalued and often not compensated.

For women in trade unions, see Philip S. Foner, *Women and the American Labor Movement* (New York: Free Press, 1982). Also, Anne Nelson, "Women in Unions," in *The American Woman 1987–1988*, edited by Sara E. Rix (New York: W. W. Norton, 1988), 232–238.

For women in the International Ladies' Garment Workers Union and the Amalgamated Clothing Workers Union, see Joan M. Jensen and Sue Davidson, *A Needle, a Bobbin, a Strike: Women Needleworkers in America* (Philadelphia, PA: Temple University Press, 1984).

On Jewish immigrant shopgirls, see Irving Howe, *World of Our Fathers* (New York: Simon and Schuster, 1976), 265–271. Howe points out that young immigrant Jewish women were faced with a dilemma. On the one hand, both American and Jewish expectations pointed in the direction of marriage and motherhood. On the other hand life was so hard that it was necessary for young women to find factory work with the hope that she would progress from shopgirl to housewife.

Nursing is an important field for professional women. An excellent study of the entire field of nursing can be found in Barbara Melosh, *The Physician's Hand: Work Culture and Conflict in American Nursing* (Philadelphia: Temple University Press, 1982). Also, see the article by Susanne Gordon, "Is There a Nurse in the House?" *The Nation*, February 13, 1995. For a discussion of various tasks and work process functions among nurses, see the article by Samuel B. Bacharach, Peter Bamberger, and Sharon C. Conley, "Work Processes, Role Conflict and Role Overload: The Case of Nurses and Engineers in the Public Sector," *Work and Occupations* 17, no. 2 (May 1990), 199–228. On the current nurse population in the United States, see the *Statistical Abstract of the United States* (Washington, DC: Bureau of the Census, 1995), Table 649, p. 411. On the current trend in nursing toward reunifying nursing tasks and enlarging the staffing of registered nurses and decreasing the auxiliaries, with its consequent enlarging and intensification of nursing work, see the article by Robert L. Brannon, "Professionalization and Work Intensification: Nursing in the Cost Containment Era," *Work and Occupations* 21, no. 2 (May 1994), 157–178. See Fred E. Katz, "Nurses," in *The Semi-Professions and Their Organizations*, edited by Amitai Etzioni (New York: Free Press, 1969), 54–78. Katz discusses whether nursing is a semi- or full profession, but as Trice points out, nursing has a body of knowledge, a code of ethics, and a set of professional skills and responsibilities, all of which are characteristic of a profession. On various aspects of nursing, see Harrison M. Trice, *Occupational Subcultures in the Workplace* (Ithaca, NY: ILR Press, 1993), 62–68, 97–98, 208–210.

On women in the clothing industry in the twentieth century, see Jensen and Davidson, *A Needle, a Bobbin, a Strike*. Also see Alice Kessler-Harris, "Organizing the Unorganizable: Three Jewish Women and Their Union," *Labor History* 17 (Winter, 1976). Also see Barbara Wertheimer, *We Were There: The Story of Working Women in America* (New York: Pantheon, 1977). On the difficult situation for women in the garment industry, see Helen I. Safa, "Runaway Shops and Female Employment: The Search for Cheap Labor," *Signs* 7, no. 2 (Winter 1981), 418–433. For a picture of Chinese women working in garment sweatshops in San Francisco, see Barbara Ehrenreich and Annette Fuentes, "Life on the Global Assembly Line," *Ms.*, January, 1981.

One of the important strike actions of women in the garment industry occurred at the Farah factory in Texas. See Laurie Coyle, Gail Hershatter, and Emily Honig, "Women at Farah: An Unfinished Story," in *A Needle, a Bobbin, a Strike*, edited by John M. Jensen and Sue Davidson (Philadelphia: Temple University Press, 1984), 227–277. Also on the Farah strike, see Philip S. Foner, *Women and the American Labor Movement*, 425–430. For a study of reactions to blue-collar work by women, see the article by Karyn A. Loscocco, "Reactions to Blue-Collar Work: A Comparison of Women and Men," *Work and Occupations* 17, no. 2 (May 1990), 152–177.

On women in blue-collar jobs, for the statistics by general category, see the *Statistical Abstract of the United States* (Washington, DC: Bureau of the Census, 1995), Table 649, p. 413. On women in the blue-collar trades, see Foner, *Women and the American Labor Movement*, 460–464, 466–475. See also Karyn A. Loscocco, "Reactions to Blue-Collar Work.

On the concentration of women in the pink-collar trades, see Louise Kapp Howe, *Pink Collar Workers: Inside the World of Women's Work* (New York: Free Press, 1977).

On women in the construction industry, see Jeffrey W. Riemer, *Hard Hats: The Work World of Construction Workers* (Beverly Hills, CA: Sage Publications, 1979), 81–100. On numbers of women in the present construction industry, see the *Statistical Abstract of the United States* (Washington, DC: Bureau of the Census, 1995), Table 649, p. 413.

For the situation of women who work in factories, see the article by Judith Buber Agassi, "Women Who Work in Factories," in *The World of the Blue Collar Workers*, edited by Irving Howe (New York: Quadrangle Books, 1972), 239–248. Agassi points out that women who enter blue-collar work enter a world defined by men and they are expected to conform to male-dominated norms that does not take into account women as mothers and wives. Agassi further points out that changing the norms of work life for working mothers may benefit them as well as our whole society, since it will benefit children and families. Agassi asks why the United States, which is the most advanced industrial nation, should be so backward in legislation and services for working mothers (245–247).

A full treatment of African-American Women in the Bell System is provided by Venus Green in her article, "Race and Technology: African American Women in the Bell System, 1945–1980," *Technology and Culture* 36, no. 2 (April 1995), S101–S172. Venus Green not only discusses the specifics of the experiences of African-American women in the Bell System, but also provides a detailed discussion of the race and gender aspects of African-American female employment. She also provides an extensive list of references to the literature on female work in the United States, along with references on work among male and female minorities.

On women and housework, two of the best sources are Juliet B. Schor, *The Overworked American*; and Ruth Schwartz Cowan, *More Work for Mother*. Also see Joseph H. Pleck, *Working Wives, Working Husbands* (Beverly Hills: Sage Publications, 1985). On the fact that women's hours of work tend to be longer than men's, see Arlie Hochschild, *The Second Shift: Working Parents and the Revolution at Home* (New York: Viking Penguin, 1989).

For a discussion on the adoption of new household technologies, see Siegfried Giedion, *Mechanization Takes Command* (New York: Oxford University Press, 1946); and Susan Strasser, *Never Done: A History of American Housework* (New York: Pantheon, 1982).

On the discussion as to whether women bring values into the workplace or whether the workplace determines women's work ethic, or both, see the article by Reba Rowe and William E. Snizek, "Gender Differences in Work Values," *Work and Occupations* 22, no. 2 (May 1995), 215–229.

For a picture of the conditions, problems, and attitudes of women in blue-collar jobs—in this case the auto industry—see Richard Feldman and Michael Betzold, *End of the Line: Autoworkers and the American Dream* (New York: Weidenfeld and Nicolson, 1988). See Chapter 2, "Dee Mueller"; Chapter 4, "Sherl Jackson and Debbie Lynn Listman"; Chapter 6, "Betty Foote." In these vignettes of women working on the auto assembly line, we find all of the issues facing female workers, both white and black, including sexual harassment, breaking into male-dominated jobs, having to deal with norms established by males, having to prove themselves, facing ambiguities of being assertive versus being accepted, and many others.

For a discussion of the female work ethic, see June Nash's book review of *Women at Work: How They're Reshaping America*, edited by Henry Myers (New York: Dow Jones Books, 1979); and Natalie J. Sokoloff, *Between Money and Love: The Dialectics of Women's Home and Market Work* (New York: Praeger, 1980). The review is in *Signs* 7, no. 2 (Winter 1981), 492–499.

On working women's attitudes toward work and labor unions, see Cynthia Costello, "Working Women's Consciousness: Traditional or Oppositional," in *To Toil the Livelong Day: America's Women at Work, 1780–1980*, edited by Carol Groneman and Mary Beth Norton (Ithaca, NY: Cornell University Press, 1987).

Work and Occupations 19, no. 4 (November 1992) devoted an entire issue to women in the workplace as it relates to sex segregation and gender stratification.

For a picture of waitressing work roles, see the article by Elaine J. Hall, "Smiling, Deferring, and Flirting: Doing Gender by giving 'Good Service,' " *Work and Occupations* 20, no. 4 (November 1993), 452–471. The author deals with both the organizational demands of the workplace along with the gendered role of the waitress as different from that of waiters. She also examines the interplay between customers and waitresses and the one-on-one interactions between waitresses and male and/or female customers. In all of these complex interrelationships gender is a crucial factor in examining how waitresses are expected to behave in order to render "good service" as part of their work tasks.

An excellent study of the relationships between the genders in the workplace is provided by Deborah Tannen, *Talking from Nine to Five* (New York: Simon and Schuster, 1994). Tannen is a linguist who studies language and the manner in which it is used habitually and ritually in the workplace to define various kinds of workplace behavior.

20

MINORITIES IN THE
TWENTIETH CENTURY

AFRICAN-AMERICANS

In 1910, 80 percent of African-Americans lived in mostly rural areas in twelve southern states. Stimulated by the pull of labor shortages during World War I, blacks migrated out of the South to the North. The building of northern urban black ghettos dates from this period. There was a pause in the migrations during the depression in the 1930s, but beginning in 1940 new and larger black migrations out of the South resumed. Between 1940 and 1970, more than four million African-Americans migrated from the South to the North. Blacks uprooted themselves from a southern, rural way of life and were cast into a northern, industrial, urban way of life. It was a traumatic social change and very difficult to adjust to. As blacks moved into the cities, whites moved to other neighborhoods and later to the suburbs, and blacks occupied the abandoned neighborhoods.

Moving North, African-Americans developed their own centers in New York, Chicago, Philadelphia, Detroit, Cleveland, St. Louis, Baltimore, and Washington, D.C. Steel, meat packing, auto manufacturing, shipbuilding, and mining were all major employers of African-Americans, though they were used in the most physically taxing, dirty, and unskilled jobs. By 1930 more blacks held blue-collar jobs than worked in agriculture. In most northern cities there was a small African-American middle class—lawyers, doctors, musicians, saloonkeepers, shopkeepers, newspaper publishers, and dressmakers. A new middle class emerged which provided services to the African-American community—ministers, newspapermen, hotel and drugstore owners, real estate and insurance agents, funeral directors, and others. African-Americans were able to create their own communities with a set of social, economic, and religious organizations that united their neighborhoods. In Harlem, African-Americans owned or managed 35 percent of the real estate in the area.

The African-American family in the early decades of the twentieth century was typically a two-parent household. Fathers headed more than four out of five black families in 1905 in New York City. As late as 1925, only 3 percent of black families in New York City were headed by a woman under twenty. The unwed, teenaged welfare mother emerged much later, after World War II.

In the 1950s, in the basic industries such as steel, auto, rubber, meat packing, and electrical equipment, jobs opened up for African-Americans. These were basic blue-collar jobs that provided good wages, job security, health and pension benefits, and vacations. They provided black men with a living wage and they permitted black families and black neighborhoods to sustain themselves and thrive. When these jobs began to disappear in the 1970s, all of the pathologies that struck the African-American communities began to appear—crime, drugs, family disintegration, and devastation of housing and communities.

With the passage of the Civil Rights Act of 1964, many of the symbols of discrimination—segregation of public facilities, denial of hotel accommodations, separate seating on public transportation, and so forth—were gone within a decade. There was optimism that the nation was moving toward greater opportunities for all groups. With the beginning of a long cycle of stagnation in economic growth, and depression of real wages in the 1970s and 1980s, the optimism of the sixties disappeared. Unemployment hit all workers during the early Reagan years and the depression of the Bush years, in the early 1990s. It struck the blacks harder as their unemployment rate was more than twice that for whites. Black teenager unemployment reached an alarming 30 to 40 percent. Blacks and whites shared concerns about crime, poor housing, drug addiction, inferior education, and above all else, about finding work that paid a decent wage and provided opportunities for a career. What the country needed was a government policy that together with private industry would have provided a plan to put the country and the poor back to work. Governments were strapped for funds in the 1990s, and being unable to balance their budgets, had no money to spend on public works or programs to educate and train workers and help them find jobs.

The African-American underclass endures because of the disappearance since 1970 of hundreds of thousands of blue-collar jobs, mainly those involving manual labor, jobs that were held by many blacks. All the other pathologies of the ghetto—soaring rates of welfare dependence, illegitimate births, teenage pregnancy, crime, and so on—are to a large degree outgrowths of the fundamental problem of no work. Rates of joblessness, out-of-wedlock births, female-headed families, welfare dependence, and serious crime were significantly lower in the 1950s and 1960s than they are today, and did not begin to rise rapidly until the 1970s when many of the blue-collar and laboring but decent-paying jobs held by blacks were wiped out.

Getting work remains a central theme among African-Americans. Black unemployment declined from a peak of 19.5 percent in 1983 to 10.4 percent in 1990, but was still twice the rate of whites. In 1994, African-Americans made up nearly 9 percent of the work force, but constituted 20 percent of the unemployed. The problem of unemployment is likely to get worse for African-Americans since many of them are in occupations that are projected to decline in the next ten years. Blacks have relatively more jobs in government than in private industry because it is more difficult to carry out discriminatory policies in government offices where actions are subject to public review. Now, with the assault on "big government" many of those jobs will be phased out. Similarly, jobs with low skill and little education requirements will also be reduced in the future, and many African-Americans occupy those positions.

In a significant article in the *New York Times Magazine* of August 18, 1996, William Julius Wilson points out that work, not welfare, is the key issue for blacks in the cities, and that if the issue is not addressed in the immediate future it will have harmful consequences for the quality of life in the cities and eventually, for the lives of all Americans. Wilson points out that work is not simply a way to make a living and support one's family. It is also a framework for daily behavior because it imposes discipline. The work ethic is something that affects all other values regarding individual responsibility, family, attitudes toward community, and individual self-esteem. Wilson describes what happened to the community of North Lawndale in Chicago (28–29). Wilson spells out a four-point program to address the issue of work among blacks: (1) Targeting education to raise the performance standards of all public schools, including those in the inner city, enlisting the support of corporations, local businesses, civil clubs, community centers, and churches, would provide students with the proper training to enter the workplace. (2) Wilson calls for a national system of child care that includes quality nursery schools, paid leave for parents of newborns, children's allowances, and a system of health care for all children. (3) Setting up information and placement centers in various parts of the inner city to provide information and to refer workers to employers. These centers would recruit inner-city workers and try to place them in jobs. They would also help to make persons who have been persistently unemployed or out of the labor force to be "job ready." (4) A new Work Progress Administration (WPA)—public works would put able-bodied people on welfare or unemployed people to work. There is much work that can be done such as building playgrounds and athletic fields, constructing parks, clean-up, slum clearance, and housing, enough work to put all those who want to work in jobs earning money. All of these programs are feasible and can be put into effect immediately if the will of the public and the politicians can be rallied.

A number of studies have attempted to analyze the disadvantages of black men and women in the labor market. One such study singled out the growth of "soft" or social skills as a factor in the racial gap in labor market outcomes. For three decades, the 1940s, 1950s, and 1960s, the gap in earnings of black and white workers was narrowing. Then, starting in the 1970s, there was a growing gap in male employment rates between whites and blacks as well as in earnings. In a study done by Philip Moss and Chris Tilly (1996), the authors found that due to competitive pressure, employers are demanding more soft skills, even in low-skill jobs. Soft skills include interaction and motivation on the job. Many managers perceive African-American men as possessing fewer soft skills than whites. Their perceptions are based on black employees and applicants, as well as media images of young blacks and cultural differences between employers and young black men. The authors suggest several remedies of the situation, including school-to-work training programs, efforts by minority contractors and public and private efforts to train black applicants for jobs rather than screening them out of jobs. (270–272).

Another study of African-American men explored the question as to why there continues to be such a large ratio between white and black unemployment, with blacks consistently showing an unemployment rate twice that of whites. Franklin D. Wilson, Marta Tienda, and Lawrence Wu (1995) found that relative high unemployment and joblessness among black men derives from residential segregation, employment in occupations subject to high turnover, and labor market discrimination. The persisting black/white unemployment ratio, even during good times, attests to the persistence of exclusionary barriers in labor markets. For inner-city blacks the problem is even worse, for employers tend to view them as uneducated, uncooperative, unstable, dishonest, and lacking motivation. Black employment is now threatened even further by the fact that a large part of their employment gains since the 1960s has resulted from increased access to public-sector employment and now there is a strong movement to reduce government employment, especially affirmative action and community and service programs that provided blacks with many jobs. Location can also be a factor in higher rates of unemployment among blacks. The relative odds of unemployment for black men who reside in the North, East, and West regions and who live in a central city or both are substantially higher than for blacks living in the South and noncentral cities or both. Residence in the central cities in the non-South raises unemployment for both blacks and whites by approximately the same level. This suggests that it is not race only that matters, but also whether one resides in a location with diminishing employment opportunities. Contractions in the absolute number of well-paying blue-collar jobs, coupled with uncertainties surrounding white-collar employment produced by corporate mergers, acquisitions, shut-downs, and downsizing to increase profitability, may once again increase the significance of race in allocating individuals to labor market positions because of intensified competition for fewer positions. The strong race gap in the relative odds of involuntary unemployment because of dismissals and layoffs point to the continuing role of discrimination in affecting the labor market outcomes of blacks.

The work ethic for low-income African-Americans is a survival ethic. It is a struggle for jobs in the first place, and for jobs that pay a decent wage. While many white workers have decent-paying jobs and can begin to think of the higher order of needs in the workplace, such as job satisfaction, autonomy, meaningful work, decision making, and so on, for many African-Americans the work ethic is the instrumental one of earning enough for subsistence and for raising the standard of living of one's family. For many African-Americans on welfare, the work ethic is also a goal, one presently shared with the new Welfare Bill just passed by Congress. But while Congress insists that welfare recipients must get off welfare and go to work, the government and private industry have failed in its obligation to provide the training and jobs so people on welfare can get off the system. The *New York Times* (1995) has spelled out how difficult it will be to get welfare recipients into the job market. They are plagued with the fact that many are not prepared for work with respect to getting to work on time, staying on the job, taking instructions from superiors, knowing how to read or do arithmetic, and so forth. Then there are those on alcohol and drugs who are totally unprepared for work. This includes both whites, who make up the majority on the welfare rolls, as well as blacks. President Clinton and others have declared the obvious fact that if welfare recipients have an obligation to society to work, then society has an equal obligation to make jobs available so they can go to work. Programs for needed training and even New Deal-type public works programs are required if the goal of turning welfare into work is going to succeed.

For the black underclass, the question of the work ethic is more serious. Many African-American youths, as well as adults, have been enmeshed in the underground economy involving drug traffic, petty crime, numbers, hustling, street vending, and other marginal forms of earning money. For these citizens the work ethic has little meaning. The promise of education and training to prepare for jobs in the mainstream is not a possibility for them. A number of programs run mainly by African-Americans have tried to reach out to gangs, to black youth, and to the underclass. Some of them have been assisted by city programs utilizing the efforts of the police, local community leaders, and black youths themselves. These programs need help and funding from the larger community and from governments at all levels. However, with Congress declaring war on the poor rather than war on poverty, the future for these programs is very much in doubt. If such programs are not forthcoming and if the underclass continues to grow, then the white majority can look forward to further disruptions, sabotage of order in white society, and a large population dedicated to destroying the social peace à la the 1960s.

For middle-class African-Americans, their work ethic is quite similar to that of white America. They seek opportunities for advancement in jobs and occupations, upward mobility in the social order, responsibility and autonomy in their workplace, and fulfillment of the higher order of work needs beyond the instrumentality of wages and salary. The work ethic of middle class African-Americans serves as a model for the other African-Americans. This is reflected in TV programs featuring African-Americans, in the advertising media directed toward African-Americans, and in the speeches and ideology of African-American political leaders in Congress and in local and state governments, as well as in the writings of many African-American intellectuals.

Race alone is not the only reason why blacks are still disadvantaged. American society as a whole has become stagnant with regard to economic opportunity that provides decent jobs with decent wages and benefits. Jobs are being created, but they are mostly low-wage, no future jobs with the exception of that small minority of 20 to 25 percent who have the best occupations in U.S. society and account for most of its wealth and income. Many Americans, white and black, feel cut off from economic opportunity and mourn the passing of traditional values that promoted the idea that hard work, individual responsibility, and dedication to community and family would result in the good life for themselves and their families.

Racism still exists and substantial inequalities, especially in economic life, persist, while the problems of the underclass are overwhelming. African-Americans will never again accept the systematic denial of their basic rights, nor will they accept the notion of knowing their place and not making waves. The belief in a right to dignity and fair treatment is now so widespread and deeply rooted, so self-evident that people of all colors would vigorously resist any effort to reinstate formalized discrimination. This consensus is a legacy of the civil rights movement of the 1960s and one that has brought about a radical transformation in the relations between whites and blacks.

Today, African-American leaders operate with a more sophisticated understanding of social causation and racial change. Race and racism are not the only structural realities that constrain the group position of African-Americans. The economy, the labor market, the distribution of jobs and opportunities by region and urban location are also critical. Given these structural imbalances, the black community cannot by itself create enough jobs to ensure economic survival and stable family life. Government and private industry must be persuaded to reallocate economic resources.

HISPANICS AND THEIR WORK ETHIC

Hispanics now constitute the second largest minority in the United States, comprising some 26 million persons as of 1995. Hispanics have a younger population than other groups in the United States, therefore their work ethic tends to reflect this factor, as the work ethic tends to be weakest among the young as compared to older adults. Language is also an issue for Hispanics, as mastering English is almost a necessity for Hispanics who wish to seek better-paying jobs or who wish to educate themselves in order to compete for entry into management and professional occupations. On the other hand, Hispanics bring with them strong family traditions and the cultural mores that stress the male as the main breadwinner and as head of the family, thus lowering the female participation rate in the labor force among Hispanic women.

Like the African-American work ethic, other than the 25 percent of African-Americans in the middle class, the Hispanic work ethic is a survival ethic, one that accepts whatever work is available to earn subsistence, without worrying about the higher needs in the workplace. There is a Hispanic professional and middle class, just as there is a black professional and middle class, where more education and higher income have permitted a more selective choice of occupations, and a work ethic that seeks satisfaction from work beyond the mere instrumental motivation of earning money for subsistence. The Hispanic middle class is still small, though it is growing, especially among the Cubans, and in certain areas of the United States where there are Latin-owned businesses such as restaurants, fruit stands, clothing stores, and mom-and-pop stores. Hispanic influence in these areas is reflected by the fact that whereas a few years ago signs would read "We Speak Spanish," they now read "We speak English."

Mexican-Americans

In 1993 there were 14,628,000 Mexican-Americans in the United States, with 6,499,000 in the labor force. There could be an additional 2 million illegal aliens from Mexico living in the United States. In 1994, the Census Bureau had a total of 26 million Hispanics in the United States, with Mexican-Americans making up more than 60 percent.

In the post–World War II years, Mexican-American workers made up the vast majority of California's agricultural workforce. Led by Cesar Chavez, a charismatic organizer, California farm workers struck the Delano vineyards early in 1965. The United Farm Workers union, built and led by Chavez, held out for five years. Chavez won a large national following and launched a national boycott against California grape growers, winning solid backing from the Catholic Church and the United Automobile Workers. The United Farm Workers won formal recognition from many growers and became an important political force in the Southwest.

Mexican-Americans were predominantly rural for many years, but have now become more urbanized than the American population as a whole. By 1970, Mexican-Americans were 85 percent urban. The outdoor manual labor of early Mexican immigrants as farm or railroad workers has given way to urban occupations. Compared to other groups emerging from an agricultural past and with no tradition of education, Mexican-Americans have more than held their own. In 1993, 11 percent of Mexican-Americans were managers and professionals, 42 percent were in white-collar occupations, 38 percent were in blue-collar jobs, and 8 percent were in farming, forestry, and fishing. Mexican-Americans have come a long way from their rural backgrounds in adapting to modern, urban America.

Puerto Ricans

By 1970, the Puerto Rican population of the United States was 1.5 million and in 1990 it was 2,738,000. The largest Puerto Rican population is in New York City, while the Northeast as a whole contains 68.6 percent of Puerto Ricans in the United States.

While fewer Puerto Rican men are in the labor force (70.2 percent) than whites (79.4 percent) and only slightly fewer than blacks (73.9 percent), few Puerto Rican women are in the labor force compared to white or black women. This might be cultural, the result of family values, or it might be due to the large numbers of small children in Puerto Rican families that keep their mothers out of the job market.

The Puerto Rican population in the United States remains one of the youngest of all ethnic groups. Puerto Ricans who are working have less experience than other working adults. They also have less education and are heavily represented among recipients of a vocational high school education. While Puerto Ricans are still behind whites in income, most Puerto Rican adults in the continental United States today are still the first generation. Given this fact, few groups in American history could claim more progress than the Puerto Ricans in as short a span of time in this country.

CHINESE-AMERICANS

Many Chinese came to the United States as contract laborers or with money borrowed from Chinese-American organizations that assumed a supervisory role over them in the United States. The Chinese, though physically smaller than Americans, were hard workers in agriculture, railroad building, and other taxing manual labor. They worked cheaply and lived frugally, saving money out of what was considered a pittance by American standards. These very virtues, however, made the Chinese feared and hated as competitors for jobs by white workers. By 1870, there were 63,000 Chinese in the United States, almost all on the West Coast. Most Chinese still live on the West Coast and in the West, more than 52 percent.

The Chinese were tolerated in occupations urgently needed but that white men were reluctant to fill—cooks and laundrymen in mining camps or as domestic servants in cities. Early Chinese-Americans were also agricultural field laborers, working long hours for low pay. By the mid-1880s, Chinese made up more than half the farm labor in California. With the passage of time, the Chinese either left or were driven out of mining camps, agricultural field labor, and even railroad gangs. They typically settled in cities in California and some dispersed eastward. For several decades their principal occupation was as laundrymen or working in or operating Chinese restaurants. As late as 1920, more than half of all employed Chinese in the United States worked either in laundries or restaurants. Laundries were more numerous than restaurants because laundries required little capital to start and required less knowledge of English to conduct. Though restricted to two main kinds of work, Chinese-Americans succeeded so that the Chinese hand laundry became an American institution, as did Chinese restaurants.

With the passage of years, the few Chinese women in the United States produced a small second generation of children and these children slightly eased the sex imbalance that remained up through World War II. Modification of the immigration laws in 1930 permitted some small numbers of wives from China to join their husbands. The repeal of the Chinese Exclusion Act of 1882 in 1943 and new legislation in 1945 helped ease the sex imbalance and permitted more normal family life to develop among Chinese-Americans. The bulk of the new Chinese immigration was female and concentrated among young people of marriageable years.

Isolated Chinese-Americans, especially of the younger generation who were American born and therefore citizens, were sent to college and became professionals. These pioneers provided examples and arguments against stereotyping. As of 1940, only 3 percent of Chinese-Americans in California were in the professions, while 8 percent of whites were. By 1950, the Chinese percentage was 6 percent and by 1960, it was 18 percent, passing that of the whites who were at 15 percent. Much of their initial economic rise was not in professions in the larger society but in businesses in Chinatown. Lack of access to banks and other financial institutions in the larger society could not prevent Chinese-American businesses from being established in Chinatowns, where they pooled their resources and set up rotating credit associations. The labor shortages of World War II opened up many new job opportunities for the Chinese-Americans, as it did for African-Americans and other ethnic groups. Their diligent work habits proved to be a decisive advantage in the labor market once the discriminatory barriers came down. By 1960, there were fewer Chinese-Americans in manual occupations than in the professions and in business.

Chinese-Americans today have higher incomes than average Americans and higher occupational status. One-fourth of all employed Chinese-Americans are working in scientific and professional fields. They have risen to this position despite some of the harshest discrimination and violence faced by any immigrants to the United States. When confined to certain occupations they succeeded in those occupations and when opportunity later opened for them they spread out to other areas. Much of Chinese-American prosperity is due to the simple fact that they work harder and have more education than others. Asian academics, scientists, and engineers typically have significantly higher qualifications than either blacks or whites, that is, a higher percentage have Ph.D.s and have their degrees from the higher ranked universities. They also publish more, relatively, than either blacks or whites.

While Chinese-Americans as a group are prosperous and well educated, China-towns have pockets of poverty and illiteracy. This is due to sharp internal differences in length of time in this country. Descendants of the Chinese-Americans who immigrated a long time ago have maintained Chinese values and have acculturated to American society with remarkable success. More recent Hong Kong Chinese are from more diverse cultural origins and acquired Western values and styles in Hong Kong without having acquired the skills to prosper in the American economy. Foreign-born Chinese men in the United States earn incomes one-fourth lower than native-born Chinese-American men with the same education. While the older Hong Kong Chinese work hard to sustain and advance themselves, Hong Kong Chinese youths often react with resentment and antisocial behavior. There are also large numbers of Chinese men and women being recruited to work in garment sweat-shops in New York City and San Francisco. Many of these shops are owned by Chinese-Americans, and Chinese networks to the mainland are used to recruit illegal immigrants under the most brutal forms of exploitation.

Families remain strong among Chinese-Americans. Almost 90 percent of all Chinese-American families have both husband and wife present. Nearly 80 percent of Chinese-American males in their mid-thirties to mid-forties are married and living with their wives. In contrast to the high rates of intermarriage during the era of great sex imbalance, 87 percent of Chinese men today are married to Chinese women. Less than 10 percent of Chinese-Americans are divorced. As a group, Chinese-Americans have integrated into American society occupationally, while retaining their own values and ethnic identity. It has been no small achievement against great odds.

JAPANESE-AMERICANS

The history of Japanese-Americans is a story of tragedy and triumph. Few people came to America predisposed to be good Americans and few met such repeated rebuffs and barriers, including the barrier of internment camps that Japanese-

Americans were able to overcome and achieve broad success socially, economically, and politically.

The Japanese were initially welcomed in Hawaii and in the United States. They were a preselected group of healthy young men of good reputation and they made excellent workers in the hard labor of Hawaiian sugarcane plantations. On the mainland about 40 percent began as agricultural laborers, while the rest worked at strenuous laboring tasks on railroads and in mines, lumber mills, canneries, meat-packing plants and at similar arduous occupations. In these occupations, the Japanese accepted low pay, long hours, and difficult working conditions. The Japanese migrants were marvels of thrift as well as industry, saving small amounts from wages that were low by American standards, but high by the standards of Japan. With thrift and industry, many Japanese moved up from the ranks of labor to that of businessmen and farmers.

A majority of employed Japanese males were farmers as late as 1940. By 1940, about a third of all commercial truck crops grown in California were produced by Japanese-Americans. In addition to their success in agriculture, Japanese-Americans became celebrated in California for their skillful work in the related field of contract gardening. The Japanese gardener became an institution among white middle-class homeowners, whose lawns and yards he tended on weekly visits. It was a small business that required little capital and yet offered independence for the Japanese gardener. As early as 1928, there were 1,300 Japanese gardeners in southern California alone. Another offshoot of Japanese-American success in agriculture was the Japanese produce market dealing with the output of Japanese farms. The Japanese also moved into other ventures not connected with the soil. By 1919, almost half of the hotels and one quarter of the grocery stores in Seattle were owned by Japanese. In Los Angeles they owned dry cleaners, lunch counters, and fisheries, as well as cheap hotels. Many of the Japanese-American enterprises went far beyond what could be supported by the ethnic community alone. Like Chinese-Americans, Japanese-Americans made use of revolving credit associations to pool funds to finance new businesses. The principal occupations of more than 90 percent of the issei immigrants were in farming, business, and blue-collar work. Professional and clerical workers were only 10 percent of the issei. In short, the initial economic rise of Japanese-Americans was not due to education nor was it in occupations requiring education. After the issei had achieved a measure of economic success they were able to send their children—the nisei—on to higher education and from there into the professions and other occupations requiring formal training.

Japanese families were extremely stable. Very few divorces ever occurred. The children were strictly controlled. Their well-being was paramount to the parents who often sacrificed greatly for their children's future. Japanese children in the public schools were notable for their obedience, politeness, and hard work and were welcomed by their teachers. Japanese-American communities were noted for their lack of crime, juvenile delinquency, or other forms of social pathology. The rare individual who continued to defy community norms could find himself shipped back to Japan rather than being allowed to tarnish the image of Japanese-Americans in the larger society. Unbridled individualism was not part of the Japanese system of values that stressed the well-being of the community over that of the individual.

On December 7, 1941, Japan launched a massive surprise attack on Pearl Harbor, Hawaii, and inflicted devastating damage to the American fleet stationed there. It propelled the United States into World War II and set in motion American anger against Japan and Japanese-Americans. In February, 1942, at the urging of the military commanders on the West Coast, who argued that the Japanese constituted a danger to the security of the country, President Roosevelt signed Executive Order 9066. It gave the army the power, without warrants, indictments, or hearings, to arrest every Japanese-American on the West Coast—110,000 men, women, and children—and to take them from their homes and transport them to ten detention camps in the interior regions of the West and keep them there in prison camps. In 1944, the Supreme Court upheld the forced evacuation on grounds of military necessity. The move was supported by nativists and racists in California, who had long resented successful Japanese merchants, fishermen, and fruit and vegetable farmers. Set in isolated, barren locations, surrounded by barbed wire and armed guards, inmates lived in overcrowded barracks, barely divided into one-room enclosures and furnished only with cots, blankets, and bare light bulbs.

The impact on Japanese-Americans was devastating. There were forced, hasty sales of homes, furniture, and other belongings before Japanese-Americans were shipped off to internment. Businesses built over a lifetime of hard work had to be liquidated in a few weeks. The loss per family was estimated at $10,000. The total loss was estimated at $400,000,000 at 1942 price levels. Added to the financial losses were the many personal tragedies of forced uprooting and internment.

In January, 1943, the U.S. Army began to recruit nisei. Despite the anomaly of the situation and the bitterness of interned Japanese youth, most of those eligible seized the opportunity to prove their loyalty in combat. More than 300,000 Japanese-Americans fought in World War II. Separate Japanese-American units fought in the European theater and were sent into some of the bloodiest fighting of the war in 1943. The all–Japanese-American 442nd Regimental Combat Unit emerged as the most decorated American combat unit of World War II.

In the postwar period, the nisei advanced rapidly as a result of their education and the lifting of occupational restrictions. As early as 1940, Japanese-Americans had more education than whites, and the gap widened over the next decade. The college degrees of Japanese-Americans were mostly in engineering, the sciences, and business administration. By 1969, the average personal income of Japanese-Americans was 11 percent above the national average and average family income was 32 percent above the national average.

In 1990, there were 848,000 Japanese-Americans in the United States. About a third live in Hawaii and another third live in California. Although they began in the United States as agricultural laborers and tenant farmers, 90 percent of Japanese-Americans today live in urban areas. The high income of Japanese-Americans is a remarkable achievement for a group that had to face decades of discriminatory laws and practices. Furthermore, they had to start all over again after losing virtually everything during their internment in World War II. The economic achievements of

Japanese-Americans today are due primarily to their strong work ethic and to their higher than average levels of education. Historically, the Japanese-Americans' rise came in occupations requiring little or no education—farming, contract gardening, small-business ownership—and only after the issei had succeeded in these fields were they able to send the nisei off to college to pursue professional careers.

CONCLUSION

The history of American ethnic and minority groups is ultimately the history of the American people, that is, it is the history of a complex aggregate of diverse groups and individuals. It is not a morality play based on the notion that one group is any better or worse than another. The history and work patterns of ethnic and minority groups is a story of similar patterns and profound differences, of much pain and adversity, and of great pride and achievement. America is the story of many heritages, but above all else it is the story of an undaunted spirit and belief in progress that has resulted in amazing advances in human culture.

BIBLIOGRAPHICAL ESSAY

For a historical survey of African-Americans in the workplace and in society in general, see Philip S. Foner, *Organized Labor and the Black Worker, 1619–1974* (New York: Praeger Publishers, 1974). On African-American workers, see Philip S. Foner and Ronald L. Lewis, eds., *Black Workers: A Documentary History from Colonial Times to the Present* (Philadelphia: Temple University Press, 1989). For the twentieth century, see Sections 5, 6, 7, and 8. A number of facts in this chapter are from Thomas Sowell, *Ethnic America: A History* (New York: Basic Books, 1981). For a detailed view of black history on the basis of its sources, see Herbert Aptheker, *Documentary History of African-Americans*, 7 vols., various dates (Secaucus, NY: Citadel Press). Also see Milton Cantor, *Black Labor in America* (Westport, CT: Negro Universities Press, 1969).

On the movement out of the South during World War I, see W. T. B. Williams, "Negro Migration in 1916–1917," in *Black Workers*, edited by Philip S. Foner and Ronald L. Lewis, 304–323.

On Booker T. Washington's statement about blacks in the South always being able to find work and their shock in finding the opposite in the North, see Booker T. Washington, "The Negro and the Labor Unions," in Foner and Lewis, eds., *Black Workers*, 285–286. On the changing status of blacks as they moved North, see James Weldon Johnson, "The Changing Status of Negro Labor," in Foner and Lewis, eds. *Black Workers*, 352–353. In that report, Johnson states: "Heretofore the Negro has had two choices—that of living in the South where most of his manhood and civil rights were denied him, but where economically his condition was secure; or that of living in the North where his rights were guaranteed him, but where his economic conditions was always precarious" (353).

On the use of blacks as strikebreakers and the use of divide-and-conquer policies of management with regard to white and black workers, see David M. Gordon, Richard Edwards, and Michael Reich, *Segmented Work, Divided Workers: The Historical Transformation of Labor in the United States* (Cambridge: Cambridge University Press, 1982), 152–153.

For a discussion of jobs available to blacks after they moved North during the great migration of World War I and afterward, see Joshua Freeman et al., *Who Built America: Working People and the Nation's Economy, Politics, Culture and Society.* Vol. 2 (New York: Pantheon Books, 1992), 241–243, 301–302.

Thomas Sowell discusses the African-American family and education among blacks in the early part of the twentieth century in his book, *Ethnic America: A History* (New York: Basic Books, 1981), 213–215. For a history of the black family in the early decades of the twentieth century, see Herbert Gutman, *The Black Family in Slavery and Freedom, 1750–1925* (New York: Vintage Books, 1977). On black workers during the 1930s, see Freeman et al., *Who Built America,* 305–306, 405–410; also Foner and Lewis, eds., *Black Workers,* 385–386, 459–461.

For black's in labor unions, see Robert H. Zeiger, *American Workers, American Unions, 1920-1985* (Baltimore, MD: Johns Hopkins University Press, 1986), 4–5, 51–53, 67, 75, 80–83, 98, 123, 133, 143–145, 170–182. On blacks in labor unions, also see Foner and Lewis, eds., *Black Workers,* 507–523. For a discussion of blacks on the welfare roles and the economic background to the rise of welfare among African-Americans, see Gordon, Edwards, and Reich, *Segmented Work, Divided Workers,* 208–209.

Tom Wicker, journalist for the *New York Times,* discusses the affirmative action program and the need for it to redress past discrimination against blacks. See "Reverse Discrimination," *New York Times,* July 2, 1979.

The William Julius Wilson article, "Work," is from the *New York Times Magazine,* August 18, 1996, 26–30, 40, 48, 52–54.

For figures on the numbers of minorities in the United States, see the *Statistical Abstract of the United States* (Washington, DC: Bureau of the Census, 1995), Tables 22 and 23, pp. 22, 24. For projections of population growth into the twenty-first century, see Table 25, p. 26.

On occupational inequality, see William Issel, *Social Change in the United States, 1945–1983* (New York: Schocken Books, 1987), 153–190. Also see Richard H. Hall, *Sociology of Work* (Thousand Oaks, CA: Pine Forge Press, 1994), 253–272. Also see, Eleanor Holmes Norton, "Minority Workers of Tomorrow," in *Work in the 21st Century: The American Society for Personnel Administration* (New York: Hippocrene Books, 1984), 65–76.

The Philip Moss and Chris Tilly reference is to a study on soft skills and its effcts on black men's employment problems, "Soft Skills and Race," *Work and Occupations* 23, no. 3 (August 1996), 252–276.

For the reference to Franklin D. Wilson, Marta Tienda, and Lawrence Wu, see "Race and Unemployment: Labor Market Experiences of Black and White Men, 1968–1988," *Work and Occupations* 22, no. 3 (August 1995), 245–270.

The *New York Times* (1995) reference is to the article "Up From Welfare: It's Harder and Harder," April 16, 1995, 4.

For statistics on Hispanic-Americans, see in the *Statistical Abstract of the United States* (Washington, DC: Bureau of the Census, 1995) the following: Table 53, p. 51, "Social and Economic Characteristics of the Hispanic Population, 1993"; Table 649, p. 411, "Employed Civilians, by Occupation, Sex, Race and Hispanic Origin, 1983 and 1994"; Table 663, p. 422, "Unemployed and Unemployment Rates, by Education Attainment, Sex, Race and Hispanic Origin: 1992 to 1994"; Table 1121, p. 682 for Hispanic farm workers; Table 653, p. 416 for Hispanic employment by industry, "Employment by Industry, 1970 to 1994."

For the history of Mexican-Americans and Puerto Ricans in the United States, along with their social and economic fortunes and their participation in the workforce, see Thomas

Sowell, *Ethnic America*, 227–272. Also see William Issel, *Social Change*, 153–170.

On the exploitation of illegal Mexican immigrants and their employment as farm workers, see Freeman et al., *Who Built America*, 514–517, 564–565; also see Richard Edwards, *Contested Terrain* (New York: Basic Books, 1979), 187–188. On the growth of the Hispanic middle-class, see Freeman et al., *Who Builit America*, 644.

For a history of Chinese-Americans and Japanese-Americans, see Thomas Sowell, *Ethnic America*, 133–182. On the employment of Chinese for the building of western railroads, see John Hoyt Williams, *A Great and Shining Road: The Epic Story of the Transcontinental Railroad* (New York: Times Books, 1988), 93–100, 113–118, 159–187, 203–238.

For a description of the hardships experienced by Japanese-Americans and their struggles against the injustices inflicted upon them by the U.S. government, see Michi Weglyn, *Years of Infamy: The Untold Story of America's Concentration Camps* (New York: William Morrow, 1976).

For statistics on Asian-Americans and Pacific Islanders by population and distribution by region, see, *Statistical Abstract of the United States* (Washington, DC: Bureau of the Census, 1995), Table 31, p. 31, "Resident Population by Region, Race and Hispanic Origin, 1990." On educational attainment by Asian-Americans, see Table 238, p. 157, "Educational Attainment by Race and Ethnicity, 1960 to 1994." On income of Asian-Americans, see Table 729, p. 472, "Money Income of Households—Percent Distribution by Income Level, Race, and Hispanic Origin, 1993."

21

CONCLUSION

It is both logical and fitting that this book conclude with an evaluation of the American work ethic as we face the future in the twenty-first century. The work ethic will be a significant element in changes that will occur, though what these changes will be and how Americans will react to them cannot be predicted. There are dim outlines of what the changes will be, given the trends in information technology, but how quickly the new technology will be implemented and how corporations, the work force, and the government will adapt to the changes is uncertain. The press and the politicians speak glibly about the work ethic, but as indicated throughout this book there is no one work ethic. The work ethic is multidimensional, a dynamic concept that changes over time and that varies according to occupation, management ideology, ethnic perspective, class position, and level of income.

When we talk about the work ethic we talk about life. Ask what the purpose of work is about and we ask what life is about since the two are intertwined. Not that work is everything there is to life. But it is central to the quality of life and affects significantly our nonwork activities and life's possibilities. If leisure is defined as all human activities not associated with earning a living, then leisure and work are interactive, mutually compensating, and reciprocally reinforcing.

One problem regarding the work ethic is that those in charge of enterprises and institutions that put people to work are often people who have never been part of the work process. They are mostly financial experts, business school graduates, and number crunchers. Usually, they are not even engineers or scientists. They care not about nor do they know how things are made, how work is performed, who works, and why they work. Corporate executives are mainly, even exclusively, concerned with the bottom line, that is how much profit is made each year, since that is what affects their stock and their position in the stock market. All the current talk about improving the workplace, about making work more meaningful to workers, and about improving the work ethic must confront the constraint of the bottom line. Those who crunch the numbers and who largely are responsible for job market recruitment are removed from the reality of work for most Americans and are not likely to provide the leadership required to humanize the workplace of the future. If this is not a viable goal for American culture then it could be that in the future we will simply accept that work is a burden to be suffered for eight hours a day, and that real life begins when work ends.

Work involves people in an objective process that leads to concrete products and concrete services. It cannot be effective if it does not take account of concrete reality. Work does not lie. It results in a real product or service. If the United States, or any other culture, is going to examine its own reality, it must confront the nature of work and the current work ethic. Not that one work ethic fits all people. But we had better get a handle on what motivates people to work productively if we are to preserve our past achievements in creating a culture of material abundance.

Work is an activity that leads to change. The materials of our physical environment are acquired with the use of tools or machines, and they are transformed into products that are useful to human beings. They are more than useful. They are survival goods that feed, clothe, and house human beings who must both interact with and be protected from nature. Work is physical effort, along with motion, hand-and-eye coordination, and mental concentration. It is both individual and collective. Work is a means to an end, but it can be satisfying and an end in itself. There is the work of physical effort and the work of knowledge. Nay more. Without knowledge there is no work, for technical knowledge in society is the precondition for knowing how to proceed with work and what to work on. There is also the work of truth discovery, directed toward inquiry into humans and nature.

There is also the work dedicated to maintaining the social order. This involves the work of governing, teaching, policing, and the work of preserving institutions such as religion, the family, and the community. Thus, we can conclude that work is conducted on three levels: First, and perhaps most important because it creates the necessities of life, there is manual, physical work that leads to products and goods. Second, there is the work of maintaining the social order that gives us our government, education, the family, and health. And finally, there is the pure work of the mind that leads to the discovery of truth and the works of art, literature, music, and science.

A strong work ethic is an integral part of past American history. For the Puritans who migrated to New England, for the craftsmen, farmers, and laborers who helped in the struggle for independence, for the adventurous folk who settled the West, for the small and large entrepreneurs that founded small and large businesses, for the millions of citizens and immigrants who built the infrastructure and industrial base of the county, hard work was the ticket to survival and success. Most worked because they had to, but many others worked harder and longer than was necessary to provide themselves and their families with a comfortable life. For many Americans hard work took on a value and a worth of its own, separate from the role of providing income. They created a work ethic based on the belief that work is virtuous and fulfilling and that it provides self-esteem for the worker no matter what the nature of his or her work.

The work ethic can take on different meanings depending on whose work ethic is being viewed. The work ethic can be seen as value in work achieved by workers themselves, often unspoken, such as the craftsman's ethic of workmanship, or the factory worker's pride in being part of a collective making steel or automobiles. But the work ethic can be an ideological tool in the hands of proprietors who need workers to show up for work and work hard. The entrepreneur who owned his own business or enterprise can believe in hard work, thrift, and industry as the path to wealth, prestige, and self-esteem. But what motivation could the factory worker, the unskilled poor, the common laborer, have for working hard? It would not lead to wealth, prestige, and self-esteem if his or her wages were so low it would barely cover subsistence goods. Thus, the work ethic is complicated by ideological differences in motivation between those who must work and those who put others to work so they can reap profits. In the final analysis work is a necessity because without it one cannot subsist.

In the modern era, since the 1930s, the idea of the social safety net took hold in the United States. In the past society took no responsibility for anyone who could not find work or was unable to work for one reason or another. Today, the obligation to work is still a dominant ideology, as evidence by the passage of the Welfare Reform Bill of 1996. What is not yet dominant is the reciprocal obligation of society to provide jobs for all who wish to work. Such an obligation can only be undertaken by the joint efforts of private corporations and government since they are the main employers of labor in the workplace.

Michael Maccoby (1983) has identified five aspects of the work ethic. The first is the traditional and classic Protestant work ethic that stresses frugality and hard work as the road to success in life and salvation after life. It applied to a time in America when most people were farmers and mechanics and therefore had control over their own work. It was part of the classic work ethic of nineteenth century proprietors' ideology that Rodgers has identified and discussed in detail (1974).

The second aspect of the work ethic identified by Maccoby is the craft ethic based on pride in workmanship and the maintenance of self-reliance and independence in one's own work. It applied to the colonial period in American history when craftsmen were a significant sector of the American work force. It was still important up to the end of the nineteenth century. From the time after the Civil War when the United States began to industrialize on a large scale, craftsmen as a significant factor in the workplace began to decline. The process took a long time and was probably not completed until after World War I. Craftsmen are still important today in the construction industry and in machine shops and among individual entrepreneurs, but they have been overwhelmed and outnumbered by factory operatives and white-collar workers and professionals.

A third work ethic, based on an entrepreneurial ethic, exists in America, as attested by the more than 12 million small businesses that are operating. It is an ethic that believes in working for oneself rather than for others. In contrast with the moderate, leisurely paced work and frugality of the traditional craftsman and small shopkeepers of the past, the present-day entrepreneur is a risk taker who must work long hours and must be tough and competitive. Her or his reward is independence, control over his or her own work and the possibility of growth. The drawbacks are that in today's society it is hard for the small businessperson to prosper in the face of costly and complicated regulations, high taxes, and competition from large corporations.

A fourth dimension of the work ethic is the notion of career that depends on administrative rather than entrepreneurial skills. Rather than hoping to establish their own businesses, these people seeks jobs in large organizations—in business, government, and the professions. Their goal is to move up in the organization toward increased responsibility and status. This ethic belongs particularly to professionals and technicians who make their living by solving problems and providing services. As more young people enter the work force with college educations, these people expect the workplace to be a meritocracy where anyone who demonstrates skills and abilities should be able to rise in the organization. They believe that talent and hard work should earn success and promotions. Many of these people were shocked during the downsizing period of the 1980s and 1990s when many management and professional employees who had given lifetime service to corporations were mustered out. They had to wait a long time to be re-employed and most took jobs at lower salaries. Today, many of those with a career ethic suffer from anxiety, worrying about the security of their jobs, about constantly being judged and evaluated, and about the competitiveness and unfriendliness of organizational life.

A fifth work ethic identified by Maccoby is the self-fulfillment ethic. A growing number of young, educated people are concerned with personal growth and the enjoyment of life at both work and leisure. They want interesting work and satisfying emotional relationships at work, characterized by kindness, sympathy, understanding, and generosity. These people are troubled by the fact that they have to prove their worth in organizations by following the career ethic and sacrificing other satisfactions in life—family, integrity, and meaningful leisure. The challenge of the future will be whether managers of enterprises and institutions will be able to elevate the motivation to work by providing opportunities for mental stimulation and emotional satisfaction as well as career advancement in the workplace.

I want to add a sixth dimension to Maccoby's five—a work ethic based on the notion of succeeding in the face of great odds, of overcoming obstacles and difficulties. It derives from American history when the majority of the population were independent farmers and craftsmen. Independence and self-reliance were strong elements in that value system and it has carried through to modern times. It was part of the western movement and the frontier and has been preserved in American literature. Even for factory workers, independence, self-reliance, and overcoming difficulties and obstacles are important. The formation of unions was in part a movement designed to provide workers with some measure of independence, dignity, and self-respect in the face of adversity as well as powerful and authoritarian corporations. It enabled workers on the shop floor and on the picket line to assert their own rights and to resist the arbitrary power of employers. This element of dignity and assertion of human self-respect was as important, or even more so, than the basic issues of wages and hours as American workers formed their own trade union organizations.

The United States, in an amazingly short time in the twentieth century, went from being an industrial society in which the driving engine was mass-produced products at falling prices, buttressed by a work force that could buy back the products, to a service and consumer society, driven by a highly productive economy that could release people from direct production and pay them well enough so they could buy the products and services of manufacturing, service, and leisure industries. We are now in the period where new high-tech methods of production are changing the workplace and worker motivation. While we need to create new jobs to fulfill the expectations of a better-educated society we find our education system in great difficulty as it takes the hit for balancing budgets. Education is the key to worker motivation and training for future technologies that require new modes of thinking and more flexibility to cope with the changing workplace. We need not only to adequately fund education but we need to change the way we learn to increase our capacity to live with and adapt to changes in our total environment.

In the early 1970s, the reinterpretation of the work ethic took hold as theoreticians of work recognized that workers had higher orders of needs besides economic ones. A higher percentage of college-educated persons was joining the work force. By 1976, one out of four persons, ages 25 to 29, had received a bachelor's degree, compared to one in twenty in that age group in 1940. The number of professionals doubled and the number of administrators increased by 42 percent. This new class of educated workers emphasized self-fulfillment and demanded greater challenges in the workplace. Growing affluence enabled the middle class to consume things that were formerly reserved for the upper classes—homes, cars, stocks, appliances, travel, tennis. The middle class continued to accept the work ethic and disseminate its values, stressing family, hard work, and industry. However, in the last twenty years it has become more difficult for the middle class to hold on to its social position and many have lost ground. Hence, the revolt against big government. People now believe government is the cause of their problems, particularly high taxes that deprive them of income needed for their families and the education of their children. But it is really jobs and earning a decent income from work that is the problem, and government can play an important role in helping to create jobs, something it has done in the past.

The new work ethic, the one most appropriate for the future workplace, involves giving workers more autonomy and more participation in decision making. New management theory seeks to organize workers into teams that share skills and are able to respond quickly and flexibly to changes in product making as the marketplace changes. Enterprises will need to be flexible and mobile to compete successfully at home and abroad. Mass production, hierarchical control, and information from the top down are cumbersome methods that cannot react quickly to changing consumer demand. Workers fit for only one task or skill are not going to be adaptive in future high-tech workplaces. Workers will need to upgrade their skills if they wish to remain at their jobs or advance themselves. Companies will need workers who can tolerate rapid changes. At the same time, workers will have to be offered more than just economic rewards if they are to remain loyal to their employers and committed to their work.

The work ethic and its precepts of commitment, workmanship, and discipline may be worth cultivating as a means to the good life. The essential reality of the work ethic is that a constructive adjustment to work is an important precondition for personal, social, and economic well-being. But work ethic precepts are best cultivated not by moralizing and ideology, but by jobs that provide good wages along with humane management. This is not to lessen the importance of ideology. But by and large, unless the work ethic is credibly associated with valued outcomes, work ethic ideology may be counterproductive and generate cynicism and a sense of betrayal. The work ethic has to pay off, not just in monetary terms, but also in work that has meaning and provides self-respect and self-fulfillment.

For one hundred years, from 1870 to 1970, the United States created an industrial culture based on power and energy, a physical and technological power that put machines and labor into motion. The result was an enormous increase in the output and distribution of material goods, with its consequent advance in the American standard of living. What is considered near the poverty line today would have been near luxury in 1900. Starting in the 1960s and 1970s, American culture tilted in the direction of information and knowledge. It was as if America for a hundred years was creating a physical structure based on energy, capable of prodigious feats of productivity. Now and into the future we are creating a system to control the physical structure, a control system based on information, technology, and computers. We created the skeleton of industrial might in the past. Now, we are creating the brain to make the skeleton self-actuating. Yet we still need the muscles and brains of working people to make the system work. The entire question as to who will work on what is a combination of individual and collective decisions, or more precisely, the summing up of a multitude of individual decisions.

Life becomes simple when we get down to basics. When we do we see what unites us. And what unites us as human beings is our ability to create products and services through the work of our hands and minds.

The real heroes of American history are the unsung heroes, the anonymous working people who built this country. They are heroes because they are anonymous. They have not been made into celebrities with phony, vulgar exaggerations, with sensation rather than fact, with myth rather than reality. The hard work of the craftsman, the nurse, the machinist, the teacher, the fireman, the assembly-line worker, and all the others who have created our society have provided the basis for social happiness. They will never get into the news but what they do is what makes our society function and live.

BIBLIOGRAPHICAL ESSAY

The five dimensions of the work ethic discussed in this chapter are from Michael Maccoby, "The Managerial Work Ethic in America," in *The Work Ethic—A Critical Analysis*, edited by Jack Barbarsh, Robert J. Lampman, Sar A. Levitan, Gus Tyler (Madison, WI: Industrial Relations Research Association, 1983), 183–196.

The reference to Rodgers is Daniel T. Rodgers, *The Work Ethic in Industrial America, 1850–1920* (Chicago: University of Chicago Press, 1974).

INDEX

ABOUT THE AUTHOR

HERBERT APPLEBAUM, who received his Ph.D. from SUNY—Buffalo, is the author of five previous books on work, including, most recently, *Colonial Americans at Work* (1996). He has been active in the construction industry, both as a worker and in management positions. His other books include *Royal Blue: The Culture of Construction Workers* (1981), *Work in Non-Market and Transitional Societies* (1984), *Work in Market and Industrial Societies* (1984), *Perspectives in Cultural Anthropology* (1987), and *The Concept of Work: Ancient, Medieval and Modern* (1992).

ISBN 0-313-30677-X

90000>

EAN

9 780313 306778

HARDCOVER BAR CODE